RESOLUTION OF INNER CONFLICT
An Introduction to
Psychoanalytic Therapy

Frank Auld
Marvin Hyman

American Psychological Association
Washington, DC

First printing June 1991
Second printing October 1992

Published by
American Psychological Association
750 First Street, NE
Washington, DC 20002

Copies may be ordered from
APA Order Department
P.O. Box 2710
Hyattsville, MD 20784

Cover designed by Debra E. Riffe
Typeset by Harper Graphics, Waldorf, MD
Printed by Edwards Brothers, Inc., Ann Arbor, MI
Technical editing and production coordinated by Linda J. Beverly

Library of Congress Cataloging-in-Publication Data

Auld, Frank, 1923–
    Resolution of inner conflict : an introduction to psychoanalytic therapy / Frank Auld, Marvin Hyman.
        p.   cm.
    Includes bibliographical references.
    ISBN 1-55798-116-7
    1. Psychoanalysis. I. Hyman, Marvin, 1926–   . II. Title.
    [DNLM: 1. Conflcit (Psychology) 2. Psychoanalytic
Interpretation. 3. Psychoanalytic Therapy.   WM 460.6 A924r]
    RC504.A95   1991
    616.89'17--dc20
    DNLM/DLC
                                                                    91-4620

Printed in the United States of America.

To
Elinor and Betty

Contents

Introduction

Why Another Book on Psychotherapy?

Introduction: Why Another Book on Psychotherapy?

Why, you ask, another book on psychotherapy? We have wondered about this too and believe that we owe you an answer. First of all, we have found in teaching psychoanalytic therapy to graduate students of clinical psychology that we were not satisfied with the available textbooks. We found some of them—such as Greenson's *The Technique and Practice of Psychoanalysis* (1967)—to be admirable presentations of analytic technique, but to assume too much sophistication of the reader. O. Fenichel's admirable *Problems of Psychoanalytic Technique* (1941) is so condensed in its prose that the beginner can hardly begin to comprehend the multifarious implications of each sentence.

Other books are ideally suited to the student's level, are written in an attractive style, but do not cover in a comprehensive way all of the topics that, in our opinion, an introductory book should cover. Malan's *Individual Psychotherapy and the Science of Psychodynamics* (1979) does an excellent job of capturing the reader's attention with well-presented episodes from daily life that illustrate psychodynamic processes. Malan brilliantly summarizes the main principles of therapy with his device of the two triangles—the triangle of person (therapist, others, parents [or past]) and the triangle of conflict (defense, anxiety, hidden feeling). Yet we miss a discussion of other important points that we have included in this book. Menninger's and Holzman's *Theory of Psychoanalytic Technique* (1973) is in our opinion a fine book but incomplete.

Some books, we must confess, we find lacking because we believe that the author has at some points abandoned sound principles—or, at least, has laid himself or herself open to misunderstandings. Basch's *Doing Psychotherapy* (1980), which one of the authors used for several years as a textbook in his therapy course, is an example of an admirable book that is slightly flawed by the author's leaving the *impression* that the therapist can and should decide what is best for his or her patient. We believe that Basch, in appealing to Kohut's therapeutic strategies as rationale for how he handled two of his illustrative cases, leaves the impression with beginners that he took an impermissible authoritarian attitude toward these two patients. (Basch, of course, had no intention of justifying an authoritarian attitude.) Thus, we proposed to write a book that would be accessible to the beginning therapist, would deal with the nuts-and-bolts of therapy as well as with the concepts that give a framework for the therapy, and would adhere to what we believe are sound principles: the principles of an *autonomous psychotherapy* (to use T. Szasz's, 1974a, apt phrase).

Our Approach to Doing Psychotherapy

Our approach to doing psychotherapy is grounded on two assumptions: (a) that the problems our patients bring to us, if these problems require psychotherapy to deal with, involve a wish–defense *conflict,* and (b) that this conflict was learned in the interactions that the patient experienced with others (especially with parents) in the past and is now lived out in the patient's *relationships* to others in the present. The others in the present are basically those with whom the patient is involved in daily life; but the same patterns of relating are also brought into the patient's relationship with the therapist. We are, in essence, taking the same approach to theorizing about therapy that L. Luborsky and his associates have taken in their use of the concept, *core conflictual relationship theme* (see Luborsky, 1984; Luborsky & Crits-Christoph, 1990; Luborsky, Crits-Christoph, Mintz, & Auerbach, 1988). Our approach is also, we believe, in keeping with D. Malan's formulation of "the two triangles" (in his *Individual Psychotherapy and the Science of Psychodynamics,* 1979; see especially pp. 80, 92–94).

These formulations are clearly derived from Freud's views on how to treat patients with neurotic conflicts, as he developed these ideas at the turn of the century (cf. Waelder, 1960, pp. 35ff.). It might be supposed, therefore, that the therapy we are describing applies only to persons experiencing neurotic conflicts and not to persons with character disorders, borderline disorders, psychoses, or some other kind of psychopathology. We do not accept any such limitation on the scope of psychoanalytic therapy. On the contrary, we believe that the basic approach of psychoanalytic therapy—the exploration of the person's stream of thinking and feeling, with the aim of understanding it, thereby enabling that person to change his or her pattern of living in the world if that is what the person wants—applies to anyone whose distresses arise from psychological causes. Should brain damage or hyperthyroidism or some other "biological" process lie behind the patient's distress, the psychoanalytic approach will not avail.

Therapy of Patients Who Do Not Suffer From Neuroses

We are not arguing that no modifications in technique are required when the patient has a character problem or has psychotic symptoms. Waelder (1960), who was mostly pessimistic about applying psychoanalysis to character disorder or psychosis, wrote as follows:

> In dealing with pathological conditions other than psychoneuroses, psychoanalysis, as the causal treatment of the neuroses, can do one of two things: it can either search for the neurotic features which may yet be hidden in the picture of other afflictions and single them out for attack, or it can try to stimulate a patient to the production of a neurosis and then treat its product. (p. 218)

We believe that what can be achieved by finding the features that are neurotic and "singling them out for attack" is far more than Waelder believed.

Are we, in adhering to the basic concepts of conflict and relationship themes, old-fashioned, uninformed about current advances in ego psychology, and neglectful of the impact of the cultural milieu (especially, of family dynamics) on the patient's functioning? In Chapter 17 of this book we address these questions. We believe that the attentive reader will find also, in early chapters of this book, that we were aware of these issues and that we have taken a position on each of these questions. We think that the reader will come to see that where we have rejected currently fashionable formulations, it was not because we were unaware of the issues, but because we had come to a different judgment than other authors.

Our book, then, presents a "classical" psychoanalytic approach to therapy, focusing on the problems of the human being that derive from conflict. We do not give explicit, systematic attention to the modifications of technique that are suitable when one deals with persons who are severely regressed (such as those who are behaving psychotically), persons who are addicted to alcohol or another drug, persons who have committed a sexual offense, or persons who have been found guilty of some other criminal offense. There are plenty of books that purport to tell therapists how to treat these various kinds of patients. Believing that we cannot do justice within the framework of an introductory book to the question of how one modifies technique to deal with these varied kinds of persons, we encourage the reader—after reading this book—to turn to more specialized books. (We cannot refrain from recommending here the superb book by Karon and VandenBos [1981], *Psychotherapy of Schizophrenia: The Treatment of Choice*.)

Expectations That We Will Not Meet

It is likely that a reader who is new to psychoanalysis will expect that this book will describe a therapy in which the patient lies on the couch, comes for therapy five times a week, is encouraged by the therapist to "talk about your childhood," and continues in the therapy for 3, 5, or 10 years. We will meet none of these expectations.

We believe that whether the patient lies on the couch or not is not the distinguishing characteristic of psychoanalysis. Like Freud (1914a, p. 16), we believe the qualifying features are (a) whether the therapist deals with unconscious processes and/or repression and (b) whether the transference is understood and dealt with appropriately. Later (see chapter 5), we discuss at greater length whether and when one uses the couch.

We point out (in chapter 5) that psychoanalytic therapy can be done within the framework of once-a-week or twice-a-week frequency, although we argue that the therapy goes better with more frequent meetings. We believe that therapy that is essentially psychoanalytic can be done, with some patients, within a much shorter time span than 5–10 years. By dint of necessity (we guess, because the National Health Service will subsidize only brief treatments), Malan and his associates in England (see Malan, 1963, 1976) have done brief psychotherapy that is psychoanalytic in its approach. In Canada, Davanloo (1978a) has developed a distinctive style of doing brief, psychoanalytic therapy. In Boston, Sifneos (1972, 1979) and Mann (1973), as well as Deutsch and Murphy (1955), have developed ways of doing psychodynamic therapy briefly. Strupp and Binder (1984) have not only developed techniques for doing dynamic psychotherapy in a briefer time-span, they and their colleagues have done extensive research to validate their methods. Finally, we cite L. Luborsky (1984), whose codification of psychoanalytic therapy embraces therapies of varying lengths—some of them relatively brief (see also Luborsky et al., 1988).

As to the misunderstanding that the psychoanalytic therapist instructs the patient to "talk about your childhood," here we can say only that in psychoanalytic therapy the therapist is deeply committed to discovering what the patient is experiencing—right now—in the therapy room. More than any other kind of psychotherapy, psychoanalytic therapy deals with the here-and-now. (We feel some regret that Perls—see Perls, 1947 and Perls, Hefferline, & Goodman, 1951—saw fit to misrepresent psychoanalysis in order to promote gestalt therapy. We believe that Perls's suggestions about promoting greater access to the emotions through technical modifications deserve to be considered on their merits, rather than to be supported by specious arguments.)

Transference is, of course, the patient's *current* experience of the therapist, and it is pivotal in the analytic process. How patients come to see that in order to understand current experiences on which the analysis is focusing, fantasies that originally developed earlier in their life must be understood is a story that we will tell in a later chapter.

A Preview of the Book

Our book starts with an orientation to psychotherapy—an explanation of what it is all about. Chapters 2 and 3 present a theoretical grounding for the reader and an overview of the therapeutic process. Chapter 4 tells how to conduct the initial interview—surely the first thing the beginning therapist should know.

Our ordering of topics in the next few chapters expresses our view of their relative importance. We believe that the therapist, before making interpretations, before providing support, before anything else is done must create an appropriate structure for the therapy. In doing this, the therapist has to appreciate that his or her own responses to the patient are critical to the therapeutic work. We then turn to considering what Freud considered to be crucial processes in the therapy (he devoted separate papers in his series on technique to these topics), resistance and transference.

Chapters 10 and 11 form a pair. Chapter 10, "Understanding Communications From the Unconscious," is obviously logically prior to the activity of chapter 11, making interpretations. Interpretation, of course, is the distinctive activity of the psychoanalytic therapist (as Greenson, 1967, pointed out, "analysis" [i.e., interpretive work] distinguishes psychoanalysis from suggestive therapy).

Yet interpretation is not all there is to psychoanalytic therapy; the relationship with the therapist, the working alliance, is equally important. Luborsky (1984) was moved to call psychoanalytic therapy, as done at the Menninger Clinic, as done by Luborsky and his associates, "supportive-expressive" therapy. The "supportive" part is what we talk about in chapter 12.

Freud's interest in dreams is well known, as is his classic work *The Interpretation of Dreams* (1900). In doing therapy, Freud gave the interpretation of dreams an important role; this can be seen, for example, in his lecture on analytic therapy in his *Introductory Lectures* (Freud, 1917, p. 456). Thus we have a chapter on dream interpretation (chapter 13). Its placement in the book, however, expresses our conviction that interpreting dreams is not essential to doing psychoanalytic therapy.

Next we turn to considering the results of therapy (which one would naturally consider at a later time). In chapter 14, the changes produced by therapy are discussed and in chapter 15, when and how to terminate therapy is discussed.

Our penultimate chapter is quite different from all the others. It acknowledges the issues that feminist writers have raised about the differences between the personality development of girls and of boys, and addresses itself to the impact that these differences may have on the psychotherapy of women and of men.

Finally, in chapter 17, we have tried to put our approach in the context of the new developments in theorizing about psychodynamics and psychopathology. Such developments include ego psychology, object relations theory, interpersonal analysis, and other approaches that differ—or seem to differ—from classical psychoanalytic theory.

Why Read This Book and How to Do It

In sum, this is a book on the technique of psychoanalytic therapy. The reader can reasonably expect to learn from it what can be learned from a book about how to do psychotherapy. Just as a marriage manual cannot teach the most important things about sex—these must be learned through personal experience—so we cannot teach some of the essential skills for doing psychotherapy. But for teaching what can be taught in a book, we hold ourselves accountable. Later, we will say what else besides knowledge acquired from books is needed to learn therapy (see pp. 8–9).

Throughout, we will make suggestions for dealing with problems that we have seen arise in the work of beginning therapists. We will try to answer the questions, "How do you . . .?" and "What do you do when . . .?" Although we hope to be of practical help, we will provide sufficient theoretical orientation that the reader can appreciate the reasons for our recommendations. To this end, we have given the book a framework (mainly a sequential one) in which the process of treatment can be understood. Finally, we try to preview for the student what he or she will experience as a therapist by providing real examples of therapeutic encounters.

Background Needed to Read This Book

In order to profit from reading this book the reader should have a thorough understanding of the fundamentals of psychoanalysis. We think of the material that C. Brenner presents in his *An Elementary Textbook of Psychoanalysis* (1973) as basic. The reader should know and understand this material (moreover, the references cited by Brenner at the end of each chapter are quite helpful). Perhaps the reader should also know a bit about psychotherapy in general—for example, the kind of material that is presented by Colby in *A Primer for Psychotherapists* (1951).

Contact with clinical material, especially with therapy cases, is highly desirable. The benefit to be gained by reading this book depends on the reader's sophistication with therapy. We have not attempted to write for those who are just becoming exposed to clinical problems, but rather for those who, building on a beginner's knowledge of the clinical field, are seeking to acquire skill in doing therapy.

Books Supplementing This Book

Although we hope that you will read the rest of this book and will find it a highly useful introduction to psychoanalytic therapy, we believe that you may also be interested in reading all or part of some other good books on therapy. We will mention a few of the many books that are available.

Authors on the technique of psychoanalytic therapy were slow to get off the mark, probably because they felt that it would be presumptuous of them to write books on therapy when S. Freud himself had not published a book on the subject. Two early and outstanding books did appear, however: one by E. Glover, the other by O. Fenichel.

Fenichel's book (1941), which is based on his lectures at the Berlin Psychoanalytic Institute, is a classic. Its only serious fault is that Fenichel expresses himself so compactly that the beginning student is at a loss to appreciate the implications of the book's sparse prose. The novice reader lacks the background and the experience to fill in the skeletal statements. Examples are needed; the implications of theoretical points must be appreciated; personal experience must have persuaded one that the events Fenichel alludes to really do happen.

The other outstanding early book on technique, by E. Glover (1955/1928), like the Fenichel book assumes more-than-a-beginner's sophistication. Glover gives us excellent examples to demonstrate the principles he is discussing, but the examples demand a good deal of clinical sophistication in the reader. We believe his book to be a sound one, but too advanced for most graduate students in clinical psychology or first- or second-year residents in psychiatry.

Recently, there has been a spate of excellent books on technique. Among these we particularly call the reader's attention to D. Malan's *Individual Psychotherapy and the Science of Psychodynamics* (1979) and to L. Luborsky's *Principles of Psychoanalytic Psychotherapy: A Manual for Supportive-Expressive Treatment* (1984). For a searching examination of the relationship between theory and technique, we recommend C. Brenner's *Psychoanalytic Technique and Psychic Conflict* (1976). Finally, to those who are interested in the validation of psychoanalysis—both of its general theory and of its theory of therapy—we commend to their attention the writings of Edelson (1984, 1988), Grünbaum (1984), Kline (1984), and Luborsky and his associates (1988).

An Overview of Therapy Training

We picture the process of learning to do psychotherapy as one of continuous, graded development. Concurrent with reading books, one should be doing therapy under supervision—close, hour-by-hour supervision. Later, one should get broader experience in working with patients, an experience involving continued supervision. (Not all of the later supervision need be so close as the first supervision.) Learning should continue throughout one's career as a clinician. Good therapy is done by people who are continuing to learn.

Our Approach to Instructing the Reader

A final observation: We do not offer a set of rules nor can we give the reader explicit and detailed instructions for carrying out therapy, instructions that can be routinely applied in every case. The evaluation of a patient is not a routine matter; rather, it requires judgment by the therapist. The therapist's evaluation, if it is appropriate, is made to a total gestalt, unique for each patient. Therefore one can't offer cookbook rules such as, "If the patient is reluctant to lie down, say, 'You are afraid of allowing yourself the relaxation, the freedom of expressing your emotions, that you anticipate would happen if you lay down.' " Such an interpretation may be correct for some patients who don't want to lie down and wrong for others. It may be a timely interpretation for some of the patients for whom it is true but premature to say to others. Therefore, we repeat that we cannot give simple rules about what to say in any particular situation.

We must also admit that this book by itself is not sufficient to teach anyone how to do psychotherapy. We expect that this book will be used concurrently with actual experience as a therapist and that its necessarily skeletal character will be fleshed out by material from the reader's practical experience.

Chapter 1

Orientation: Why Do We Do Psychoanalytic Therapy?

1 ———————————————————————————————

Before answering why we do psychotherapy, we must ask: What leads persons into psychological difficulty? How does the answer to that question tell us something about how to help them out of the difficulty?

Defining Neurosis

Psychoanalytic therapy was developed as a way of treating neurosis. Accordingly, we ask what neurosis is. Here we are concerned first of all with what it "looks like," what it is descriptively. (Later we will consider a theory of how neurosis comes about.)

We like R. Waelder's (1960, p. 35) definition: "Neurosis is a circumscribed affliction of an otherwise normal person who is in contact with the world and adequately adjusted except for a limited area; those afflicted with neurosis have feelings, anxieties, thoughts or impulses, or carry out actions, which they *feel as ego-alien but which they cannot help* feeling, thinking, or doing." Let us consider, part by part, this rather complex definition. First, the reader should notice that Waelder points out that on the whole, persons with neuroses adapt reasonably well to the world around them. They develop well in most aspects of their lives; they learn how to earn a living, are reasonably successful in school, and get along with other persons fairly well most of the time. Yet there are problems in their lives.

These problems may involve overt actions or they may involve *feeling* or *thinking*. Waelder has embraced the whole range of possible behaviors of human beings, and he has divided this behavior along more or less commonsense lines. Waelder points out that these problematic responses (feelings, thoughts, actions) are unwanted by the person exhibiting them. That is what he means by *ego-alien*—the feeling, the thought, or the action is disowned by the person, who views it as unacceptable.

Yet the person cannot refrain from making this unwanted, disowned response. It is a strange state of affairs, is it not, when the person making a response asserts that it is unwelcome? As we are striving to explain what we (as clinicians or as scientists) observe of the patient's behavior, the unwanted feelings (e.g., anxiety or depression) cause us no great problem, because we can easily view them as an unwanted consequence of the stream of behavior. Physical symptoms such as headaches, vomiting, vaginismus, or impotence seem to make sense, because (without the least understanding of their cause) we can assume that they are caused by something outside the person. Our tolerance for assimilating the patient's irrationality into our explanatory system, without paying any attention to its strangeness, breaks down, however, when we look at obsessive thoughts (thoughts that the person has, but does not want to have), compulsive actions, and phobias (supposedly senseless fears). We lay this paradox before the reader, although we cannot disarm it by a short and simple explanation.

The Neurotic Paradox

There is, as we can now appreciate, a paradox in the behavior of individuals experiencing neuroses: They are responding in a manner that is unwanted, that is, in a way that causes suffering. The alcoholic damages relationships with others, personal effectiveness, physical health, or all of these, and yet cannot refrain from drinking. The person who suffers from panic attacks is limited in independence, handicapped in the work place and in social interactions, and yet cannot stop feeling afraid. The compulsive cannot refrain from the actions that are known to be senseless. In each instance, we would expect (from the well-accepted principles of learning that we all learned in our introductory psychology course) that the maladaptive responses would be eliminated because they do not lead to reinforcement. Yet these unwanted responses persist.

Why is the ineffective behavior not unlearned? The authors believe that the most important reason for the lack of unlearning is the existence of hidden reinforcements for the persisting behavior. But beyond this, we believe that there are barriers to the person's carrying out extinction trials, that is, to trying out the ineffective behavior under circumstances that could demonstrate to him or her the inappropriateness of the behavior. Some of the barriers to extinction training consist of mental operations that shield the person from reexperiencing a trauma. Finally, we note that even external events that should count as evidence of safety and of expected gratification are dismissed by the patient as not counting.

Two psychologists, O. H. Mowrer and A. D. Ullman (1945), offered the following explanation of why ineffective behavior persists: They pointed out that the effectiveness of a reward is reduced the longer the reward is delayed. They pointed out, too, that the effectiveness of a punishment in attaching fear to the cues produced by performing a response is reduced more, the longer the punishment is administered after the performance of the response. It follows from these principles, Mowrer and Ullman argued, that if a reward for a response comes immediately but a punishment for the same response is long delayed, the reward will control the subject's response, and the punishment will have little impact. Accordingly, when a person makes a response that has very damaging effects on his or her adaptation, but the damage (the punishment) occurs after considerable delay, it may well occur that this maladaptive response will persist.

As Dollard and Miller (1950) wrote: "In short, the immediate effects of a moderate reduction in drive can be stronger than those of a much greater increase in pain that occurs long afterwards. Thus the strengthening effect of an immediate weak reinforcement on a symptom such as drinking may be much greater than the deterring effect of a much stronger but delayed punishment, which often also occurs in the presence of a considerably different set of cues" (pp. 187–188).

The Psychoanalytic Explanation of Neurosis

We believe that scholars in the field of abnormal psychology generally agree that the descriptive definition of neurosis given in earlier paragraphs is appropriate. Regardless of their theoretical orientation, they would say that a person having any of these symptomatic responses suffers from neurosis. What scholars do not agree on is what causes these symptoms. As for us, we have adopted the psychoanalytic theory of neurosis as the basis for our understanding of neurotic behavior and for our approach to changing that behavior.

Again we find R. Waelder's (1960) statement cogent. He says that the basic propositions of the psychoanalytic explanation of neurosis are as follows:

1. that psychoneuroses are due to an inner conflict between an impulse and the interconnected rest of the personality, the so-called "ego";
2. that in the case of neurosis, the conflict has not been solved in favor of one or the other side, nor by a suitable compromise, but has . . . become unconscious through a process called "repression";
3. that the repression, however, has been unsuccessful . . . and that the repressed impulse has found its way back into conscious manifestations in disguised form (return of the repressed). (pp. 36–37)

Thus, when we speak of neurotic conflict from a psychodynamic point of view, we refer to an individual's repressed wishes, desires, urges, and the like; the dangers that the person links to those wishes; the anxiety that accompanies the experience of danger; the defenses—including repression—that have been mobilized to block the expression of the forbidden wish in consciousness or in behavior directly; and the compromise formations that the person creates both to express the hidden wish or impulse in disguised derivatives and to keep the repressed wish-defense conflict out of awareness. Such compromises take the form of symptoms, character traits, parapraxes (errors), and other psychopathological formations of everyday life. The compromises, we should recognize, provide these persons with a synthetic handling of the forces of the inward-looking part of their psychic life; this synthesis is sometimes achieved at the cost of a disturbed adaptation to the outer world.

How One Restores Adaptive Functioning

If one takes seriously the theory that Waelder outlined, it is clear that one could try to restore adaptive functioning in any one of three ways: (a) One could strengthen the repression, (b) one could reduce the drive, or (c) one could somehow increase the direct gratification that the patient was obtaining, or offer substitutes for that direct gratification. The moral exhortations that various authorities, including priests, ministers, and other religious teachers, made to those seeking their counsel (in the days before psychotherapy) generally followed the first strategy. The authority figure urged the troubled person to abandon his or her striving for socially condemned gratifications. If the person hearing this exhortation was sufficiently frightened by the dire consequences that the authority promised for disobedience, the conflict might be relieved, because the repression would become strong enough to keep the unruly impulse in check. Even today, some authorities make use of this strategy. (We have even known so-called psychotherapists who used it.)

It is likely that some of the psychotropic drugs now used by psychiatrists reduce the drives that compose the patient's conflict. For example, persons suffering from what the *Diagnostic and Statistical Manual of Mental Disorders* (*DSM-III-R*) calls *panic disorder* may be impelled to make angry, hostile responses, yet have strong inhibitions against carrying these impulses into action. If a drug could interfere with the mobilization of the anger, it could greatly reduce the intensity of the conflict, thereby preventing the responses that had been learned to the cues of the anxiety component of the conflict. The person would become less afraid and would have less need to avoid the situations in which unconscious anger had been provoked. Our speculation about the mechanism by which some drugs alleviate a panic disorder is just that, a speculation; but it may serve to illustrate how medication could influence what psychologists call *drive*.

Psychotherapists cannot (at least, cannot if they are at all wise) offer gratifications directly to their patients. But they can offer permission to their patients to be more expressive of impulse (of course, in those situations where it is appropriate to be more expressive). They might suggest to a patient that even though he or she is unable to have the desired childlike dependence on a parent or parent-substitute, the patient can lean on friends or spouse to a reasonable degree. The patient's guilt about allowing himself or herself reasonable gratifications can be reduced, through the therapist's (or other authority's) expression of opinion. In so far as the therapist or other authority has prestige in the patient's eyes, such suggestive interventions of the therapist may be helpful. Yet one has to wonder why the therapist would have any special role as a benign authority, that is, why the patient would not have already found a benign authority (such as a compassionate priest, a warmhearted teacher), and one that costs a great deal less than a therapist.

Paradoxically, psychoanalytic therapy restores adaptive functioning by none of these means (although it may, indeed, use the third strategy as a minor part of its approach). Instead, the way in which psychoanalysis restores adaptive functioning is by undoing the repression, in order to allow the patient to attempt a new resolution of the conflict. Once the repression has been undone, the patient can decide whether to renounce gratification of impulse (akin to the first strategy), whether to allow gratification of impulse (akin to the third strategy), or whether to try some combination of these two strategies, and to modify the kind of gratification one will accept. We may point out, in passing, that using drugs for the reduction of drive is a response that we, as therapists, don't have to teach our patients; too many patients have learned to do that on their own.

To sum up: Psychoanalysis aims at letting the person decide what he or she wants. It does this by making the unconscious conscious, so that the person himself or herself can make that decision.

Is Psychoanalysis Suitable Only for Those With Neuroses?

In arguing that psychoanalytic therapy is a rational procedure that is based on a theory of how the suffering human being came to have problems in living, we have relied on the psychoanalytic theory of neurosis as our theory and have tried to show how the strategy of undoing repressions in order to resolve the neurotic conflict meshes with that theory of how the problems in living originated. Because our exposition so far has dealt only with the therapy of neurosis, the reader might well draw the conclusion that the therapy we are describing and explaining applies only to those with neuroses, and the reader might well expect that a quite different approach would be needed in order to work with persons who have a character disorder, a borderline disorder, a narcissistic disorder, a schizophrenia, or a major depressive disorder. We will explain why we believe that psychoanalytic therapy of the kind we are writing about is suitable for a far broader range of patients than those who suffer from neuroses.

The Postulates of Psychoanalysis

To show that psychoanalytic therapy is applicable to a broader range of persons than those with neuroses, we need first to discuss a number of assumptions that underlie the clinical method of psychoanalysis. We do this in order to argue that the core of this clinical method—using associations to discover the operation of unconscious processes—can be applied to every human being, not only to those who are experiencing neuroses.

Our discussion of these assumptions will not be exhaustive. Because our focus is necessarily on how to do therapy, the reader will have to look elsewhere for an adequate discussion of these postulates. We want to point out, nevertheless, that the postulates of psychoanalysis include at least the following:

1. the proposition that later mental structures have to be explained by earlier experiences, by a turning back to the past;
2. the concept of psychic continuity;
3. the proposition that mental life has meaning;
4. the principle of determinism, the conviction that nothing that happens is accidental;
5. the concept of instinct (i.e., of the source of motivation in bodily processes); and
6. the concept of the unconscious (necessary because conscious experience leaves gaps in mental life, which unconscious processes bridge).

We owe this list to D. Rapaport (1944/1967) and to H. Shevrin, who brought Rapaport's thinking to our attention. The reader will find a fuller discussion of these ideas in Rapaport's paper, especially on pages 186–192.

To these postulates of psychoanalytic theory, intended by Rapaport as guides to clinical method, a seventh could be added: *Access to unconscious functioning comes about through the associative process.* Therapeutic technique is built on this premise, and the applicability of the psychoanalytic approach to various kinds of patients relies on the hypothesis: In so far as the psychodynamics of this person can be elucidated by pursuing his or her associations, the therapist and the patient, working together, can understand the patient and have a constructive effect on the patient's life.

Accordingly, we recommend that whenever psychodynamic processes are contributing to problematic behavior, the therapist and the patient make an empirical test of whether psychoanalytic therapy can work, rather than allowing themselves to be guided by the patient's diagnosis which, after all, only tells us what the symptoms are.

How Does One Undo Repressions?

Although the whole of our book will be devoted to answering this question, we can provide a very brief answer in this paragraph. The psychoanalytic therapist, first, instructs the patient to speak whatever comes to mind. This task is called *free association*, because the patient does not respond to specific prompts of the therapist but is, instead, free to say whatever he or she wishes. Second, the therapist observes that the patient falters in the attempt to express what is on his mind or what is on her mind because the patient has to work against the force of repression in trying to express unconscious contents. The therapist helps the patient to overcome this counterforce by interpreting resistance. (We will give a more detailed definition and explanation of resistance in chapter 8.) Third, the therapist observes and interprets transference—the responses of the patient to the therapist that are inappropriate to the actual behavior of the therapist. (Transference will be discussed in greater detail in chapter 9.)

In order to encourage free association and help the patient overcome resistance and understand transference, the therapist (a) listens; (b) confronts, clarifies, and interprets; (c) knows when to talk and when not to; and (d) knows how to understand the patient's communications. The therapist needs to acquire (a) a background of knowledge of psychopathology and psychodynamics; (b) an ability to empathize, to observe, to make use of his or her own personal responses; (c) a knowledge of the technical maneuvers appropriate to various situations in the therapy; and (d) a sufficient amount of practice in applying the background knowledge, the personal responses, and the technical maneuvers to specific cases. In the chapters that follow, we explain how the therapist does these things.

Can One Learn Psychotherapy by Having It?

Glover tells us (1955, p. 5) that there is a rather vague tradition that a full understanding of technique can be acquired by a psychoanalytic candidate through the training analysis. A similar assumption is made by many psychologists, whether their theoretical persuasion is psychoanalytic, Sullivanian, client-centered, or otherwise. Glover contends—and we agree—that the experience of having therapy is not a sufficient training in therapeutic technique. One's own therapy surely did not expose all of the situations that can arise in the therapy of patients who differ greatly from each other in character structure and therefore in defenses, in kinds of expression of transference, and in modes of resistance. Nor is the task of learning about oneself through psychotherapy entirely compatible with observing the therapist's technique: As a patient, one has to be involved in dealing with one's own experience; one cannot have sufficient objectivity in observing the therapist's actions, nor can one identify sufficiently with the therapist to learn the role of therapist. To the degree that one does identify with the therapist and does learn to imitate his or her technique, one may copy bad points as well as good; one may also copy personal idiosyncrasies and non-essentials as well as generally valid and necessary procedures.

Having therapy oneself, moreover, does not present the learner with a systematic canvass of the technical problems that a therapist needs to know about. Nor are the questions of technique posed as technical issues; indeed, they should not be. The patient's attention should be on understanding and resolving her or his emotional difficulties, not on observing the technical difficulties of the therapist.

The Value of Personal Therapy

Having said all this to warn against relying on an experience of therapy to teach one technique, we strongly urge that those who wish to become good psychotherapists seek out therapy for themselves. We believe, however, that "successful" or "completed" therapy for oneself can hardly be imposed as a condition for the awarding of a certificate or a degree attesting to competence in doing therapy. Such a requirement is absurd, because therapy that is based on the tenets of psychoanalysis leaves freedom to the patient to choose a course of life, to settle unconscious conflicts in the way that suits his or her own dispositions. To state it in a different way, psychoanalytic therapy is interpretive rather than suggestive. To permit such self-determination, the therapist has to avoid holding any real-life power over the patient; real-life dealings with the patient outside of the therapeutic relationship are to be avoided. If the therapist becomes involved with the patient outside of his or her role as therapist, there will always be an area of unconscious interaction that cannot be interpreted, that cannot be demonstrated as stemming from the patient's transferred unconscious attitudes. For example, a candidate in a psychoanalytic institute whose progress in therapy is reported to the education committee of the institute by an analyst is bound to feel under some pressure to please the analyst. To say that this desire to please stems in part from unconscious trends deriving from early childhood is no doubt to express a truth, but it is to express a truth that can hardly be demonstrated by the training analyst to the candidate under the circumstances of the required psychoanalysis.

If those interested in learning psychotherapy need to have therapy themselves, yet it does not work well to require that they get therapy with a therapist who also has influence over decisions about training, are there alternative ways of bringing about a situation in which those who learn therapy also get therapy? We see two ways in which this purpose can be achieved. First, it is possible to make no requirement about the trainee's own therapy, instead hold the trainee responsible for dealing effectively with patients and for being free of the hindrances of unanalyzed countertransferences. (In chapter 9 we define and discuss countertransference.) The trainee in the course of work with patients would discover that his or her own personal difficulties stood in the way of effective work with patients, and he or she would at that point understand the need for personal therapy. Second, it is possible to require each trainee to get therapy but to take pains to separate the therapy from the training organization. The student's teachers and supervisors would receive no reports from the therapist, and the check on the adequacy of the therapy would be the student's ability to do clinical work effectively, unhampered by personal difficulties.

We realize that situations may arise in which it is not feasible to make a sharp separation between the student's therapy and training, as can occur when training is attempted in a city that has only a few qualified therapists. In such a city the same therapist must both supervise and do therapy with the students whom he or she supervises, if therapy and supervision are to be done at all. Under such conditions, we believe, it is better for the student to get therapy from the supervisor than not to get it at all.

Before leaving the topic of the student's personal therapy, we want to comment on the effect that the atmosphere of a training center has on personal therapy by students. There are psychological and psychiatric training centers—graduate programs in clinical psychology, psychiatric residency programs, psychology internships, and postdoctoral training centers—in which it is almost taken for granted that every student will get personal therapy, in which students know that most of their fellow students have had or are having an experience of therapy for themselves, and in which the staff have all had personal therapy. The atmosphere created by these circumstances makes it easy for the student to seek out therapy, and it reduces the feelings of stigma and the apprehensions about being thought inadequate because the student seeks therapy, which the student might otherwise have. At the other extreme there are centers where students seek therapy only infrequently, where most of those who seek therapy have serious emotional difficulties, where few if any of the staff have had therapy, and where the staff is likely to look with disfavor and suspicion on a student's interest in getting therapy, especially if the therapy is psychoanalytic. We believe that an atmosphere conducive to the student's getting therapy leads to better clinical training than one less conducive to this.

Unfortunately, it is our impression that most clinical psychology graduate programs are more hostile than friendly toward their students' getting personal therapy. It seems that there is a widespread belief among psychology professors that therapy can be taught as a theoretical matter (i.e., as a technique derived from some theory of therapy) separable from the student's own character. It is, we think, not sufficiently recognized that the student's personality will determine, more than any other factor, whether he or she will be able to recognize psychodynamic events in the therapeutic interaction. Nor is it sufficiently recognized that the understanding of therapeutic concepts is somewhat dependent on experience; that one cannot fully understand what is meant by *transference, resistance, insight, reassurance,* and *countertransference* without having had experience in being a patient.

Is There a Conflict Between Therapeutic Skill and Scientific Objectivity?

We have encountered a number of graduate students who were under the impression that there is a conflict between therapeutic skill and scientific objectivity. They believed that a good therapist would float with the material presented by the patient, respond to that material intuitively, and avoid thinking about clinical matters with intellectual rigor for fear of destroying a delicate clinical sensitivity. We have tried to disabuse these students of their prejudices.

To be sure, we believe that one must be committed to the therapeutic approach that one has adopted if one is to be at all effective in using it. If the reader is to try doing psychoanalytic therapy, we urge him or her to commit to it wholeheartedly, at least until this approach is found to be wanting.

We have observed, however, that the best analytic clinicians are those who insist on evidence, who want to learn from the patient, and who do not make premature formulations. In short, their approach to the clinical material is highly empirical. Among writers who have adopted such an empirical approach we are impressed especially by Malan (1979) and Nemiah (1961).

We believe that the student who is interested in learning the concepts of psychoanalysis can know these concepts adequately only by seeing their exemplifications. A nominal definition of *resistance, transference,* or *obsession* is, in our opinion, not sufficient; one needs to be able to point to examples of these phenomena.

Only after becoming steeped in psychoanalytic ideas through seeing their clinical exemplifications will one be in a position to make an adequate test of the truth of psychoanalytic propositions. In our view, then, one would want to learn to be a good clinician in order to be able to prove or disprove the fascinating hypotheses of psychoanalysis. We picture clinical skill and good scientific work as proceeding hand in hand.

Conclusion

Before proceeding with the discussion of personality theory, let us end this orientation with a brief review of our main points:

1. Psychoanalytic therapy was developed to treat *neurosis.*
2. Neurosis occurs as a limited phenomenon, afflicting an otherwise functional, adequately adjusted individual. It presents as feelings, thoughts, anxieties, or behaviors that the individual feels to be *ego-alien,* but over which she or he has little or no control.
3. The paradox of neurosis involves the perpetuation of an unwanted behavior or of unwanted states of mind or affect.
4. The ego-alien behavior is not unlearned, because there are hidden (i.e., unconscious) reinforcements for that behavior.
5. Psychoanalytic therapy restores adaptive functioning by undoing *repression* and thereby allowing the patient to regain a certain degree of control.
6. Psychoanalysis can be suitable for a broader range of patients than those who experience neuroses.
7. Among the assumptions that underlie the psychoanalytic clinical method are the following propositions: (a) later (including current) mental structures are to be explained by earlier experience; (b) operating within the human personality are psychic continuity, drives, and the unconscious; and (c) access to the unconscious comes through the associative process.
8. The psychoanalyst helps the patient overcome the counterforce of *repression* and understand *transference* through *interpretation.*

9. The psychoanalyst cannot learn the complexities of psychotherapy merely by undergoing therapy himself or herself, but the personal experience of undergoing therapy can be of the greatest value in his or her work.

10. The best psychotherapists take a highly empirical approach to the clinical material presented by patients and do not make interpretations that are not justified by the current material.

Chapter 2

Personality Theory: Framework for Therapy

2 ———————————————————————————————

Psychopathology

We define neurosis as disordered behavior characterized by (a) suffering of the patient, (b) behavior that is maladaptive because of repression, and (c) responses that partially gratify, but do not adequately gratify, the unconscious strivings that are repressed. Suffering is caused by the conflicts that persons with neuroses bear. We intend to remind the reader that the ungratified drives involved in these conflicts cause the patient pain. In speaking of repression we call the reader's attention to the fact that by definition neurotic conflict is an inner conflict. The ordinary suffering of life, brought about by external events, is not to be called neurosis. The hungry peasant in China, the sorrowing man whose father has just died, the worker thrown out of his job by automation—these people are not, by reason of their suffering, afflicted by neuroses. We would say they had neuroses only if an inner conflict had caused their suffering and only if their adaptation to the environment were, because of repression, less satisfactory to them than the circumstances would allow. For the individual experiencing a neurosis, conflict resolution in the form of symptoms is expensive, it costs him or her a great deal. Among the symptoms of neuroses, we count not only physical ailments such as headaches and gastric ulcers (when determined by psychological events) but also such mental and behavioral responses as excessive anxiety, depression, obsessional thoughts, sexual inhibitions, irritability and unreasonable aggression, overdependence, and work inhibitions.

Neurosis involves ineffective behavior that, despite its unsuitability, persists. Whereas the principles of reinforcement and extinction of behavior would lead us to expect that behavior that is maladaptive will be unlearned, the neurotic behavior is not unlearned (see chapter 1).

The Childhood Neurosis

It is our view that every adult affected by neurosis suffered from an *infantile* (early childhood) neurosis during childhood. We picture the structure of this infantile neurosis in this way: An infantile wish, that is, a pregenital sexual wish, was stimulated in the child. It was not possible for the child to get complete gratification of this wish, both because the circumstances would not permit gratification and because the child would have been too frightened at complete gratification; he or she was, at least in part, frustrated. To protect the self against unbearably intense stimulation (either from unsatisfied drive or from the anticipated punitive consequences of gratifying a drive), the child developed a defensive mental system. The defensive system served all of the following purposes: (a) It expressed the infantile wish, (b) it minimized the anxiety bestirred by the wish, and (c) it maintained repression. The repression, of course, is the exclusion from consciousness of the wish; such exclusion is necessary if anxiety is to be held in check, since consciousness of the wish creates a more intense experience of anxiety. Note that in order to accomplish purposes (a) and (b) simultaneously, the defensive system has to be involved in some sort of compromise between opposing tendencies.

Because the child had to be protected against unbearably intense stimulation, a defensive system developed. The defensive system, with its repression of some crucial aspects of the child's struggle to achieve both gratification of drives and safety, imposes a penalty (a cost) on the efficiency of the young child's adaptation to the world, and to herself or himself. Repression entails the blocking of the verbal, secondary-process system of thought. Different, usually less efficient modes of thinking, dominated by primary process, remain. (It might be said, however, that repression is seldom complete; therefore the degree to which the child is forced back on a more archaic mode of thinking will differ among children and will vary from time to time in the same child, depending on which aspects of the child's conflicts are touched on.)

The child is left with a less efficient way of thinking about problems. Handicapped by repression while struggling to solve personal problems, the child blunderingly makes the same kind of mistake over and over. How can the child stop doing this? Secondary-process thought, with its qualities of foresight and flexibility, has been denied him or her. These blind struggles, these repeated attempts to master a conflict that originated in an early-childhood trauma, are said to be evidences of a *repetition compulsion*. A lucid explanation of the importance of such repetitions is presented in Kubie's classic paper, "The Repetitive Core of the Neurosis" (1941).

The Importance of Fantasy

We point out here, because it has such important implications for all of what follows in this book, that the actual events that take place in the child's life are not all that matters. What matters even more is what the child makes of these events, how he or she understands the events and processes them mentally. For brevity, we call this experiencing of what happens *fantasy*, because we want to emphasize that what matters is the inner experience rather than the outer behavior as seen by an observer. Furthermore, the residue of this early experience in the person's later life (the impact of the relationships of the child with his or her parents, for example) cannot provide the therapist with a dependable way of inferring what in fact occurred to the person during childhood. The therapist is in no position to reconstruct reality confidently.

The child's understanding of what is happening to him or her is very likely to be faulty, because the child's conception of action and its consequences is immature. Piaget has shown the limitations in the child's understanding of reality. We know, for example, that the child knows the importance of size before appreciating the significance of value, that the child is disposed to believe that bigger is better. Children believe their parents are better than themselves because parents are bigger. No doubt parents have some advantages from being bigger (greater strength, for example) but it by no means follows that parents are in every way "better." Yet children may believe that that is so.

We would point out, too, that the traumas that the child experiences prove damaging not only because of the amount of excitation that the traumatic stimulation produces, but also because of the dangers that have previously been associatively linked to these stimuli. Thus if one supposes that the child's external environment (the objective facts) provide a sufficient basis for understanding the impact of early relationships on the child's psychological development, one is very mistaken.

Neurosis and Outcome of Conflict

The experiencing in childhood of such an infantile neurosis makes a person more susceptible to the breaking out of neurosis during adult life, because the defensive system is inefficient in giving adequate gratification. Thus in adult life when for any one of a number of reasons the strength of repression is weakened or the strength of the drives is increased, the result will be an adult neurosis. Neurosis, then, is a result of a relative weakening of repression which allows a *return of the repressed.* The symptoms of adult neurosis are (as Waelder pointed out) a compromise between the repressed strivings, now returning after having been unstably repressed, and the defensive forces that hold these strivings in check.

Still, the symptom is not a complete failure of adaptation. It is the best bargain that the individual can make with mental resources limited by repression; the individual tries to gratify the infantile wish while still satisfying defensive forces. It is a compromise between drive and defense. However, we call it a symptom because it is not a very efficient compromise; it offers too little drive-gratification, with too much suffering and too great an expenditure of energy in the conflict between the drives and the inhibiting forces.

Psychoneurosis and character neurosis. When symptoms seem strange to the individual and not in keeping with what is truly wanted, when they cause considerable suffering, they may be spoken of as being *ego-alien.* If, however, the person's symptomatic behavior seems acceptable to him or her, or at any rate seems not to be causing so much suffering that he or she would risk giving up this behavior, these symptoms can be called *ego-syntonic.* Ego-syntonic symptoms may consist of character traits and behavioral dispositions, of the typical ways in which a person relates to other persons; therefore such symptomatic behavior may be less obvious than psychosomatic reactions, depression, or anxiety. The difficulties of persons whose symptoms are ego-syntonic are frequently mostly characterological; and so one speaks of the disorder which these persons exhibit as *character neurosis.*

It makes a great deal of difference whether the individual's symptoms are mainly ego-syntonic or mainly ego-alien; for without motivation to change, the individual is not a good candidate for psychotherapy. Waelder (1960) contends that people are only treatable by insight psychotherapy to the degree that they are psychoneurotic (as opposed to character-neurotic). He asserts that the person with character neurosis can be successfully treated only if there is some remnant of motivation with which one can work, through which one can slowly make the person dissatisfied with these character symptoms. Becoming dissatisfied, the patient then gives up these symptoms and develops ordinary symptoms. In other words, the person turns into a psychoneurotic.

There is, then, an ego-split in the psychoneurotic person, an area of relatively free, relatively adaptive functioning that exists alongside an area of disability and ineffective adaptation. The therapist seeks to ally herself or himself with the adaptively functioning part of the patient's personality.

The cost of neurosis.   Though a symptom is the best attempt at adaptation that the person is able to make, we should still inquire into how costly an adaptation it is. Because (as we have already said) the symptom is an inefficient adaptation, we are not surprised that it fails to be effective in gratifying drive or in defending against drive-expression. When it fails to provide adequate defense, anxiety breaks out; and so, paradoxically, a person who cannot gratify sexual and aggressive drives very well suffers more than most persons from anxiety about gratifying them. This inefficient adaptation denies individuals experiencing a neurosis many of the joys of living that a more normal adaptation would allow. Not only are possible gratifications passed up, but resources are spent in unconscious conflict, which results in all kinds of suffering. Finally, achievements are much less than the individual's talents and opportunities would otherwise make possible; effective use of energies is inhibited.

Understanding the Patient's Behavior

In order to understand the patient's behavior, we make two assumptions: (a) The assumption of psychic *determinism*, and (b) the assumption that *the current neurosis is a new edition of an infantile neurosis*. What does it mean to say, as psychoanalysis does, that all mental life, all behavior, is determined, that we reject coincidence, happenstance, and meaninglessness in mental events? It means more than that we as scientists must assume regularities, and therefore any scientific study of behavior must find lawfulness in its subject matter. Such an assertion would be hardly more than a definition of our field of study and our method. It means less than that every mental event is determined by a prior mental event. For we recognize that pollen as well as psychic stress can lead to sneezing, that cold weather can make one feel cold in the same way that a sense that someone is treating us coldly can make us shiver. No, *psychic determinism* cannot mean either of these two things; rather, as Salmon (1959) has pointed out, this principle is an assertion about the content of what determines mental life. The principle might be stated as follows: When constitutional, bodily mechanisms are insufficient to explain behavior, and at the same time the individual's conscious account of his or her actions is inadequate to explain them, we assert that there must be an unconscious determining process. Applying this assumption to the therapeutic situation, we assert that all behavior in therapy is (a) heuristic, (b) meaningful, and (c) highly specific as communication.

Behavior as Heuristic

We say that behavior of the patient in therapy is heuristic because we find it to be the source of our knowledge about the patient and of the patient's knowledge of self. What we have from the patient's lips is not an unevaluatable, uncheckable report of what happened or what was experienced in another situation; rather, the patient gives us directly, by acting within the therapy, the material that we need to develop knowledge about him or her. We can take hold of the patient's verbal reports and other actions and learn from them, because we are assuming the principle of psychic determinism.

Behavior as Meaningful

The behavior of the patient is meaningful, not accidental, not random. We submit that this statement is a postulate subject to empirical test rather than an unverifiable assumption. If we act in accordance with this postulate in interpreting the patient's behavior, we find that we do come to understand his or her behavior.

If we may use an example from a number of years ago, when society prescribed much more rigidly than it does now how people are expected to dress, we can illustrate the importance of paying close attention to seemingly minor changes in the patient's self-presentation. When, for the first time in a therapy that had been going on for more than two years, a young woman patient wore slacks to the therapy session, the therapist delved into the meaning behind this choice of costume. We do not consider this patient's choice of what to wear to be accidental or meaningless.

As another example, we might consider a patient who had been clean-shaven during the first 3 months of his therapy who appeared, following a 2-week interruption of the therapy for his vacation trip, with the first growth of a beard. His decision to begin at that time to grow a beard cannot be considered accidental. He and the therapist needed to explore how this decision was related to other mental events in the patient's life.

Behavior as Communication

Finally, the patient's behavior is highly specific as communication. To continue with the example cited earlier, the patient's wearing the slacks may be unconsciously intended to tell the therapist, "I feel I'm getting too close to you; I want to draw back. I don't want you to notice me as a woman; I want you to treat me like a brother. I'd be terrified to take a receptive, feminine role toward you, with you as an attacking man. Moreover, I can be just as much a man as you . . . and it's safer to be a man than a woman." Needless to say, we do not know all of these meanings of the patient's behavior all at once; we are asserting only that these meanings are there to be found, that they are expressed in the patient's behavior.

Our assumption that the current neurosis is a new edition of the infantile neurosis means that we look for a specific content in the patient's behavior, that is, that we are guided by certain general hypotheses in formulating for ourselves an explanation of the patient's behavior in the therapy. This assumption implies, first, that the patient's behavior toward the therapist is a repetition, or an attempt at repetition, of emotional relationships experienced with important persons in early childhood, and, second, that the defensive forces that drove the neurotic conflict out of awareness are still active, keeping these conflicts out of consciousness. Thus we find in the therapeutic situation repetitions of emotional relationships that the patient had experienced in childhood (*transference*) and hindrances to the undoing of repression (*resistance*).[1]

---

[1]We have provided only a sketch of the psychoanalytic theory of personality and psychopathology. The reader may want to supplement our discussion by reading such books as C. Brenner's *An Elementary Textbook of Psychoanalysis* (1973), R. Waelder's *Basic Theory of Psychoanalysis* (1960), and O. Fenichel's *The Psychoanalytic Theory of Neurosis* (1945).

Chapter 3

Basic Principles of Psychoanalytic Therapy

3

The Goals of Psychoanalytic Therapy

The person affected by neurosis behaves maladaptively because of repression. It is the aim of psychoanalytic therapy to enable such a person to behave more adaptively, through undoing the repressions. Another way of stating this aim is to say that the aim of therapy is structural change in the personality. As Freud (1933a) put it, "Where id was, there ego shall be" (p. 80). The ego is to be modified, to be enlarged, to be made capable of dealing with conflicts it had formerly repressed. The greater capacity of the ego will be shown in increased mastery of life actions, especially of emotions, in the greater employment of rational thinking (which takes place through the operation of the verbal system), and in increased self-understanding. These changes lead to greater happiness, to more efficient adaptation, and to the abolishing of symptoms.

We acknowledge that there are other ways (besides structural change) by which one could achieve greater happiness, more efficient adaptation, and the removal of symptoms. However, unless these effects come about as a result of structural changes in the personality (which depend, in turn, on an understanding of transference and of resistance) the process should not be called psychoanalytic therapy.

When therapy is successful the patient knows it through the greater satisfactions that are experienced. We recall a woman who out of her great need for care and love always felt starved, who literally expected that her husband would not give her enough money to buy the family groceries for the week, and who felt that her husband's and her children's demands for affection were robbing her of food she needed for herself. As a result of psychotherapy this woman found more direct ways of expressing her wish to be cared for.

After therapy, when she wanted affection from her husband she asked for it, when she wanted his caresses she snuggled up to him, when she wanted his help in putting up some curtain rods she asked him to help, and when she wanted him to take her to the store she asked. Before therapy, such relatively direct and effective means of achieving satisfaction were impossible; after therapy, they replaced the indirect and ineffective techniques she had been using. Describing the situation theoretically, we would say that the patient came to make use of more adaptive derivatives of the basic unconscious conflicts.

The Therapeutic Situation

The goals of the therapy are achieved through a unique relationship between the therapist and the patient. We call this relationship unique because it is different from friendship, from the relationships between husband and wife, parent and child, employer and employee, priest and parishioner, teacher and pupil, or doctor and patient. Though it has something in common with these relationships, it is lacking in the exchange of rewarding actions, in the bread and butter of emotional reciprocity that are found in other human relationships. For psychoanalytic therapy is limited to the task of understanding the patient's living and through this, helping the patient to live more adaptively. Adherence to this aim leads the therapist to create a very special situation, one not lacking in human warmth or emotional exchange, but one that is extremely unusual in the kind of warmth and exchange. At this point we call the reader's attention to this situation's peculiarity; fuller discussion must wait until the chapter on the therapeutic relationship (see chapter 12).

The Therapeutic Process

In this unique situation the suffering caused by neurosis motivates the patient to cooperate with the therapist in achieving the goals of the therapy. The adaptive aspects of mental functioning enable the patient to cooperate. To use a metaphor, we can speak of the cooperation of the healthy portion of the patient's ego. The patient tells about herself or himself, giving conscious cooperation in the achievement of the aim of the therapy.

As this is being done we are surprised to see that the patient often acts in a way that is intended to prevent further self-discovery. We call this opposition to the therapeutic process—an opposition that is mostly unconscious—*resistance*. With a deeper understanding of what the patient is doing, we come to realize that although the patient believes that self-discovery is being prevented, this is not fully achieved, for the patient's actions are also communicative. When resistance arises, the therapist must intervene, calling the patient's attention to the resistance and showing him or her the purposes that it serves. By demonstrating the purpose of the resistance, the therapist makes it possible for the patient to consider whether this defense is still necessary. Such an intervention is called *interpretation*.

We notice, too, that as the patient tries to cooperate, becoming more involved in the therapeutic situation, reactions inappropriate to what the therapist has done and said occur. The patient's actions and feelings earlier in his or her life, toward parents and others, are determining the patient's current actions. What the therapist does may, of course, lend some support to the patient's attitudes, but it is not a sufficient explanation for them. To illustrate: A young woman patient complained that the therapist in pointing out her fear of passivity had "pushed" her in the previous session. As a matter of fact, the therapist could not have been more gentle in the interpretations. But the therapist *had* made interpretations, and the patient was predisposed to respond to any intervention of the therapist as though it was a coercion, because she had been so used to being coerced in childhood. The phenomenon we are describing is called *transference*. It may be noted that transference forms the focus for the most important resistances and that it reveals all of the important unconscious attitudes of the patient.

When all of the vital unconscious conflicts of the patient become focused on the therapist—a result that is brought about gradually in the course of successful therapy—we may speak of a *transference neurosis*. Transference responses occur from the very beginning of therapy, but a transference neurosis does not exist until all of the unconscious conflicts are expressing themselves principally through the transference.

We have said that the aim of psychoanalytic therapy is to enable the patient to behave more adaptively *by undoing repressions*. How are the repressions undone? They are undone by helping the patient to make conscious what has been unconscious. How does the therapist help? Principally, the therapist helps through making interpretations. As we understand the therapeutic process, the patient does not improve because she or he senses the warmth and concern of the therapist and in this warm atmosphere is able to "grow." Rather, the patient is driven by personal suffering to cooperate with the therapist. The therapist instructs the patient to verbalize all thoughts freely—a process which, if carried out fully, is bound to bring about undoing of repressions. But as the patient tries to speak freely, resistances arise. Because of their established relationship and the warm atmosphere of therapy, it is at this point that the therapist dares to make interpretations of resistance.

Thus we picture the interaction of the strong and positive therapeutic relationship and the therapist's work of interpretation as follows: The warm relationship is needed to make the pain of self-discovery bearable for the patient. The warm relationship is the necessary context for the interpretive actions of the therapist, because interpretations necessarily involve some narcissistic affront to the patient; it is as though the therapist had said, "I know something about you that you don't know." We must reserve a full discussion of how the interpretive processes work until the chapter on interpretation (chapter 11).

We do wish, however, to take a few words at this point to comment on the role of historical reconstruction in psychotherapy. We hold that reconstruction of the events in the patient's childhood, divorced from the emotional accompaniments of the patient's experience in these situations and separated from the current expressions of the conflicts that were active in these situations, is of no value. We assert that the therapist should always be dealing with the "current flow of material," with what is preconscious or about to become so (see Fenichel, 1941). As the therapist and patient faithfully stay with the current flow of material, they are inevitably led back to those childhood experiences that are related to current expressions of the same conflicts. As the patient reexperiences the earlier happenings, understanding of these earlier experiences and of current, related experiences is deepened. We commend to the reader the excellent discussion of historical reconstruction by Wetzler (1985).

Finally, what of the choice between strengthening defenses and overcoming repression? As we have said, psychoanalytic therapy works by helping the patient to overcome repressions, unstable repressions which have not worked successfully to hold impulses completely in check but have allowed an indirect expression of impulse, in the form of symptoms. In the disordered adaptation that we call *neurosis* there are three conceivable ways of helping persons afflicted by neurosis to arrive at satisfactory solutions to their conflicts: (a) One can reduce the strength of the drives, (b) one can strengthen defensive forces, and (c) one can undo repression.

The first approach would require the capacity to influence the patient's physiological processes, perhaps through the administration of drugs. Although it is sometimes appropriate and valuable to approach the problem in this way, to do so is not to do psychotherapy, it does not work through psychological methods.

The second approach is, in general, that of suggestive psychotherapies. We would add, however, that suggestive therapies usually contain a mixture of strengthening defenses and giving permission for freer gratification of impulse.

The third approach, undoing the current repression and replacing it by a gratification of the drive or by a more suitable defense, is the approach of psychoanalysis. Undoing the repression will not always lead to gratification of the drive; it is, however, the aim of the analytic therapist to replace the repression by a tolerant acceptance of drive-gratification or by a renunciation that is firm and stable. (See Fenichel, 1941, pp. 15–16, for a discussion of these points.)

What Does the Therapist Do?

So far we have described the patient's activity in the therapy, emphasizing the reasons for cooperation, the inevitable resistance, and the transference. Although we have said that the therapist interprets, we may have left the impression that the therapist is relatively passive. Nothing could be farther from the truth. The effective therapist is intensely active, though this intensity cannot be judged by how much is said.

The therapist does at least the following things: He or she listens to the patient in a special way—with friendly interest, with acceptance and lack of condemnation, and with an active attempt to understand the meaning of the patient's communications. The therapist is alert to communications that express the patient's unconscious wishes and fears. Such communications are indirect because of the anxiety that is attached to unconscious motives. The therapist responds appropriately in a timely fashion to make the patient aware of the patient's communications and of the feeling state that underlies them. All of this demands an intense involvement of the therapist and an active intervention whenever it is appropriate to pose questions, to clarify feelings, to reassure, or to interpret.

Methodological Principles in Psychodynamic Therapy

Our discussion to this point has made clear that there are half a dozen methodological principles underlying psychoanalytic therapy. They can be summarized as follows:

1. The focus of the treatment is the elucidation of unconscious mental activities.
2. Everything that occurs in the therapy situation is psychically determined.
3. Discontinuities between a person's intention and his actions or verbalizations signal the working of unconscious factors.
4. The patient's lifelong repetition of the original conflict, and resolution of the conflict, is expressed in the therapy as transference.
5. Association constitutes the primary, if not the only, means by which the therapist and the patient learn about the hidden, unconscious activities.

6. Interpretation, rather than attachment, is the essential curative factor. Attachment provides the context in which interpretation can be implemented.

The Result of Psychotherapy

When the ego has been restored and extended, the person can get more satisfactions. It is this more adequate satisfaction, including more adequate sexual satisfaction, that basically maintains an adequate adaptive posture. The effects of catharsis or of suggestion are transient, but structural change in the ego brings lasting relief. Structural change brings with it the capacity of the person to deal with new increases in tension and to find ways of either gratifying the drives or renouncing their gratification. Catharsis reduces, in the immediate therapeutic situation, the feeling of guilt associated with the conflict. For a time after a cathartic expression the patient feels better. Then drives build, conflicts reappear in the situations of everyday life, and the patient has no way of dealing with these events because the ego has not been permanently modified.

Similarly, suggestive therapy cannot be expected to have the same kind of long-term effect as a therapy that modifies the ego. Suggestion can be expected to help only to the degree that the new modes of satisfaction adopted by the person responding to the suggestion are a slightly better compromise between impulses and defense than the original symptoms.

Thus we can appreciate that it is not prurience at all that causes psychoanalysts to insist that a satisfying sexual life is an essential of the aimed-for resolution of neurosis. These sexual satisfactions (including affectionate attachments as well as coitus) are what cement together the adaptive behavior and ensure its stability over the long run. It is the existence of these basic satisfactions that makes it possible for a person to work effectively, have creative activities, and show concern for society's welfare. Therefore it matters a great deal to the patient, to the therapist, and to society, whether the patient achieves a satisfying resolution to instinctual conflicts.

Chapter 4

The Initial Interview: Assumptions, Purposes, and Techniques

4

The initial interview provides the therapist with the first opportunity to interact with the prospective patient for more than a few minutes. The encounter in the initial interview will largely determine, for both participants, how they will interact with each other during the rest of the therapy. Therefore we need to look carefully at how the therapist should handle this session.

What the Patient Knows or Imagines
Before the Initial Interview

Although the initial interview begins when the patient comes into the therapist's office, the reactions of the participants to each other began earlier, during the communications that preceded the interview. Consider, for example, a patient who is consulting a therapist in private practice. How did the patient learn of the therapist? Was the patient referred by a professional or by a friend? Did the patient learn about the therapist in some other way, for example, by hearing the therapist give a lecture or by taking a course taught by the therapist? Has the patient inquired about the therapist, and if so, what questions were asked? Were the patient's inquiries focused on the therapist's formal qualifications, or did they take a more personal turn? And what of the responses? Did they describe the therapist accurately and objectively or did they express some bias, favorable or unfavorable? Although the therapist will not be aware of all (or of many) of the answers to these questions, what should be kept in mind is that the patient's demeanor is determined by the information about the therapist acquired earlier.

Even for the patient seen in a clinic, this kind of previously acquired information plays a part in his or her reactions to the therapist. Did an intake worker give the therapist's name to the patient and, if so, how? Did the patient come for the interview after receiving a letter from the therapist and, if so, what was the tone of the letter, what was its wording? How was the therapist described to the patient; as psychotherapist, as staff member, as psychologist, as psychiatrist, as student, or as trainee?

To illustrate how events preceding the initial interview influence it, we will discuss the encounter of a therapist with a patient who had been, some time before the therapy began, a student in a course the therapist taught. During the interview the patient complained that he couldn't find a direction for his life; then he said that he objected to the laissez-faire attitude the therapist had shown as a teacher. The course would have been much better, the patient continued, if there had been more formal lectures and fewer class discussions. The discussions, he felt, got out of hand. As the therapist understood these complaints, the patient was expressing a concern that the therapist would be too laissez-faire in the treatment and would not direct and control the patient's life as the patient wanted him to do. The interactions between therapist and patient that preceded the therapy provided the patient with material for expressing this concern.

When the patient and the therapist talk to each other before the initial interview in order to arrange for the first appointment, this contact provides both of them with material that they can use to make judgments about the other person. The judgments are shaped not only by realistic considerations but also by the participants' unconscious needs. For example, a young man calls the therapist saying that it is urgent that he be seen as soon as possible. When the therapist offers him an appointment within the week, he plaintively asks whether she can't see him sooner. If the therapist then offers the prospective patient an earlier time, this willingness to agree to his request will provide material for certain reactions by the patient. In our example, the therapist does, after considerable study of her appointment book, manage to offer the patient an earlier appointment; when she does, she is amazed to hear him say, "Oh, that's the night I bowl; I can't come then."

The Therapist's Prior Expectations About the Patient

Just as previous information about the therapist shapes the patient's anticipations about the initial interview, so does prior information shape the therapist's expectations. At the very least, the therapist is pleased that a patient has come along; this will enable the therapist to do his or her chosen work. Therapists' responses are shaped by a host of factors, conscious and unconscious: the motives for doing this kind of work (including, perhaps, the need to earn money); their attitude toward themselves and their competence; their status in the institution in which they work and in the professional community; and their knowledge and understanding of the ways in which these factors affect their professional functioning and their responses to patients.

To return to the example of the young man who was planning to go bowling: There are many reactions that the therapist may have to such an utterance of her patient. These reactions are bound to influence the therapist's expectations of how the patient will present himself in the initial interview. We do not decry the therapist's propensity to develop expectations of what the patient will do; these human reactions are an essential ingredient of the work that the therapist does, they are the stuff of which clinical intuition is made. We recommend that the therapist be aware of these reactions and anticipations so that they can be used effectively in clinical work. These reactions and anticipations will not, we hope, become a source of actions that serve only the therapist's needs, not the patient's.

Anxieties About Therapy: An Example

Therapists sometimes have patients ask them in the initial interview, "What is the difference between a psychologist and a psychiatrist?" Usually, it turns out, one should translate this question into, "Do you have the qualifications to help me?" Paradoxically, the question may express a wish that the therapist does not have the qualifications to help, a fear that he or she will help. That fear derives from the patient's expectation that being helped will involve an anguishing experience. Impelled by this fear the patient looks for acceptable ways to avoid getting help; and, of course, it is acceptable to avoid help if one believes that the therapist is not competent. Accordingly, patients seize on the therapist's professional designation— as psychologist, for instance—as a way of expressing such a fear of help. They could just as well choose some other way of expressing the fear.

Assumptions of the Initial Interview

Even though we are confident that each patient comes to the initial interview with a set of conscious and unconscious attitudes toward therapy and the therapist, we know that often we cannot decipher these attitudes very well in that initial interview. We may not be able to do so even in the first several interviews. Because each patient responds in an individual way, we can give no general rules for what one should expect. Nevertheless there are some principles that we can offer that will help the therapist to make sense of the initial encounter.

The First Assumption: The Patient's Distress

Once the patient has made arrangements to meet with the therapist, it is justifiable to assume that this was done because of the psychic distress that the patient is experiencing. Although patients sometimes declare that they have come to therapy out of curiosity or out of a desire to experience first-hand what they have heard their friends talk about or have seen depicted in movies, if the therapist probes deeply enough, more personal and therapeutically relevant reasons for the patient's coming will be found. Our commitment to determinism requires us to assume that a person who comes to a therapist of his or her own free will must need to consult a therapist, even though other reasons for coming are offered.

Internal and external sources of distress.   The patient may not come to the therapy because self-dissatisfaction is experienced. Rather, the patient may come because of the distress of uncontrollable, external pressures; this distress is attributed wholly to what is external and no personal responsibility for the disturbing events is felt. The patient is self-presented as helpless (i.e., like a child who comes to the parent to have a splinter removed from a finger). Just as the child may not feel that he or she had anything to do with the splinter's getting in the finger in the first place, so the patient may not feel any responsibility for his or her distress.

The kinds of external pressure that patients experience are myriad. We give two examples of patients who defined their problems in terms of external pressures. The first example involves a man of 32 who came to a firm of personnel consultants to have his abilities and his career plans evaluated. He said that he wanted to speed up his advancement in his career, even though he had already been reasonably successful. When the personnel consultants gave him a battery of tests they discovered evidence for a rather severe psychological disturbance. In the lengthy counseling that followed the testing, the consultants told their client that they had found this evidence of a serious problem, and they recommended that he get psychotherapy. Despite the efforts that the personnel consultants had made to inform the patient about his disturbance, the patient presented himself in the initial interview as bewildered about why he should be seeing a psychotherapist. He said that he had come only because the personnel consultants had made a referral; he asserted that he was satisfied with his life, except for his mild unhappiness with how slowly his career was advancing. He maintained that he would never have considered psychotherapy if therapy had not been urgently recommended to him by his career consultant. Because it had been, however, he professed to be willing to do whatever was necessary "to remedy my defects."

Another man, 32 years old, was brought to the initial interview by his wife, who had called to make the appointment. The wife, who was seen separately, reported behavior by her husband that seemed to indicate that he sorely needed treatment. When the therapist talked to the husband, however, this man reported that he had come only because his wife had insisted on it; she had threatened to leave him if he did not come. He was interested in entering treatment only because doing so would satisfy his wife. He insisted, moreover, that he felt no need of help; he had no confidence whatsoever in the ability of a psychotherapist to provide help.

In presenting these examples we have sidestepped the question of whether the therapist had the impression that these prospective patients were seriously disturbed and could profit from therapy. We neglected this point in order to emphasize the fact that the patients' professed motives for getting therapy were not necessarily related to the reality of their psychological situation. Therefore these motives have to be evaluated separately. We are sure that every reader of this book knows many persons who, in his or her opinion, realistically need and would benefit from psychotherapy. Yet the conviction of another that a person needs psychotherapy is never so important as the patient's feeling within herself or himself that help is needed.

We do not intend to suggest that a patient who comes to therapy professing that external pressures were the reason for needing therapy, is therefore an unsuitable candidate for treatment. Exploration beyond the initial interview will often show that the patient is willing and able to participate effectively in the psychotherapy, even though the patient was initially unaware of unhappiness with any area of his or her functioning. The man in the first example entered therapy on a trial basis. By the eighth interview he was deeply involved in the therapy and committed to the treatment process. The patient of the second example, however, never became an active participant in the therapy, although he stayed in therapy for some months. His fear of what the treatment might bring made him unable to participate in it. The fear found expression in various ways. For example, he involved himself in avoidable automobile accidents as a way of preventing himself from coming to therapy sessions and as a way of saying, in action, "Psychotherapy is as dangerous as an automobile accident."

Most psychotherapists would describe the ideal patient as one who seeks psychotherapy because he or she is frightened, distressed, and wants help for some disturbing feeling or behavior that is producing unhappiness. Sometimes the disturbance has produced a specific symptom that distresses the patient. More often, the patient professes unhappiness about some more or less vague disturbances in daily life (e.g., the inability to function effectively in school, on the job, or in the marriage relationship). A frequently heard complaint is, "I just can't seem to do what I have to do (or want to do)."

Without deciding whether the unhappy patient that therapists prefer is indeed the ideal patient, we draw the reader's attention to the assumption we set out previously: There is some reason for the patient's coming, whether he or she is aware of it or not. The therapist can get clues from the initial interview about the kinds of internal pressures that the patient is experiencing. Such information provides a starting point for the therapy.

The Second Assumption: The Patient's Goals

We assume that, speaking broadly, patients come to therapy seeking relief from their distress. They hope that psychotherapy will somehow remove the cause of their distress (i.e., that external pressures on them will be made to disappear or that symptoms and life dissatisfactions will be lessened or removed). The expectations of patients about what therapy will achieve are usually colored by their previous experiences with the healing professions. When seen by the family doctor, the patient expects the physician to assume total responsibility for providing the help. Accordingly, the patient is likely in the psychotherapy situation to initially expect that the therapist will provide a prescription for changing his or her life or those aspects of life about which he or she is unhappy.

Less often, patients coming for therapy are already able to verbalize their goal of attaining greater understanding of themselves or are able to embrace an aim that indicates a sophisticated concept of psychotherapy. The patients who do this frequently have been in psychotherapy before or have read about psychotherapy or taken psychology courses. The therapist is inclined to be impressed with this apparent understanding of the purposes of therapy. A course of treatment closely paralleling his or her theoretical ideal of how therapy ought to proceed is envisioned. Such expectations are rarely, if ever, fulfilled. That a patient seems to have a good deal of knowledge about psychotherapeutic processes and goals is no guarantee that intellectual comprehension is accompanied by an understanding of what it means, emotionally, to "understand oneself." On the contrary, it is more likely that this sort of patient has used this intellectual understanding as a defense against the anxiety that would be experienced were he or she truly aware of the specific feelings that underlie the current difficulties.

The therapist must be aware, therefore, that no matter how winningly the patient states goals for the therapy, no matter how intent he or she seems on getting help, no matter how sophisticated a front is put forth, the patient's formulations are always at least partly a consequence of the defenses that the patient finds necessary. These defenses stem from the emotional conflict that needs resolution and from the patient's concerns about entering therapy.

The authors have never encountered a patient who did not manifest anxiety, early in the therapy, about what might occur during the treatment. This anxiety usually is first detected through the analysis of some manifestation of resistance. For example, a patient may speak of the experience of a friend who became worse in therapy rather than better. In that way the patient expressed the concern of being harmed.

It follows from our conceptualization of the dynamic processes at work in emotional problems that such resistance and anxiety are to be expected. The assumption that behavioral and emotional difficulties stem from the patient's attempt to maintain certain conflicts in repression leads us to believe that even though this attempt may produce an inadequate adaptation, the patient prefers the result to the experiencing of anxiety that would occur if the repressed material entered consciousness. The patient must therefore resist any endeavor to lessen the repression and to facilitate admitting to awareness thoughts and feelings related to the conflict. The patient will have to resist even though he or she is trying to fulfill his or her responsibilities in the therapy—trying to be a "good" patient. Unconsciously the patient considers the therapist an enemy—the advocate of the repressed material. For this reason we find the analysis of resistance playing a dominant role in the therapeutic process.

Purposes of the Initial Interview

Each patient, then, comes to a psychotherapist because he or she wants help with some distressing internal or external situation that is causing some disruption in his or her life. One purpose of the initial interview is to enable the therapist to determine whether through therapy such help can be provided.

A first step in arriving at a judgment about whether therapy can help involves considering how appropriate to psychotherapy the problem that the patient presents is. Sometimes the professionals who make referrals misunderstand the purposes and the limitations of psychotherapy; as a result, they make inappropriate referrals. It is up to the therapist to find out, in the initial interview, whether the problem is one suited to psychotherapy.

We illustrate the necessity for such a judgment with the case of a 20-year-old woman who came to the initial interview complaining that after 2 years of college work she found herself dissatisfied with her grades and her progress. During the interview she revealed that she did poorly in those courses where the subject matter did not interest her. She said that she had not chosen a major and she could not make plans for a postcollege career because she could not find out what the educational requirements were for the several possible careers that she was interested in. A friend of her family, a pathologist, had referred her to the psychotherapist; the pathologist viewed this woman's problems as being the kind that are sometimes helped by psychologists. The referrer did not make any distinction between a "psychologist" and a "psychotherapist," possibly because of the common confusion about the activities and functions of the various professions whose titles include the prefix "psych."

Because the interviewer believed that this young woman's problems could best be dealt with by a vocational counselor, the patient was referred to the counseling service of the university she was attending. To be sure, the psychotherapist could have explored at some length the reasons for this woman's neglecting to make important life decisions. It would be reasonable to consider the neglect to be symptomatic of an emotional conflict. The more cautious conclusion, however, is that she was in trouble because of naivete and lack of specific information. That hypothesis should be tested before one encourages this woman to spend the time, effort, and money needed for psychotherapy.

We cannot stress too much the importance of an accurate, realistic determination of how appropriate for psychotherapy the problem presented by the patient is. Commitment to arriving at an honest judgment on this matter may, of course, be difficult when it is so fashionable nowadays to view all behavior as being determined by underlying psychological dynamics and to leap to the conclusion that because all behavior has unconscious determinants, behavioral difficulties are therefore always best dealt with by exploring and uncovering unconscious processes. By this reasoning one would believe psychotherapy to be the treatment of choice for a bewildering variety of human ills, ranging from reading difficulties through spontaneous abortions of pregnancy to a wavering religious belief. The trend to prescribe psychotherapy for every problem is pervasive. It is strengthened by the greater psychological sophistication of more and more people. Nevertheless, the therapist has a responsibility to reject the popular view that for every human problem "it's all in your head," and focus instead on arriving at a truthful answer—for the benefit of the patient and the therapist—to the question of whether psychotherapy can be of help to the person being interviewed.[1]

Importance of the Therapist's Skill

In deciding who is appropriate for therapy one must take into account the competence and experience of the therapist. No problem is appropriate for psychotherapy if the therapist lacks sufficient skill or experience pertinent to that patient and to the condition to be treated. We can define certain broad areas of training, skill, and experience that tell us whether the therapist is competent for the work at hand. For example, the professional who is trained only to work with children cannot appropriately be considered anything more than a novice in doing therapy with adults. It follows that the evaluation of the appropriateness of the problem must include a modest, realistic evaluation by the therapist of his or her own competency in the specific situation.

In deciding whether to recommend psychotherapy for a patient, the therapist must be able to answer two questions affirmatively: "Is this patient presenting a problem that, in my judgment, is best helped by psychotherapy?" and "Do I have the competence to provide adequately the psychotherapy I recommend?" It is to be

---

[1]It is neither feasible nor appropriate here to list the conditions that have been reported in the literature to have been helped substantially by psychotherapy. The kinds of problems helped by psychotherapy are no doubt as varied as the kinds of human beings in the world. Not wanting, however, to leave the reader without any guidance, we call the reader's attention to the recommendations of D. Malan (1979) about which patients can be expected to do well in the kind of brief psychotherapy practiced at the Tavistock Clinic, to L. Luborsky's summary (1984, pp. 54–57) of what we know about selecting patients for psychoanalytic therapy, and to H. Davanloo's statement (1978b, pp. 9–34) on how to select patients for short-term dynamic psychotherapy. We are, however, not entirely satisfied with the conclusions these authors have reached. For example, Malan would exclude deeply depressed patients, especially those who have intense oral needs. It is true that his brief therapy seems inappropriate for them; yet they might do well in a long-term therapy, if that is available. Most experts advise against working with psychotic patients, at least against working with them interpretively; yet our experience, and that of Karon (see Karon and VandenBos, 1981), is that at times one can do highly effective interpretive therapy with persons suffering from schizophrenia.

hoped that whatever answers the therapist gives to these questions are unbiased by personal needs, by financial considerations, or by caseload size.

The Distress of the Patient

Besides deciding whether the patient's problem is suited to psychotherapy, the interviewer needs to appraise how much distress the patient is experiencing. Here we are not concerned with what kind of distress there is but with how much. How much the patient wants treatment matters more than why it is wanted. Many studies have shown that the majority of patients who begin psychotherapy stay for fewer than 10 sessions. Would the record be so dismal if clinicians were more selective in whom they accepted? Experienced clinicians know that many patients seem to want therapy at first but lack the ability to persevere in the work; apparently these patients find the distress from their psychological disturbance more tolerable than the stress of psychotherapeutic work. Because abortive therapeutic attempts waste the patient's money and time and the therapist's time, if we could reduce the number of such foreshortened cases by insisting on strong motivation in any patient who is accepted, we should do so.

To make an accurate judgment of the patient's distress (and, one infers, motivation for treatment) we need to consider both the patient's psychological state and behavior patterns in real-life situations. We need to notice how much anxiety is shown in the initial interview, how aware the patient is of this anxiety, and how unhappy he or she is. Rather than relying on the patient's judgment about how much distress is being experienced (because unhappiness may be denied even in the face of all kinds of indirect evidence) we should pay attention to what kind of realistic sacrifices the patient is willing to make in order to get therapy. Clues to factors that will motivate the patient to make these sacrifices come from statements about the price that is being paid in decreased effectiveness as a result of neurotic adaptations; the length of time that the symptoms have been put up with and the patient's reasons for tolerating them; and the efforts that have been made to get help and the reasons for the failure of these attempts. All of these may be considered behavioral indices of the distress that the patient may not be able to declare verbally in the initial interview but which nevertheless is present and is serving to motivate cooperation.

As the therapist assesses motivation for treatment, the therapist must take into account not only the forces leading to cooperation but also those supporting avoidance of treatment. The person who says, "I need and want help, but . . ." is well known; we should not view such a person as one who really lacks motivation for therapy while giving lip service to it. Rather, the therapist has the more complex task of evaluating the motivation toward, and the avoidance of, therapy. We find these conflicting elements in every patient. Thus we ask: Granting the patient's distress and the desire for help, to what degree will contrary motivations influence, inhibit, or prevent treatment?

An illustrative case may clarify this point. A 29-year-old man consulted a psychotherapist for help with his impotence, a condition that he said had existed for 6 years. The patient reported that because numerous medical consultations had proved to be of no benefit, he came to the conclusion that his symptom must have its origin in some psychological disturbance. He described himself as unhappy, miserable, and frightened about his impotence; he said that he desperately wanted to do something about it. Because further discussion confirmed the genuineness of his distress and because he seemed a suitable candidate for psychotherapy, the interviewer recommended psychotherapy to him. Upon hearing the recommendation the patient pondered it briefly, then asked about alternatives. First, he asked the interviewer's opinion about tranquilizers; he wondered whether his impotence might not be dealt with by his taking a tranquilizer before attempting intercourse. Second, he inquired about hypnotic suggestion. It was then clear to the interviewer that, notwithstanding the patient's desire for help, the patient was trying to avoid psychotherapy. When the therapist raised this issue the patient said that he was avoiding therapy because one could not tell how long it would take to be effective; but he did acknowledge that he had doubts whether he wanted to explore his emotional life. The interviewer then suggested that the patient think over the recommendation and call the therapist back if he decided to try psychotherapy.

In this case the interviewer made the judgment that the patient's anxiety about treatment (and about all that treatment implied) outweighed his genuine desire for help. To put it more bluntly, the therapist believed that the patient was at that time too frightened to undertake therapy, even though the patient needed it. To be sure, the interviewer may have been mistaken in this judgment; it may well be that further interviews would have helped the patient to come to terms with his anxiety, enabling him to participate effectively in therapy. There are no absolute criteria, no hard-and-fast guidelines. Yet the therapist has to make a decision one way or the other.

Psychodynamic Assessment of the Patient

During the initial interview, the therapist needs to assess the psychodynamic functioning of the patient. Although all of the therapy (if it follows psychoanalytic principles) constitutes a continuing evaluation of psychodynamics, the focus here is on those dynamic processes relevant to deciding whether the patient should have therapy and, if so, how the therapist should begin the therapy. It is not necessary at this point—or desirable—for the therapist to attempt a complete dynamic formulation of the case. Obviously, that is impossible. Rather, the focus should be on evaluating those factors relevant to the evaluation *for* therapy. We list now some of the more important aspects of the patient's psychic life that need to be evaluated (but this is not an exhaustive list of such aspects).

In the last analysis, treatment by psychoanalytic principles relies on the patient to treat himself or herself with the assistance of the therapist. The patient must *experience* in the therapy, and at the same time come to observe this experiencing. We are describing, of course, what has been called "a therapeutic ego-split." The patient has to be capable of such a separation of function, or of such an oscillation between the two attitudes of the ego. Thus in evaluating the patient the interviewer asks, "Does this person have enough ego-strength for the work of psychotherapy?"

In arriving at the answer to the question the therapist would want to consider such factors as (a) the nature of the patient's relation to reality, including the adequacy of reality-testing; (b) the quantity and quality of the patient's control over his or her instinctual impulses; (c) the manner in which the patient relates to the therapist, and the implications of this for the quality of the patient's object relations; and (d) the degree of ego and instinctual regression that can be inferred from the symptoms manifested and the manner in which the patient lives his or her life. On the basis of the answers that the therapist gives to these questions about the patient's ego-strength, well-reasoned, practical decisions regarding how to handle the therapy can be made. The therapist has other judgments to make, beyond the basic one of whether to accept the patient for therapy; there have to be decisions about how frequently to see the patient, about whether to use the chair or the couch, and about the manner and timing of interpretations.

In the initial interview the therapist will, of course, find out about matters besides the patient's ego-strength, for example, the level of fixation in psychosexual development, and intrasystemic and intersystemic conflicts. The therapist is glad to know these things but does not need to consider them in detail in order to decide whether the patient is suited for psychotherapy. Saul (1958) recommended that the therapist, early in the therapy, obtain a systematic, dynamically oriented history; this history would include information about first dreams and earliest memories. Our experience makes us feel that getting such a history overstructures the interview, causing the patient to learn to expect that throughout the therapy the therapist will provide the focus for what is talked about. We recommend that the therapist be alert in the initial interview primarily to psychodynamics bearing on evaluating the patient for treatment. Other dynamics should not be probed; if other information comes out, this should be filed away for future reference when it is needed.

Evaluating the Patient's Ability to Work in Therapy

In order for psychoanalytic therapy to occur, the patient must do three things: come, talk, and understand. In judging the patient's suitability for therapy, the therapist considers the patient's ability to do these things. We have already written about how to judge whether the patient will come; here we focus on the patient's verbal and conceptual abilities.

Psychoanalytic therapy makes a fundamental demand on the patient: "Say what comes to mind." This demand—known as the "basic rule," "the main rule of psychoanalysis" (Freud, 1910a, p. 33), or "the fundamental rule of psychoanalysis" (Freud, 1912, p. 107)—requires that the patient, as completely as possible, report aloud every element that enters into consciousness. Thus to do therapy the patient must have the ability to adhere to this, at least minimally; if his or her verbal skills stand in the way of doing it, the therapist will not be able to assume that departures from the rule express resistance. When the therapist has reason to doubt the patient's ability to put the content of consciousness into words, the therapist will be frustrated by the lack of success achieved in attempting to understand the patient's silences, hesitations in speech, and choice of words.

Nor is the problem of understanding resistance the only difficulty when a patient cannot readily verbalize thoughts. It is only through the verbal communication of associations, fantasies, dreams, or images that the patient can provide the therapist—and himself or herself—clues to the unconscious determinants of psychic functioning. As significant as nonverbal communication is, it cannot serve as more than an adjunct to verbal communication.

For these reasons it is essential for the therapist to assess the ability of the patient to communicate verbally. The best indication of the patient's verbal ability is provided by the responses given in the interview. The therapist should want to know: How does the patient respond to my comments? Do reactions to my observations, comments, or questions demonstrate the patient's ability to transmute conscious thoughts into spoken utterances?

Some writers have argued that psychotherapy based on free association can be used only with verbally skilled persons. The present writers believe, however, that most persons possess the needed verbal ability for therapy to some degree. As a practical matter, of course, it may be too costly for a person who has great trouble expressing herself or himself in words to engage in psychoanalytic therapy; it will simply take too long to do the therapy.

Every therapist has encountered some patients who, after describing their psychic difficulties in the initial interview, lapse into silence, apparently unable to give further expression to their thoughts. For many such patients one can reasonably conclude that anxiety makes their silence necessary. For some of them, however, the exercise of speaking thoughts aloud is so alien to them, they are so unused to doing it, that it will take a long time for them to learn to speak their thoughts fluently. Thus the patient's lapsing into silence compels the therapist to decide (a) whether the communication difficulty stems from anxiety or from lack of practice and, when it stems from lack of practice, (b) whether it is advisable to accept the patient for this kind of therapy that requires a greater level of verbal skill than is now possessed, or instead recommend a kind of therapy that demands less skill in verbalization.

Ability to conceptualize, a related but not identical skill, is also required of the patient who participates in psychoanalytic therapy. Because this kind of therapy focuses on the dynamics of the patient's inner life, the patient and the therapist together must consider how the inner processes find expression in the patient's verbalizations. When the therapist makes comments and interpretations, basing these on assumptions about determinism, metaphoric communication, defense, resistance, and the like, the patient may find these responses to his or her verbalizations strange and new. For example, a patient, early in treatment, complained bitterly that she was getting nowhere in the therapeutic work. The therapist pointed out (appropriately, we believe) that the complaint probably expressed a *wish* of the patient that she would get nowhere. The therapist explained that if the patient could count on getting nowhere, her fear of the consequences of achieving something in the therapy (e.g., exploring frightening feelings) would be greatly reduced. To understand concepts like this—in which the therapist, as one patient put it, "twists things around in odd ways"—requires not only that the patient be emotionally free to think, but also have the substantial ability to conceptualize.

In order to make a judgment about the patient's ability to conceptualize, the therapist can in the initial interview make some trial interpretations. These are interpretations that deal with rather obvious dynamics evident in the patient's verbalizations. When the therapist makes such minimal interpretations, the patient gets a sample of therapeutic work (and proof that the therapist understands), and the therapist has a chance to see how the patient responds to interpretations.

Diagnostic Impressions

Another purpose of the first interview is the development of diagnostic impressions. The reader should be warned that by "diagnosis" we do not intend a description of the patient's symptoms (the definition of diagnosis in the *DSM-III-R*) but an elucidation of current dynamics and of etiology. We are too well aware of the meager guidance for therapeutic decisions provided by the classification schemes.

At the same time, we do not subscribe to the outright rejection of all diagnosis that some writers, especially those adhering to client-centered therapy, advocate. These writers have argued that diagnosis is of dubious value, if not in fact harmful. They have emphasized that each person is unique. They believe that the therapist's putting the patient into one or another category hinders his or her sensitivity to the unique processes at work in the patient and blinds him or her to the idiosyncratic way that the patient expresses personal needs and fears. If these concerns about diagnosis were justified, we too would oppose it. We believe, however, that diagnosis need not be a static pigeonholing of a patient, that it can be a broad, summary statement of psychodynamic status. From such a summarization one can derive working hypotheses about this unique patient.

For example, let us assume that we have given a patient the working diagnosis *depressive neurosis*. If this term only summarized a collection of symptoms, the effort of arriving at the diagnosis would be fruitless. Furthermore, if assigning this label to the patient results in the therapist's making inappropriate, incorrect interpretations concerning, say, "incorporation of an ambivalent object," we would have grave reservations about the value of diagnosing. If, on the contrary, such a diagnosis enables the therapist to make use of his or her knowledge of depression and depressive persons to come to some greater understanding of this particular patient and of this patient's particular dynamics, then diagnosing is worthwhile.

We illustrate this by citing a 40-year-old man who, as the therapist observed him in the initial interview, was unquestionably clinically depressed. In subsequent interviews early in the therapy, he continued to be depressed. He complained bitterly that he was punishing the members of his family by being utterly inadequate as a father and a husband. To support this assertion he cited numerous instances of how he had (he said) caused his son to become a mixed-up kid; he had reacted with exaggerated anger to minor infractions of family rules by the son. The therapist, instead of waiting for the patient to provide clues about what was overdetermining these associations, could immediately form hypotheses about the dynamics of the behavior that the patient was describing and about his inclination to blame himself. The therapist knew that depressive reactions often derive from a person's attempt to deal with the feelings provoked by separations from someone with whom the person has had a close tie. Making use of this knowledge, framing the hypothesis that such a process had occurred in this patient's living, materially helped the therapist to understand the associations that the patient presented. It also helped the therapist to understand the quality of the developing transference and to be sensitive to the way this patient dealt with anxiety about closeness to others. It enabled the therapist to speculate about the structure of the infantile neurosis, even though confirming (or disconfirming) information could only be gotten later. Finally, when the therapist allowed the interpretations of the patient's current emotional responses to be guided by this hypothesis (as well as by the therapist's intuitive responses to the patient), the interpretations resulted in the patient's disparaging himself much less and getting along much better with his family. It also had the result that the patient produced associations that confirmed and elaborated the hypothesis.

Thus we believe that making a working diagnosis and using it flexibly and creatively (not neglecting the specific, idiosyncratic facts about the patient) considerably aids the work of the therapy. Of course, sometimes the therapist has no choice about making a diagnosis, it is a requirement of the clinic in which he or she works. Furthermore, honesty requires the clinician to admit that many clinical judgments are implicitly diagnoses, whether or not explicit labels are used. We are diagnosing when we make such judgments as "I believe this patient cannot tolerate the abstinence required by psychoanalytic therapy" or "This person deals with anxiety by discharging it through impulsive actions." We conclude that couching clinical, pragmatic decisions in terms of diagnostic labels is justified if the therapist finds it congenial to think this way.

In some cases, the therapist may want to have a formal psychological assessment or a physical examination of the patient. When this information is desired, the following questions arise: Who should do the assessment or the physical examination? Should every aspect of the results be communicated to the patient? Are such evaluations necessary? Taking the last issue first, we would raise the question whether the information obtained in such evaluations is relevant to the therapy. For example, when one uses information obtained from psychological testing, one is, we believe, working on assumptions that directly contradict the basis of psychoanalytic therapy. In psychoanalytic therapy one's basic position is: The material of the therapy is what the patient presents to the therapist in the therapy session. The patient and the therapist *together* have to explore and attempt to understand the meaning of this material, in the course of the treatment. To introduce into this situation material that has not been derived from the patient's verbalizations in the therapy but has come, instead, from arcane, extratherapeutic procedures, the results of which came first to the therapist, creates a great risk of reinforcing the patient's resistance-determined view that the treatment is a situation in which the therapist will read his or her mind and then deliver authoritative pronouncements. These pronouncements will, the patient hopes, cause self-understanding and provide advice about how life should be lived. Such resistance-determined perceptions are already too prevalent among our patients; we don't want to make them flourish even more by introducing a procedure that can be understood as confirming these expectations.

Yet there is the vexing question, "How much of what I know should I tell my patient?" The therapist, throughout the therapy knows more about a patient than is communicated in comments and interpretations. Indeed, the patient pays the therapist not only for knowing what to say but also for knowing what not to say. We cannot here enter into the broader question of when to say what one knows and when not to. Although this problem applies equally to communicating in therapy and communicating the results of testing, the therapeutic situation is sharply different in one regard: All of the information that the therapist has comes from what the patient has said or done in the therapy (at least, all of the information that the psychoanalytic therapist believes should be used), it does not come from sources unknown to the patient. When ready, the patient can come upon this same information through the same processes of inference and the same raw material that the therapist used. The patient need not rely on information imparted by the therapist. This strategy has great advantages. For example, it is immeasurably more meaningful to the patient for him or her to experience anxiety and label it as anxiety, rather than reaching the conclusion that she or he must be anxious because the test scores relayed by the therapist show the presence of anxiety.

Having the patient tested may create other problems as well. Knowing about the patient through a test report may hinder rather than help the therapist in the therapeutic work. Although a test report sometimes provides a broad, amazingly accurate picture of the psychodynamic patterns of the patient's current functioning, the tests do not enable one to predict the specifics of behavior, the minute-by-minute or hour-by-hour reactions of the patient in the therapy. To make that kind of prediction, the therapist has to be dedicated, alert, willing to use herself or himself as an instrument. The therapist's skills in making such specific, detailed predictions may degenerate if the therapist assumes, with false security, that the information provided through testing can substitute for what can be learned from the patient in the therapeutic interaction.

We would take a similar position about physical examinations. Let us suppose that a patient comes to the initial interview with symptoms that involve bodily functions, symptoms that may be produced by physical illness. Is it any psychotherapist's responsibility (whether the psychotherapist is a psychiatrist, a psychologist, a social worker, or some other professional) to diagnose or to get diagnosed the physical disorders of a patient? Psychotherapy is concerned solely with psychological events; the patient's physical condition, like all the other aspects of the patient's reality, is entirely his or her own responsibility. If he or she has a legal or an economic problem, it is the patient's responsibility to deal with it. That is true as well, we argue, for physical health problems. (For protection against lawsuits, however, the therapist should document *in writing* that the patient was urged to consult a physician.)

Thus we argue that the therapist's responsibility to a patient in regard to the patient's physical welfare is discharged through asking whether the patient has consulted a physician and, if so, what conclusions the physician arrived at. From the patient's report of the medical opinions he or she has been given, the therapist may conclude that the patient's problem is not amenable to psychological intervention. If so, the therapist should recommend against psychotherapy. If both physical and psychological causes are involved in the patient's problem, the therapist may judge that the physical factors so greatly outweigh the psychological ones that psychotherapy is best postponed until the physical problems have been dealt with. Even if important physical causes for the patient's suffering exist, there are times when the therapist will believe that psychotherapy is needed and will be useful nevertheless. When the patient has not sought medical advice, yet it is obvious that this needs to be done, the therapist should deal with the psychological reasons for the patient's evasion of this responsibility to himself or herself.

We do not embrace a mind–body dualism. Our recommending a division of labor between psychotherapist and medical diagnostician stems from our view that psychotherapy, when done properly, focuses only on psychological events, including those physical events that can be defined as and considered as psychological. To clarify our meaning: A broken leg in itself cannot be considered to be a psychological event (although the way in which it occurred and the patient's reaction to the injury may be considered relevant to psychology); on the other hand, the physical fatigue that a patient experiences when struggling to maintain repression is just such a psychological event.

We have presented a rather strict view of what belongs in psychotherapy and what does not. We recognize that there are occasions when one cannot reasonably follow these strict rules. For example, the policy of a hospital or a clinic may be that all patients have to have physical examinations. A therapist working in that institution may therefore have to see to it that a patient has the examination; the therapist should, if at all possible, avoid doing the examination herself or himself. This personal involvement needs to be avoided in order to keep the therapeutic relationship uncompromised (i.e., as free as possible of any reality that could confirm the patient's view that the therapist is a doer, giver, examiner, magician, or healer). In keeping with our viewpoint, we recommend that the therapist report the results of any such physical examination to the patient as soon as and as fully as possible. This must be done in order to develop and maintain, in the relationship with the patient, an atmosphere that encourages mutual trust, and to exclude the view that the therapist is omniscient, that he or she has secrets about the patient.

Importance of Reality Circumstances

The therapist also needs to evaluate the realistic circumstances of the patient and of the therapist, as these bear on the practicality and the expected effectiveness of therapy. To illustrate, we cite two women, each of whom came to an initial interview seeking help for psychological disturbances, each of whom had had psychotherapy appropriately recommended to her. Each decided to consider the recommendation and to discuss the recommendation with her husband and to tell the therapist, at the next session, whether she would come for therapy. The first patient reported that her husband had concurred in her decision to have therapy, had agreed to make the needed money for therapy fees available, volunteered to baby-sit when his wife had an appointment, and had, in general, encouraged and supported his wife in her decision to participate in treatment. The other woman reported just the opposite reaction from her husband. She said that although she wanted very much to undertake the recommended therapy, her husband vehemently and adamantly opposed her participating in any way. He refused to allow any part of their funds to be spent for this purpose, he assured her that solving her problems was simply a matter of willpower, he complained that she had not tried hard enough to master her difficulties, and he threatened her with dire consequences should she pursue treatment against his wishes. Despite his threats the patient seriously considered undertaking psychotherapy and keeping it secret from her husband.[2]

---

[2]In describing these interactions between wives and husbands we are, of course, not advocating that a married woman should give up her autonomy and allow her husband to decide whether she should have therapy. Quite the contrary: We believe that a healthy marriage relationship would involve appropriate autonomy for the wife.

Assuming that these women gave accurate accounts of how their husbands reacted to the idea of psychotherapy, it is clear that serious difficulties would arise should the second woman try to get psychotherapy. Not only would her husband's position be a practical obstacle to her pursuing therapy, but his opposition would provide a ready-made nucleus around which resistances could crystallize. Because of the husband's opposition, these resistances might be uninterpretable. This woman would then be able to assert that her distress was produced by her having to live with a vicious husband, and this belief would be a more comforting belief than the proposition that one makes one's own neurotic distress.

In the initial interview the therapist makes an assessment of whether the patient's reality is favorable for therapy. When he or she can, the therapist does what can be done to adapt to temporary circumstances that may interfere with the patient's getting therapy. Where the interfering circumstances are not temporary, it would be more appropriate for the therapist to recommend that the patient not enter into therapy until her or his reality has been altered sufficiently as to not interfere with therapy.

When the therapist considers the alternative of compromising with realities of the patient's life, he or she is obligated to make sure that he or she is not compromising with the patient's neurosis. In the example of the woman with the husband who is hostile to therapy, the patient is not helped if the therapist agrees to a fee that is set too low in order for her to conceal the therapy from her husband. Adult patients should be expected to deal with problems such as the opposition of a mate to one's therapy in a more realistic way, notwithstanding the adult's neurosis. If the patient cannot work out a realistic adaptation to the reality circumstances, the therapist should seriously question whether that patient meets the requirements for psychoanalytic therapy.

Other Purposes of the Initial Interview

Another, equally important purpose of the initial interview is to give the patient an opportunity to evaluate the therapist. Both objective and subjective factors enter into this evaluation. The patient may inquire about the therapist's training and experience. It is clearly realistic for the therapist simply to answer his or her questions; it would be ridiculous for the therapist to consider such inquiries as evidence for resistance. The patient, in considering whether to buy therapy from the therapist, has the right to consider the therapist's ability to provide it, in so far as this can be judged from the therapist's certifications, training, and experience.

Even when the patient finds no fault with the therapist's credentials he or she may, for reasons that even he or she may not understand, dislike the therapist so much that meeting with the therapist frequently and regularly would be intolerable. The therapist cannot analyze such a reaction because the patient has not yet agreed to analytic work. Thus interpretations of resistance in the initial interview, before the patient and therapist have entered into a contract to do therapy, are unwarranted. (Some interpretations [not of resistance] may be justified for the purpose of building motivation for therapy, as we discuss in chapter 6).

The patient not only assesses the therapist, but also the therapy. He or she observes how easy or how hard talking to another human being about matters that are quite private is and reacts to the explicit purposes of therapy, namely, the uncovering of feelings and wishes. Because of the anxiety that is attached to these hidden contents, the patient has previously tried to keep them hidden from herself or himself and from others. Faced with the task of exposing these contents, the patient may decide that the anticipated distress far outweighs any benefits that may obtain from this style of therapy. Accordingly, the patient may choose some other brand of therapy.

We hold that the right of the patient to assess the therapy and the therapist is inalienable. To make this right effective, the therapist is obliged to present himself or herself and the treatment as honestly and naturally as possible. No matter how much the therapist believes that the patient needs therapy, it is wrong for him or her to put forth a false image of a benevolent, omnipotent, omniscient parent who has the magic to alleviate the patient's distress. The therapist might seduce the patient into therapy by this false presentation, but the patient would not stay in therapy long after discovering that the therapist cannot deliver on these promises.

Moreover, the therapist's honest, natural demeanor helps to build a relationship between the patient and the therapist. Patients have come to expect, on the basis of everyday interactions with others, how other persons will behave; these expectations, so far as they are based on experience, can be considered realistic. Patients thus expect that others are frequently devious: people do not say what they mean, they do not always show what they feel. The patient anticipates that the ordinary rules of social life will apply in the therapy; the therapist will be as devious as anyone else. When the therapist does not meet these expectations in the initial interview, it is often a shock to the patient. Sometimes the patient is relieved by noticing this, because criticism, advice, direction, or authoritarian guidance was expected. Sometimes, however, the patient is disappointed; he or she had hoped for all of these responses. Whether the patient is happily or unhappily surprised, the remarkable behavior of the therapist (when the therapist is behaving as we believe therapists should) provides the basis for a positive, constructive relationship. Without that kind of relationship, therapy cannot go well.

Another purpose of the initial interview is to give the patient some sense of the workings of psychotherapy, thereby to enable the patient to recognize the promise that psychotherapy might hold for him or her. The therapist does this not by describing therapy in words (although this can be done if appropriate), but in action. When the therapist interprets some simple dynamic process occurring in the session, the working of therapy is shown. For example, a patient presents herself as the victim of a malevolent, sadistic husband; she also reports, without seeing any inconsistency with her claim to be a victim, having had several opportunities to get out of the marriage, but having made no effort to take advantage of them. When the therapist confronts this patient with the inconsistency, saying that her failure to take advantage of the opportunities shows that she would rather be in the marriage than out of it, the patient is intrigued by this idea and asks why she would want to perpetuate a situation that causes her so much anguish. This bestirring of curiosity can only enhance the treatment; the patient's attention has been drawn to her unconscious motivation, and the therapist has involved her in trying to understand it. If an interpretation is made early in the therapy, the interpretation must be simple and superficial, otherwise it will either arouse the patient's skepticism or will give the impression that the therapist is a mind reader who will disclose to the patient the contents of his or her mind and, therefore, a person to avoid.

Making Practical Arrangements

The initial interview is also the setting in which practical arrangements for whatever further actions therapist and patient agree on, can be made. If the therapist recommends psychotherapy, then they must make arrangements regarding the fee to be paid and regarding the times when they can meet. If the patient cannot afford the fee or cannot come when the therapist has time, alternative arrangements must be sought. If, for whatever reason, the therapist doesn't like or cannot work with the patient, then the therapist has a responsibility to make an appropriate referral.

Technique of the Initial Interview

The technique appropriate to the interview follows from the purposes that have been described in the previous pages. When the therapist schedules the initial interview, an appointment at a set time and for a scheduled time period (usually the same amount of time that is customarily devoted to a therapy session) should be offered. The therapist assumes that the prospective patient is an adult human being who is entitled to the privilege of making decisions and caring for himself or herself. The therapist greets the patient with a handshake if the patient seems inclined to shake hands. The therapist indicates to the patient where he or she may hang up a coat (if the patient is wearing one) and where he or she may sit. The therapist does not hang the coat up for the patient or seat the patient; these are social courtesies more appropriate for intimate social relationships than for professional interactions. It is not too early to show the patient that, in the interest of the treatment, certain social amenities will have to be foregone, particularly those actions that would affirm the patient's wish to have the therapist act as a solicitous, benevolent parental figure.

Importance of an Open-Ended Style of Inquiry

The data that the therapist needs from the patient can best be obtained when the therapist provides the patient as wide an opportunity as possible to present herself or himself verbally to the therapist, unconstrained by special interests of the therapist. Thus the therapist's first inquiry should be open-ended, and should provide maximal opportunity for the patient to talk at length. It is helpful, however, not to overemphasize that this is a situation in which the patient has presented himself or herself to the therapist for help with problems. One doesn't want the patient to think, "I bring my problems to the therapist, that's all I have to do; then he or she will fix me up." The therapist is interested in the patient, not in the troubles alone, except as these are an expression of the patient's living.

Thus the therapist may open the interview with a statement such as "Won't you tell me about yourself?" The therapist should avoid saying "What seems to be the trouble?" or "What problems bring you to the clinic?" When the therapist says "Won't you tell me about yourself" or, alternatively, "Tell us about yourself" he or she implicitly makes several points: (a) the therapist is inviting the patient to select (both consciously and unconsciously) how the patient will present herself or himself, (b) the therapist is challenging the expectation that she or he will ask questions of the patient, receive the answers, and then provide recommendations or prescriptions, and (c) the therapist is defining the interaction as a collaboration to which both the patient and the therapist make a contribution, and in which both of them are expected to *experience* and to *observe*. If the therapist chooses the alternate wording, "Tell *us* about yourself," she or he is communicating the idea that the patient should listen to the verbalizations as well as produce them. The therapist who chooses this form of the instruction surely does not intend it to sound kingly or pontifical, or to be an editorial "we."

However the therapist begins the interview, the patient most often responds by presenting at some length the factors that led to his or her coming to therapy. While talking, the patient will make references to the realities of his or her life and when this is done, the therapist has a chance to inquire about the facts of the patient's life (the patient's age, education, marital status, occupation, religion, family, etc.) that would serve to orient the therapist. Gathering such information in a natural context is far preferable to asking a set schedule of questions. That mechanical kind of collection of information is not necessary. Indeed, asking questions in that fashion defeats the purposes of the interview, and it negates the principle that the patient knows what is going on with him or her psychically (although this knowledge may be unconscious) and will tell the therapist if given a chance. Furthermore, such question-and-answer interchanges lead the patient to expect that all future communications will be of that sort; that expectation builds into resistance. Again, asking a schedule of questions implies that the therapist is in search of particular information, and that the patient has only to provide it, then sit back and await the therapist's diagnosis and advice, guidance, and prescription for living. To put the matter in another way: The therapist's interventions make waves. Because they do, they should be made sparingly and only with good reason.

Ordinarily the therapist does not make interpretations in the initial interview, no matter how well he or she understands the patient's dynamics. As we pointed out previously, a simple and obvious interpretation may be made in order to evaluate the patient's conceptual abilities, or to give a sample of the therapy to the patient; but as a rule, early interpretations are avoided, except to display his or her wares. On the other hand, reflection is a therapeutic tactic that can and should be used in the initial interview. One wants the patient to experience the therapist as a person who is able to understand the essence of the patient's communications, to sense the underlying thoughts and feelings even when the verbalizations are not all that clear.

We believe that the techniques of the initial interview are simple: The therapist listens and provides maximum opportunity for the patient to communicate. On the basis of what is heard, the therapist inwardly formulates judgment as to whether psychoanalytic therapy should be recommended to the patient.

When a positive recommendation (i.e., "You should involve yourself in psychotherapy") is made, the therapist has to keep in mind that the recommendation he or she is making to the patient is just that, a recommendation. It is not a prescription, not a pronouncement, not an assumption. It is offered as a recommendation so that the patient can consciously and freely decide whether or not she or he wants to follow the recommendation.

Menninger (see Menninger & Holzman, 1973) discussed at length the basic contract that is established between the patient and the therapist. In order to have a contract, both parties must be absolutely free to enter into it or to refrain from doing so; otherwise it is a contract in name only. To achieve a genuine contract, the therapist presents a recommendation to the patient in such a spirit that the patient knows that the therapist accepts his or her right to accept the proffered contract or to reject it, whatever the reasons for doing so may be.

Our view of this matter contrasts with the views of those who say that one should tell a patient authoritatively that this kind of treatment is needed. The authoritative pronouncement is frequently accompanied by dire predictions about what will happen if the prescription is not followed. A variant of the authoritarian approach is the assumption by the therapist that the patient by consulting her or him has already agreed to abide by his or her recommendations. When the therapist takes that for granted, no attempt is made to have the patient consider the recommendations explicitly and accept or reject them. Instead, such a therapist discusses arrangements concerned with schedule, payment of fees, and the like, assuming then that a contract with the patient has been concluded. Under these circumstances, even if the patient continues to appear for therapy sessions the therapist has displayed a degree of arrogance that is antithetical to the principles of psychoanalytic therapy.

The present authors have found it useful to recommend therapy to patients in words like these: "From what you have said, it sounds as though the difficulties you are experiencing are the result of feelings that you are having that you are not aware of. We have to assume this in order to explain why you find yourself continuing to do and to feel things that make you unhappy. Assuming this is true, I recommend that you try to gain an understanding of these hidden feelings and thoughts, so that you can discover how they are affecting your life. I am recommending a kind of treatment that will aim to help you acquire that understanding."

The therapist would then go on to tell the patient, explicitly, any reservations that he or she had about the advisability of the patient's becoming involved in psychotherapy and any risks from the patient's participation in psychotherapy that the therapist believed to be at all likely. It should be up to the patient *and* the therapist to decide whether the therapy is worthwhile despite these risks. We believe that the patient shares fully the responsibilities for all decisions.

The reader will notice in the proposed speech that the therapist cites as the reason for treatment the enhancing of the patient's understanding of self. The alleviation of symptoms, the bringing about of personal or behavioral change, or the altering of the patient's life is not promised.

We are not so naive as to suppose that any patient is fully able to give an informed consent to such a recommendation by the therapist. Indeed, quite a period of time may elapse before the patient understands very well the implications of agreeing to therapy. Nevertheless, to ask explicitly for an agreement by the patient enables the therapist to make clear the view that the patient is an autonomous human being, responsible for her or his own life.

The contract between therapist and patient goes beyond a simple assent to the recommendation for treatment. It entails taking on those realistic obligations that each of the parties to the contract must assume. For the therapist, making the recommendation that the patient have therapy with him or her means that the therapist is ready to assume the obligation of committing a portion of his or her skill, ability, interest, and time to that patient; that the therapist dedicates himself or herself to the therapeutic work with that patient, putting nothing else in his or her life ahead of that obligation. For the patient there is a commitment to come, to participate, and to pay, with a similar degree of dedication. The therapist's recommendation that a patient consider therapy has to be accompanied, therefore, with specifics about the fees the patient will be expected to pay and the frequency of sessions that the therapist recommends. The patient who can afford to come only once a week cannot accept a recommendation for therapy twice or three times a week. Similarly, a patient who is out of town four weeks out of every five cannot enter into a therapeutic contract that includes the recommendation that the patient be seen several times every week.

The therapist will need to present the specifics of the recommendation in words such as "This kind of therapy goes best when the patient and therapist can meet frequently, the more frequently, the better. The reason is that continuity in the therapy is important. Ideally we would meet seven days a week, fifty-two weeks a year. Realistically, however, we have to compromise this ideal, because you and I have other things to do, and because therapy costs money. But it would be well for us to arrange to meet as frequently as is realistically possible." At this point the therapist can indicate to the patient the number of hours that are available, or he or she can focus on the patient's financial situation to determine how many sessions the patient realistically can afford each week.

If the patient agrees to the recommendation to involve himself or herself in therapy, then therapist and patient together consider how to arrange therapy, taking into account the schedules of both of them. Just as the therapist expects the patient to take account of the therapist's realistic needs, so the therapist is considerate of the patient's. The principle is simple: The patient's time is no more at the disposal of the therapist than the therapist's is available at the whim of the patient. Conflict in their schedules may make it necessary to meet less frequently than both would have wished; the participants may agree, however, that they will meet more often when it becomes practical. The therapist should be aboveboard about her or his schedule and he or she has the right to expect the patient to be so as well.

Having considered these primary matters, the patient and therapist may turn to other concerns. The therapist will answer questions that the patient has about the structure of the therapy. The therapist may have forms that need to be filled out (e.g., history forms, financial forms, and address and telephone number forms). The therapist may want to ask the patient to agree to tape recording of the sessions. The therapist should present any such matters in a matter-of-fact way, just as is done when dealing with such ordinary issues as when to meet. When what the therapist asks of the patient raises issues of confidentiality, the therapist is ready to assure the patient that the material of the therapy is completely confidential; the privilege to waive this confidentiality rests wholly with the patient. If there is some item about which the therapist cannot truthfully make that statement, the item should be excluded from the therapy. We do not consider it a violation of confidentiality for a therapist to present tapes, or material derived from his or her notes on the case, to a supervisor or to professional colleagues, if the patient's identity is completely hidden.

When the Interviewer Recommends Against Therapy

A therapist may decide not to recommend psychoanalytic therapy because he or she believes the patient is not able, psychologically, to participate in such therapy. The therapist may decide against therapy because of the belief that the treatment would be so hindered by factors beyond the patient's control that therapy would not be feasible. Whatever the reasons for deciding not to recommend psychoanalytic therapy, the therapist has an obligation to communicate to the patient the reasons for the recommendation.

Having decided not to recommend psychoanalytic therapy, the therapist can, if he or she sees fit, recommend an alternative: treatment of another kind, referral to a therapist of another persuasion, or no therapy. Sometimes, indeed, the patient has come to the wrong person in choosing to consult a therapist. There is the example of a young man who came to a therapist (as he put it) "to find a friend." During the initial interview the therapist came to the conclusion that although psychological factors played a part in making it difficult for this young man to make friends, the patient was not ready at this time to explore these factors; he would be better off simply to try to find someone to be his friend. Because the therapist would not sell his friendship under the guise of offering professional services, he told the patient that he did not need therapy but would be better advised to spend his time and effort seeking friends in social situations. It happens that later on this young man did seek therapy and at the later time he was treated not for a lack of friends but for a disturbance within himself that he had by then become aware of.

Conclusion

In this chapter we started by pointing out that both the patient and the therapist come into the initial interview with expectations, some derived from information they have received about the other participant, some mainly derived from unconscious sources, about what the other participant will be like. The patient is likely, as well, to have anxieties about what the therapy will do to him or her.

We then discussed the assumptions that the psychoanalytic therapist makes as he or she enters into the initial interview: that the patient is experiencing some distress (it is better if he or she feels this as an internal pressure) and that the patient has some hope that psychotherapy can alleviate this distress. We considered the purposes of the initial interview: (a) to decide whether psychoanalytic therapy is appropriate, (b) to evaluate how distressed the patient is (it is favorable if he or she is motivated by this suffering but not overcome by the intensity of the suffering), (c) to appraise the psychodynamic functioning of the patient, (d) to evaluate the patient's ability to work in the therapy, (e) to formulate some diagnostic impressions, and (f) to consider the impact that the realistic conditions of the patient's life will have on the therapy. The initial interview also offers the patient the opportunity to size up the therapist and the therapy, offers the therapist an opportunity to start building a relationship with her or his patient, and provides the patient, through modest interpretations that the therapist makes, a sample of the therapeutic work. Finally, we dealt with some of the nuts-and-bolts of the initial interview: We pointed out the necessity in the initial interview to make practical arrangements for the therapy, and we gave some advice about the therapist's demeanor.

Chapter 5

Structure of the Therapy: Practical Arrangements

5

By the "structure" of the therapy we mean the external arrangements, including the setting in which the therapy takes place: the room used for it, the time of day, the auspices under which it takes place (say, in a clinic or in a private practice), the frequency of the sessions, the fee that has been agreed on, and the understanding about when the fee will be paid and by whom and how. The structure of the therapy, if it is maintained consistently, can provide a stable framework within which the therapist can evaluate the patient's responses. For example, if the therapist is consistently punctual in beginning the session, when the patient comes unusually early or comes late, the patient's behavior cannot be attributed to concerns about the therapist being there at the appointed time and starting on time. Having disposed of this possibility, one can assume that the patient's departing from the agreed-on arrangement expresses some inner motive.

One cannot stress too much how important it is for the therapist to maintain a steady structure for the therapy. Only in such a framework can transference be discovered, evaluated, and demonstrated to the patient. Moreover, when the therapist is ambiguous or fails to maintain a consistent structure, the patient is able to use these variations to express resistance. Concrete things that should be kept constant are discussed later in this chapter. Here we will simply emphasize the importance of consistency. We should also make clear that we do not have in mind a rock-hard rigidity. We take for granted that the therapist will show ordinary social politeness and that neutrality will not amount to a hostile coldness.

Some structure is absolutely necessary to the therapeutic work. Somehow the therapist and the patient have to be brought together at the same time and place. Orderly arrangements for this have to be made. One has to provide a furnished room that is private as well as lighted and heated. Facilities for the patient and the therapist to communicate with each other if one of them cannot keep an appointment must be made available. There must be a way to pay the therapist for his or her time; payment may be made by the patient, a clinic that is subsidized by government or by community charitable funds, a university, or a prepaid health plan.

Arrangements for Meetings

Patient and therapist must agree on the time, the length, and the frequency of the therapy sessions. As to time there is little advice we can give, except to recommend that the therapist stay within the bounds of what is customary, that is, probably not before 7 in the morning and not after 10 at night. Nor should the therapist, except in unusual circumstances and for well thought out reasons, schedule appointments on holidays or on Sundays. In keeping to what is customary the therapist holds the therapy within the framework of professional services, neither making unusual demands on patients nor going to unusual lengths to provide therapy for patients.

Length of the session may be different for different patients, depending on the convenience and comfort of the therapist and the patient. A reasonable range for sessions seems to be from half an hour to an hour and a half. A period shorter than 30 minutes does not allow time for the patient to get warmed up to the task before the session must stop, and a period longer than 90 minutes is likely to exhaust both participants. Most therapists set the length of the session at 45 or 50 minutes and schedule patients for the beginning of each hour, thus allowing them a break of 10 to 15 minutes between patients. We have known some therapists who schedule patients back-to-back, without any breathing space between patients. We believe this to be unwise.

The kind of therapy that we describe in this book, which has as its aim increased self-understanding by the patient, goes better and is more likely to have a successful outcome when the sessions are frequent. With most patients, something can be accomplished by meeting once a week. When the sessions are twice a week, the work is likely to go much better. Meeting three times a week is still better, four times are better than three, and five are better than four. The reason for this is that there is a logic implicit in the patient's associations. One thought leads to another. This stream of associations tends to be dominated by an inner, unconscious determination when the sessions are more frequent. But the frequency of sessions is limited by the time that the therapist has available, by the time the patient has available, and by the amount of money the patient can afford to pay for therapy.

Vacations and Holidays

Vacations.   Provision for vacations is part of the structure of therapy. Ideally the patient and the therapist should take their vacations at the same time. The therapist, however, cannot arrange his or her vacation schedule to suit all patients. To try to do so would allow for no vacation at all. Therefore the only realistic way to arrange vacations that coincide is for the patient to try to match the therapist's vacation schedule. If a patient should complain that this procedure amounts to an unfair double standard, the complaint has to be considered a resistance, on the grounds that the patient should expect to make some sacrifices in order to obtain the therapy that will be so valuable to him or her.

Therapists should tell their patients as far ahead of time as they can when they are planning to take a vacation. Patients can be expected to arrange a vacation at the same time if feasible, keeping in mind the principle that the fewer interruptions the therapy has, the better. If the patient cannot arrange a coincident vacation, then the therapist should accept that reality.

Holidays.   By "holiday" we mean a short (often 1 day) vacation. When a holiday falls on a day when an appointment would normally be scheduled, the therapist should remind the patient at least a couple of sessions beforehand that there will be no meeting on that day. One should offer an alternative appointment to any patient who comes as seldom as once a week, if practical. When the patient comes twice a week or more frequently, we advise the therapist not to take the initiative in proposing a makeup meeting time, but to schedule such an alternative session if the patient requests it and if the therapist can do so.

Therapist-Initiated Alterations in Structure

Cancellations

The therapist should consider the agreement to see a patient at an appointed time to be a serious obligation; this agreement should be broken only for the most urgent reasons. When it is necessary to miss an appointment, the therapist should give adequate notice to the patient and offer the patient alternate times if they are available. The patient's refusal to accept the alternate time cannot, of course, be construed as expressing resistance, because the patient's time is no more at the therapist's disposal than the therapist's is at the patient's. When practical considerations in the therapist's life, such as attending a professional meeting, are the reason for cancelling the session, he or she may wish to tell the patient the reason; when there are more personal reasons, the therapist is usually well advised not to give the reason, because the therapist's personal problems would then intrude into the patient's therapy.

If (as happens very occasionally) the therapist forgets an appointment, an apology for not keeping the appointment should be offered, but the therapist should not tell the patient about the memory lapse. When another meeting comes up, and the therapist considers that meeting to be more important than his or her session with the patient, the therapist should apologize for not keeping the appointment but should *not* tell the patient, "I considered it more important to go to the other meeting." Ordinary tact, social politeness, and the demands of the therapeutic relationship all require a certain reticence in such circumstances. (If the patient pursues the matter, the therapist naturally would have to acknowledge that for valid reasons commitments to another activity were made in place of the therapy session.) For the therapist to fail to apologize is, however, not neutral but an aggression against the patient. Finally, whenever the therapist chooses, consciously or unconsciously, to miss an appointment with the patient, this action should be the focus of self-study.

Lateness of the Therapist

Participation in psychotherapy is not a trivial endeavor. There should be nothing of greater importance in the patient's life during the span of the therapy. Because the endeavor is so serious, the therapist is obliged to show his or her belief in its importance by participating in it seriously. This should be made clear both by what is said and by what is done. An important way for the therapist to communicate this dedication to the therapy is by arriving on time for each session and ending each session on time.

When the therapist is precisely punctual in beginning and ending the sessions, the introduction of a sense of vagueness into the therapy is avoided. By avoiding vagueness the therapist deprives the patient of an opportunity to use such ambiguity in the service of resistance. For example, if the therapist begins a session five minutes early (when the patient has arrived early), in order to finish it five minutes early, then if on subsequent days the therapist starts on time the patient is enabled to interpret the change in the therapist's behavior as an indication that the therapist has changed in his or her feelings toward the patient. Even though that conclusion is more than likely a distortion, motivated by processes within the patient, the therapist's erratic behavior has made it very difficult to interpret the distorting process to the patient; the inconsistency enables the patient to slough off the therapist's interpretation of the unconscious processes.

Sometimes, despite best intentions, the therapist is late, unavoidably so. When this happens the therapist should apologize for being late and explain the reason for the lateness if it is not too personal. For instance, if an accident on the expressway tied up traffic for half an hour, the therapist might report this in the course of making an apology; but if the therapist's daughter had had a brain concussion from falling off a bicycle, and had to be rushed to the hospital, the therapist would not mention this incident to the patient. (We wonder whether the appointment would even be kept under these circumstances.) Besides apologizing, the therapist might offer the patient an opportunity to make up the missed time by extending the hour beyond the agreed on ending point. Of course, this should be done only if time is available and not be borrowed (or stolen) from the beginning of the next patient's session. When the therapist is able to continue beyond the usual end of the session, he or she should not assume that the patient should or will accept his offer. The offer should be made and then the patient's explicit agreement to extending the session solicited. If the patient cannot stay longer, the therapist cannot view a refusal to do so as resistance; it should be counted as reality. It is not helpful, in our experience, to try to make up the missed time by extending the appointment of another day. If the missed time cannot be made up, then the therapist should explicitly agree with the patient to a reduction in fee for the amount of time by which the session was shortened. The reduction should be precisely related to the time missed, not an amount arrived at through a casual approximation.

Patient-Initiated Alterations in Structure

Cancellations

On occasion patients will cancel appointments. When the patient proposes during a therapy session to cancel a subsequent appointment, it is appropriate for the therapist to inquire into the reasons for the cancellation. The therapist should avoid giving the impression that judgement has already been made as to whether the cancellation is justified or not. If the cancellation is for realistic reasons (both the patient and the therapist agree that the reasons are realistic) the therapist should assent and, if the patient so requests, arrange an alternate appointment.

When the patient does not ask for an alternate appointment, the therapist should then test the hypothesis that resistance is at work, even though the reason for the cancellation has been deemed realistic. One way of checking this hypothesis is to observe the patient's associations closely. (We can appreciate that the therapist has more available information if *he or she* does not propose a makeup for the session that is to be missed, but waits to see whether the patient will propose it.) Another way of deciding whether resistance is at work is to note the amount of lead time the patient gave when announcing the cancellation. Realistic considerations and common courtesy require that the patient give notice of the cancellation as far ahead of time as possible; when the patient does not do so, one suspects resistance.

At times patients give a reason for wanting to cancel an appointment that the therapist deems unrealistic. When this happens the therapist is well advised not to challenge the patient with his or her opinion that the cancellation is unjustified, thereby inviting debate about whether the cancellation is realistic. It is better for the therapist to examine the patient's associations that occur before and after the patient's announcing the cancellation, with a view to discovering the reasons for the patient's intention to express resistance in this way. When the therapist can understand these reasons, the unconscious factors that underlie the patient's wish to absent himself or herself from therapy should be interpreted.

After interpreting the factors leading to the patient's cancelling the session, the therapist may then declare the belief that it would be in the patient's best interests to deal with these factors in the therapy instead of acting them out through cancelling. If this is the first occasion on which the issue of cancellations has come up, the therapist should take the opportunity to establish an agreed on procedure for dealing with cancellations. In doing this the therapist would let the patient know that a specific reason for any cancellation is expected, that the patient and the therapist will discuss in the therapy any proposed cancellation (so far as practical), and that the patient will pay for sessions that are cancelled for unrealistic reasons or without sufficient notice. In setting this structure the therapist should not impose it on the patient arbitrarily. Rather, having demonstrated to the patient how cancellations can be made in the service of resistance, the therapist should then propose that they agree on a set of arrangements such as we have just described, in the best interests of the therapy. If the patient should refuse to agree (for reasons that seem unrealistic), the therapist can then deal with the refusal by interpreting the resistance that motivates it.

When a patient has missed an appointment without notifying the therapist ahead of time, the therapist can reasonably expect that the patient will call afterwards as a matter of courtesy. When the patient does not do this, the failure to do so can be considered an expression of resistance. If the patient misses the appointment without giving prior notification, then fails to call, we recommend that the therapist take no action. Unless there is some pressing reason for doing otherwise—such as the need to initiate a change in structure—the therapist should not call the patient. If, however, the patient then fails to appear for the appointment following the missed one and still has not communicated with the therapist, then we advise that the therapist call the patient during the time of the missed session. The purpose of this call is primarily to ascertain the patient's intentions about the therapy: Does he or she want to keep coming? The therapist cannot keep an appointment time open indefinitely without knowing that the patient indeed will be staying in therapy. The therapist may, by making such a call, discover the patient's reasons for not adhering to the therapeutic contract. A call that is made at such a time and under such circumstances should not have as its purpose encouraging the patient to continue treatment or to resume it; it should not be intended to seduce the patient into continuing therapy. Though the therapist may point out to such a patient that it is in the patient's best interests to talk over with the therapist any decision to quit, the therapist does not demand, order, or coerce a patient to come and talk about the decision to quit.

When a patient decides precipitously to terminate the therapy, not discussing this decision with the therapist, one should view this decision as manifesting the patient's fear of participating in the therapy and should regard the decision as the patient's way of protecting herself or himself by leaving the situation. (We are, of course, taking for granted that the therapist has behaved appropriately and has effectively carried out therapeutic work.) Having such an understanding of the dynamics, the therapist should respect the patient's judgment that the anxiety provoked by the therapy is not tolerable (assuming that the patient always knows best).

Lateness of the Patient

When the patient comes late for a session the therapist expects, as a matter of courtesy, that the patient will give an explanation for the lateness. If the patient who comes late simply apologizes for the lateness, it is appropriate for the therapist to ask, "What happened?" If, on the other hand, the patient makes no mention of the fact that he or she is late, either by apologizing or by offering an explanation, the therapist should take note of this, say nothing at that time, and make the assumption that the patient's associations will provide an explanation both for the patient's lateness and for her or his avoiding mentioning it.

Even when the patient's lateness seems fully explained by realistic circumstances, the therapist should form the hypothesis that the lateness constitutes a communication, typically a communication expressing resistance. It is as though the patient begins the session with a statement, "I want to shorten my session today," and follows that with, "I am now going to tell you the reasons for this." We recommend that the therapist deal with lateness as with any communication of the patient, by interpreting its significance when one has the information to make an interpretation, provided that the patient seems ready to respond to the interpretation by widening his or her self-knowledge; by probing for factual information when the time is not ripe for interpretation but the patient needs to have attention directed to this issue; and by neglecting the matter when other issues seem to be of overriding importance. Rarely, however, is something else more important than the patient's attitude toward the therapy or the therapist, expressed in the patient's missing a session or coming late for an appointment. Thus, although the therapist may choose to wait awhile to see whether the patient will discuss the lateness, if the patient does not bring up this matter the therapist is well advised to raise the issue. It can be raised by either asking about it directly or by interpreting associations related to it.

To show how the therapist can deal with lateness we cite an incident involving a young woman who came for a session eight minutes late, out of breath, and gasped out the apology, "Sorry I'm late. I missed the bus." The therapist asked, "Does it have any significance that you're late today?" The patient dismissed that idea by reiterating that she had missed the bus. She went on to say that she had dawdled more than usual in getting ready to come downtown to the therapist's office. She reported, too, that she had overslept; the alarm went off, but she turned it off and went back to sleep for a while. The therapist again raised the question whether her lateness had some significance. He wondered aloud whether the patient had mixed feelings about coming to therapy today. In response, the patient said that she had indeed been wondering whether the therapy was getting anywhere. Last night when she and her husband had been discussing financial matters, it had occurred to her that she could ease their financial situation by quitting therapy. The therapist then interpreted the lateness, pointing out that her coming late amounted to a compromise between coming to therapy on time and not coming at all. A discussion of the patient's attitudes toward therapy followed.

The Place of the Meeting

The therapist, of course, usually sees patients in a professional office. Sometimes it is convenient to have the office in his or her home. If this is done, it is best for the office to be separated from the living areas of the house and to be clearly a space set aside for professional work.

A waiting room of some sort is necessary, so that a patient who comes a little before the appointed time will have a place to sit down and wait. It is ideal to have an arrangement that permits the patient to enter the consulting room from the waiting room through one door, and to go out of the consulting room through another door that does not take him or her through the waiting room. With such an arrangement, the patient doesn't run into another patient when going to therapy or when leaving. Thus the privacy of the patient is protected and the confidentiality of his or her having therapy is fully guarded.

The therapy room should be soundproofed. By this we do not mean sound-*treated*; that is, having the sound deadened by acoustical tiles. Sound-treatment may add to the comfort of the room, but it does not keep people outside from hearing what is said inside the room. Sound*proofing* requires sufficiently staunch walls and doors that are thick and have tight closures. For satisfactory soundproofing it is often necessary to have special doors with rubber gaskets around the door frame. It is helpful, as a means of preventing talk in the room from being heard outside, to increase the noise level just outside the room; one can do this by installing a noisy air conditioner, an air purifier, or a radio. The noise of such apparatus tends to mask the sounds from the therapy room.

The therapist needs telephone service in the office so that patients can communicate with him or her when necessary. It is important for the therapist to be available for phone calls from patients; for example, if a patient calls to cancel an appointment or to alter the structure of the therapy arrangements in some other way, the therapist wants to be able to deal with these challenging developments as they occur, particularly if the calling patient is acting out a resistance. Therefore secretaries should not be interposed between the therapist and the patient; rather, one should instruct the secretaries to arrange for the patients to speak directly with their therapists whenever they call, whatever the reasons for their calls. In order to avoid the interruption of an ongoing therapy session, should the call come during a session, the secretary or the therapist's answering machine should instruct the caller to call back in the 10- or 15-minute space between sessions.

The question of chaperonage arises because people tend to suspect a sexual relationship when any two persons are alone together. (Bion in his *Experiences in Groups* [1959] drew attention to this unconscious assumption that two persons couldn't want to be together except for sexual purposes.) To appreciate the importance of this question one need only remember E. Jones's difficulties as he pioneered in the psychoanalytic investigation of personality (see his autobiography, *Free Associations*, 1959, pp. 150–151). Accordingly, it is helpful if the therapist can have a secretary/receptionist or can share one with other professional people. But this is not always feasible. Many therapists don't need a secretary apart from their usefulness as a chaperon. The therapist is then faced with the necessity of using his or her judgment about what is an appropriate setting and time for therapeutic work.

If the therapist uses a professional office in an office building, if the office is accessible to the public and not in an out-of-the-way location, and if scheduling of sessions adheres to the usual business times of the day (say, between 7 in the morning and 10 at night), he or she should run into little difficulty from the common expectation that two people couldn't want to be alone except for sex. The climate of opinion in the community makes a difference; the usual practices of colleagues should also influence the therapist's judgment. Such a judgment cannot be made rationally without a weighing of the whole pattern of the arrangements for therapeutic work, a weighing that permits the therapist to guess at the impact of these arrangements on the thinking and feeling of the patients, of their friends and relatives, and of the community as a whole. Some discussion of these matters has been included in the handbook, *Ethical Principles of Psychologists* (American Psychological Association, 1981), which the reader is encouraged to read.

And what of the therapy room itself? How should it be furnished and decorated, how arranged? The furnishings, we think, should be reasonably comfortable, not shabby and not overpoweringly opulent. Their style should reflect the therapist's taste and personality rather than giving an air of impersonal sterility. The therapist may provide a couch for the patient to lie down on or a chair to sit in. We believe that effective therapy can be done with the patient lying down or with the patient sitting up. We believe, further, that the therapist may well decide that for some patients the couch is preferable, for others the chair. A last word about furniture: Don't move it around unnecessarily. In advising this we are relying on the general principle previously stated, that the arrangements for the therapy should be kept as consistent as possible.

Couch or Chair?

In deciding whether to use couch or chair, the therapist can be guided by a few principles. First, the couch fosters regression. One has to decide how much one wishes to foster regression. Will regression be an advantage to a particular patient, enabling the patient to commit more fully to the therapeutic task, or will it frighten and frustrate the patient, making the work more difficult?

In making this determination, it is helpful to consider regression as both a libidinal-genetic phenomenon and an ego phenomenon. Using the couch enhances the appearance of behavior and associations indicative of pregenital libidinal organizations. For instance, using the couch makes it easier for a patient (as we have shown in some examples) to bite fingernails, to curl up in a fetal position and fall asleep during moments of anxiety, to report feeling gassy and flatulent, to knead the pubic area, or to describe incestuous fantasies. Such phenomena not only represent functioning at a pregenital level of psychosexual development but also give evidence of a relaxing of the ego controls that ordinarily enforce adherence to the reality principle. Patients on the couch are more accepting of their primary-process thinking, of a lessened control of instinctual impulses (because lying on the couch provides a measure of externally imposed control), of the expression of affects connected to current and to past experiences, and of primitivization of defenses matching the depth of the transference neurosis. Because regressive phenomena such as those just cited do occur when one uses the couch, the therapist must be confident that the patient has the ego strength and resiliency that will enable her or him to undergo a regression during the therapy session and then, at its end, bring that regression to an end as he or she walks out of the consulting room.

Second, the use of the couch does not, in our opinion, make the therapy psychoanalysis, nor does failing to use the couch make the therapy unanalytic. As we said, the depth of regression is somewhat dependent on whether the couch is used. That, in turn, has some impact on whether a transference neurosis develops, on how it develops, and on how quickly it develops. Yet a therapeutic process that is analytic in every essential respect, that involves a fully developed transference neurosis, that includes a reconstruction of the personality, can occur without the use of the couch.

What then does determine whether the therapeutic process is to be called psychoanalysis rather than called a psychotherapy based on psychoanalytic principles? We think that the dividing line should be drawn between therapies in which there is a full development of the transference neurosis (with a thorough interpretation of it) and therapies in which this is absent. Therapies with transference neurosis, thoroughly interpreted, are psychoanalysis; therapies lacking this are not.

We would mention, finally, the historical connection between use of the couch and hypnosis. As Freud said (in "On Beginning the Treatment," 1913), his use of the couch was a legacy from his use of hypnosis. Psychoanalysis grew out of the hypnotic method; we have the couch as a remnant of that now-discarded technique. Even though hypnosis has been abandoned there may still be good reasons for retaining the couch: (a) The desire to foster regression; (b) The belief that the transference will be easier to discern if the patient has fewer cues (from visual input) of what the therapist is like; (c) One may want to make it easier for the patient to associate (again, because there are fewer visual cues); and (d) The therapist may wish to avoid expending energy to control his or her facial expressions in the face-to-face situations, in order to avoid betraying or seeming to betray reaction to the patient's productions.

The Fee

The fee is an important aspect of the structure of the therapy, not only because it provides the therapist with necessary income but also because money is our society's principal way of exchanging satisfactions, transmitting the fruits of love and work, and conferring power over the environment. People know that what is worthwhile must be earned and be paid for either in the direct exchange of gratifications or in an indirect exchange, through money. Thus the fee should not be set too high or too low. If it is set too high, the fee becomes a hardship on the patient. An excessive fee may gratify the patient's masochistic tendencies, fit in with self-destructive trends, and serve to allay unconscious guilt. If the therapist is able to reduce the fee but fails to do so, and the patient knows this, the excessive fee provides a real ground for hostility toward the therapist—and such hostility could not be considered "transference." On the other hand, too low a fee makes the patient feel that the therapist's services can't be worth much. Too low a fee may make the patient feel guilty at receiving service at too low a price, and hence make him or her reluctant to express any dissatisfaction felt and reluctant to verbalize transferred hostility. Furthermore, too low a fee is a hardship on the therapist and that may make her or him resentful.

As Menninger (1958) pointed out, the basic social contract between therapist and patient is that the therapist will supply professional skill and the patient will pay the fee. The exchange between them is defined as an exchange of skill for money. Such a contract is different from such contracts as those defining friendship, love, pastoral care by clergyman for parishioner, or teaching. In these other relationships exchanges of gratifications take place that are not appropriate to the therapist-patient relationship. In the therapist-patient relationship the therapist is allowed only two main sources of gratification: the pay received from the professional work and satisfaction in doing his or her job well. (We are aware that the therapist becomes a therapist in the first place out of personal motives, such as the wish to understand herself or himself and to solve personal conflicts, the desire to help other human beings, and curiosity about the behavior of other people. If these needs are gratified in a sublimated form, their driving force can aid the therapist's adaptation to his or her professional task. But if such needs become too clamorous they can disrupt the therapist's work.)

The amount of the fee should be determined at the first meeting of the therapist with the patient; hence, setting the fee has already been discussed in the chapter on the initial interview (chapter 4). We have, however, not yet discussed when and how the fee is to be paid. As to when: The fee can be paid by the patient at each visit, at the end of each week, or at the end of the month. It probably does not matter greatly which of these arrangements is adopted. Some therapists would rather make out a bill each month and be paid at the end of each month. Some prefer to have the patient pay without billing at the end of the month. Some do not find it inconvenient to receive payments at varying times throughout the month from patients who are variously paid on a weekly or semimonthly basis; these patients prefer to pay the therapist immediately after they get their money. Even though the therapist may recognize that a request to pay right after getting one's paycheck is an expression of the patient's characterological difficulties, he or she may nonetheless accede to the request for a time if he or she thinks that doing so is in the best interests of the therapy. It is somewhat more businesslike and conducive to good record-keeping if the payment is made by check rather than in cash. Yet one cannot make a hard-and-fast rule about this.

Following a principle that applies to all matters of therapeutic structure—to minimize the opportunities for the patient or the therapist to act out—we recommend making the arrangements for setting and collecting fees as straightforward as possible. Our own practice, we think, exemplifies this: After we have agreed with the patient about how much the fee should be, we ask the patient to pay the therapist by check at the last meeting of the month (or the week or the fortnight) for the number of therapy sessions that occurred during the month. Several advantages derive from this procedure. The therapist neither has to bill the patient nor provide receipts for cash payments. The arrangement is concrete; departures from it are immediately evident. The patient is explicitly made a partner in the procedure, in that he or she has to keep a record of the meetings rather than waiting passively to be told by the therapist what is owed. When the patient uses the fee and the way of paying or not paying it as vehicles for resistance and transference, this procedure ensures that the fee and its payment automatically become an integral part of the treatment.

In those situations where administrative policy requires that the patient pay someone besides the therapist (e.g., a secretary or a cashier) the therapist must keep informed of the status of the patient's account. She or he should know when the patient has paid, how much the patient has paid, and when the patient has departed from the arrangement that was agreed to. The therapist must know this because it is such an important aspect of the relationship between the patient and herself or himself. Through paying or not paying the patient expresses feelings about the therapy and the therapist.

When the patient does not pay, the nonpayment must be discussed in the therapy. If the patient raises the issue, asking whether he or she can delay paying or pay less, the therapist should evaluate whether the patient is responding realistically to the circumstances of personal life or is acting out a neurotic conflict. If there is a permanent reduction in the patient's ability to pay for therapy, one should consider which of several courses of action is best under the circumstances: (a) lowering the fee, (b) referring the patient to a therapy clinic (assuming that the patient is being seen in private practice), or (c) accepting a hiatus in treatment that will last until the patient is able to afford therapy again. In a more temporary situation, one can allow the patient to propose a plan for paying for part of or all of current therapy at a time in the future when financial resources will permit him or her to pay. In any case the therapist should be ever alert to the therapeutic implications of the patient's request that the therapist reduce the fee, accept a delayed payment, or serve as a banker to the patient (in effect, making him or her a loan).

Occasionally a patient will report forgetting to bring a check to the treatment session at which she or he had agreed to pay. Of course, the therapist has to deal with the reasons for the "forgetting;" practically, the therapist may agree to the patient's paying at the following session or (if there will be a prolonged interruption such as a vacation period) to the patient's mailing the check. Some patients try to extend their appointments by writing the check after the therapist has indicated that the session has come to an end. Rather than participating in such acting out, the therapist should indicate that the patient can pay at the next session and discuss then why he or she waited until after the session was over to write the check. Some patients "forget" their pens and ask to borrow one from the therapist. One should deal with this action, too, as a communication within the therapy.

If the patient fails to pay but does not raise the issue of payment, the therapist has to deal with this expression of unconscious forces. The patient's failing to pay at the expected time is a communication by action rather than by words. It is as though the patient has said, "I am not going to pay at this time." Accordingly, one must recognize the issue of nonpayment as one that is fundamental to the therapeutic relationship, not a matter that is extraneous to its central thrust. The therapist's approach to dealing with a patient's failing to pay (while not mentioning it) should reflect the importance of this action to the therapy. One way of dealing with the nonpayment is to make the assumption that the associations of the patient in the session of the absent payment, and perhaps the associations in the next session as well, will provide elaborations and explanations of the reasons for not paying and for not mentioning this nonpayment. Guided by this assumption, the therapist would listen to the material, arrive at an understanding of the motivation for nonpayment, make an interpretation based on this understanding, and then come to an agreement with the patient about whether realistically the patient can pay immediately or must delay paying. If the therapist does not understand the motivation for the patient's not paying, this matter should be brought up at the beginning of a therapy session, inquiring about the reasons for the nonpayment and the reasons for the patient's not raising the issue.

When the therapist and the patient have agreed on a fee that was set in accordance with the patient's ability to pay, the therapist may at times ask whether a change in the patient's financial status justifies a change in the fee. We have already discussed how to deal with lowering the fee; we emphasize that raising the fee when it is appropriate to do so is equally important, for doing so maintains the reality of the therapeutic structure. If the patient raises the point that her or his financial status has improved and suggests increasing the fee, the therapist should examine with the patient the realities of the patient's situation, arriving at a realistic agreement to increase the fee if that is appropriate, or not to do so if that is appropriate. If the patient does not raise the issue, the therapist should at the beginning of a therapy session mention that it would be important to discuss the fee in order to ascertain whether it is still appropriate. The therapist has a right to expect that the patient will join in a realistic exploration of his or her financial situation and will agree to an appropriate fee. Any other posture by the patient would be a matter for study and interpretation. The principle to be followed is that the fee is a part of the contract; it is not imposed by the therapist on the patient in an authoritarian way.

Payment by Relatives

The integrity of the therapeutic relationship is maintained only if the therapist deals with the patient alone and considers her or his contract to be with the patient. To illustrate: A colleague of the authors had as a patient a priest who was a member of a religious order whose local community was paying the bill for the therapy. At one point in the therapy the priest's superior, becoming concerned about what seemed to be a developing manic phase in the patient's life, called the therapist to ask advice about the kind of assignment that would be wise as a way of suppressing manic excitement. The therapist believed that she could not manage the patient's life through advice to the superior *and* maintain a relationship of trust and openness with the patient himself. Acting on this belief, she refused to give advice to the priest's superior, insisting that discussion of the suitability of work assignments would have to be between priest and superior, without the involvement of the therapist. The patient would then remain in charge of his life and be responsible for it.

The therapist involves herself or himself with the realities of the patient's life as little as possible. Ideally suggestions to the patient on how to get the money for therapy are not given nor does the therapist intervene directly in order to get money for therapy from a third party. The therapist does not collect money from a husband for a wife's therapy nor investigate what the insurance company will cover and negotiate with them to obtain payment for the patient's psychotherapy. Rather, the therapist guards his or her position of neutrality and the separation from the realities of the patient's life by involving himself or herself in the patient's life as little as possible. A bill that must be turned over to a spouse, parent, or insurance company is presented for payment to the patient by the therapist.

Records of Fees and Visits

Because the payment of fees is so important an avenue for the expression of unconscious communications by the patient, it is critical that the therapist be literally up-to-the-minute in regard to the patient's attendance at therapy sessions, payment of fees, and departures from what has been agreed on in regard to these two aspects of treatment. We recommend, therefore, that the therapist keep a daily calendar or daybook at hand in which she or he records not only the patient's attendance at each scheduled meeting but also latenesses, missed and cancelled appointments, and amounts paid and when, as well as reminders to inform patients of coming holidays, vacations, and other occasions for the therapist to miss appointments. This daily record should supplement a permanent, continuing record of each patient's visits and payments (recorded by date). The therapist may also need other information for the conduct of his or her business affairs.

Those therapists who work in a clinic where records are kept by a secretary or a clerk are well advised to keep their own daybook in addition to the clinic's records. Moreover, the therapist working in such an organization should make sure that the records kept by the agency agree with hers or his; there should be no discrepancy between the agency's view of what the patient owes and the therapist's view of it. The therapist must do what is possible to assure that the agency's records are no less up-to-the-minute than his or her own.

Chapter 6

Instructions to the Patient: How and When the Therapist Educates

In order to do his or her part in the therapy, the patient has to be an active and informed partner in the therapeutic process. The patient therefore has to know the general principles by which the therapy works and how they are applied. The patient learns this both by participating in the therapy and by paying heed to what the therapist tells him or her about the therapeutic process. In this chapter we indicate how the patient learns about the therapy in these ways.

Therapist–Patient Interaction

Taking into account only therapeutic technique, one would consider a therapist–patient interaction in which the therapist did nothing but listen and interpret as ideal. The opposite of this ideal would be an interaction in which the therapist was actively involved in the realities of the patient's life as the patient reported them, neglecting to treat these "realities" as expressions of fantasies that the patient was having. Tarachow (1963) drew a sharp distinction between these two positions; we recommend his book for an extended discussion of this point. It must be admitted that if this technical ideal were to be achieved, the result would be a totally inhuman, mechanical kind of therapy. Therapists therefore must recognize that they are involved as human beings with their patients, even though they do not, for the most part, involve themselves with patients as "real objects" (to use Tarachow's terminology).

As we say in chapter 7, the therapist's humanness should enter into the therapy situation at various times: when congratulating the patient about a realistic triumph or when consoling the patient for a realistic loss, for example. This human involvement of therapist with patient, though it may be a deviation from what some authors consider to be a technical ideal, can be considered the catalytic agent that enables the therapy to proceed. It enables the patient to tolerate that abstinence that is imposed, most of the time, by the therapist's just listening and interpreting. R. Sterba (personal communication, 1962) has offered an analogy to make this principle better understood: Distilled water will not transmit an electrical current. There must be impurities in the water before it can conduct electricity. Justifiably, therefore, Sterba decries the "parameter phobia" (cf. Eissler, 1953) that so afflicts many therapists and causes them to be inhuman in the pursuit of a technical ideal.

In the therapist-patient interaction both participants must recognize the importance of abstaining, to a considerable degree, from the kinds of exchanges that are so much a part of everyday social life. Because the patient, when first coming into therapy, is not aware of the necessity for this abstinence, the therapist is obliged to instruct him or her about it through example, explicit educative comments, and interpretations. When the patient indicates that she or he would like a relationship with the therapist that goes beyond the limits that the rule of abstinence imposes, the therapist must interpret this as a resistance-motivated desire to change the interaction from a therapeutic relationship to something else.

We recommend that the therapist take a natural attitude posture: polite and courteous but lacking in some of the amenities that are usual in social intercourse. The following discussion will explain this recommendation.

The therapist's courtesy is the kind of response that saves him or her from boorishness and lack of feeling. When the patient has experienced a significant loss, the therapist is responsive, recognizing the patient's sadness. When the patient has had a triumph (e.g., a musician's highly successful recital), the therapist offers congratulations. When vacations are going to occur, the therapist gives ample warning to the patient. When the therapist has inconvenienced the patient, she or he apologizes (with or without an explanation, as we mentioned in chapter 4).

However, the therapist also maintains reserve. Though friendly, he or she does not give the amenities of friendship. In particular, the therapist avoids physical contact, does not help patients on with their coats, nor light their cigarettes. The therapist may shake the patient's hand at the beginning of therapy and, of course, at the very last session. The therapist does not shake the patient's hand at every session. As with all rules, this one too has its exceptions. If a patient falls down, the therapist helps the patient to get up, regardless of the motivation for the fall. If a patient makes it a practice to offer his or her hand at the beginning and end of every session, the therapist may choose to shake it until the significance of this action is understood and the therapist is able to interpret it.

Usually the therapist avoids using the patient's first name. She is "Mrs. Smith" rather than "Mary" and he is "Mr. Jones" rather than "John." The principle here is that the therapist seeks to communicate to the patient the conviction that the patient is an adult, autonomous individual deserving of the respect that is the right of such an individual. One of the authors treated a patient who referred to himself only as "Johnny," never as "Mr. Jones." Indeed, this patient communicated to the therapist both implicitly and explicitly, when the therapist called him "Mr. Jones," that Mr. Jones was his father, he was Johnny. If the therapist had addressed the patient as Johnny, he would have seemed to agree with the patient's neurotically determined view of himself. To that extent the therapist would have become an ally of the patient's neurosis.

The therapist ideally is natural, human, and direct rather than stiff and distant; yet he or she avoids overidentification with the patient. We call the reader's attention to our discussion in chapter 4 of the therapist's constant oscillation between experiencing and observing. Overidentification involves too much emphasis on experiencing, too little on observing. Nevertheless, the therapist has to somehow capture the experience of the patient's reactions; furthermore, the therapist should, at times, openly express empathy rather than keeping it inside. The therapist should show genuine interest, a concern going beyond the contract of the therapist with the patient, a truly human attitude (see Szasz, 1956).

Freud (1915a) stated: "The treatment must be carried out in abstinence; I do not mean physical abstinence alone, nor yet the deprivation of everything that the patient desires, for perhaps no sick person could tolerate this" (p. 165). What was Freud talking about? He was not referring to the patient's sexual life in general; rather, he was talking about the satisfactions that the patient strives for in the therapy. He was recommending that the therapist not provide these wished-for satisfactions. He recognized, however, that the therapist does, and must, provide some modest satisfactions for the patient (". . . nor yet the deprivation of everything that the patient desires"). It is our position that the degree to which it is appropriate for the therapist to provide these gratifications that the patient demands is determined by the nature of the patient's ego resources and their organization. The patient with certain kinds of ego functions will demonstrate empirically that he or she can stand more frustration and more privation in the therapeutic situation. These patients will have the capacity for delay, secondary-process thinking, and draining off tensions in effective activities of daily life, thus enabling them to tolerate this privation. The patient with another kind of ego functioning needs more help from the therapist. Thus interpretations of unconscious impulses are held in abeyance until the patient is ready to approach such material.

Similarly, resistant wishes and fears, such as a patient's anticipation of going crazy if he or she allows himself or herself to participate fully and freely in the work of the therapy, may require the therapist not only to interpret these wishes and fears (saying, for example, "It is comforting to feel that you will go crazy because if that were so, it would be wise for you to leave therapy") but also directly oppose them at times (saying, for example, "Because we can understand why it's necessary for you to anticipate going crazy, we can also clearly recognize that this anticipation has no merit as a prediction").

One of the authors worked for a time with a very troubled young woman who had great difficulty in mustering even the energy to get to the therapy sessions. Despite high intelligence and education as a professional person, she would on most days sit at home in her apartment, surrounded by disorderly stacks of newspapers and magazines and piles of unwashed clothes. She felt that her husband couldn't care less about her, except for wanting her to provide him with clean shirts. She and her husband had not had sexual intercourse for two or three years. As she sat in the apartment alone she often felt that her body was heavy enough for two people; indeed, felt that there *were* two of her, one on top of the other, weighing her down. And sometimes, when she did muster the energy to do a load of washing in the basement, she would hear the superintendent going down to the basement immediately afterwards, as though what the patient had done had to be repeated or checked on. The patient thought that the landlady must be thinking her thoughts after her.

When this young woman came in one day for her therapy session dripping wet (there had been an unexpected rain), the therapist didn't hesitate to express concern about her having been caught in the rain, didn't hesitate to offer help to her in getting dried off (she refused the offer, saying that only her hair was really wet because her raincoat had protected the rest of her), and didn't hesitate to light her cigarette when she couldn't find a dry match. The therapist's solicitude was, of course, in violation of any absolute rule of abstinence. It is justified, however, not only as a decent thing to do under unusual circumstances, but also because it provided the patient the wherewithal to participate in the therapeutic work at a stressful moment.

Even when a patient does not require special consideration at particular moments, there are times when the therapist appropriately offers direct gratifications. When a woman patient picks up her handbag to leave the therapy session and tips the purse over, spilling all the contents on the floor, it is appropriate for the therapist to help her pick up the scattered contents, rather than standing stiffly by. This action can be interpreted later. Similarly, if a patient getting up from the couch to leave a session falls flat on his face, the therapist should help him get up and then interpret the falling down as a physical communication of wishes and conflicts active in the patient's mental life.

The therapist's abstinence includes refraining from joining with the patient in activities outside of the therapy unless such social or professional involvement is quite unavoidable. It was a mistake, for example, for a colleague of ours to ask a patient to plan and to execute the landscaping of his new house, even though the therapist needed the landscaping to be done and the patient was in the nursery business. The arrangement offered the patient the opportunity to express through action rather than through communication in the therapy sessions current transference feelings. These feelings happened to include deep hostility toward the therapist. Needless to say, the landscaping was abominable.

What if one meets the patient outside of the therapy setting by chance? Our rule is that the interaction should be kept to a minimum. If a patient turns up at a cocktail party to which one has been invited, one need not flee to another room or leave the party prematurely. But neither should one seek the patient out or, if introduced to her or him, encourage a lengthy conversation. While sending a son off to summer camp, one of the authors happened to come upon a patient at the Greyhound bus station. The author said hello, the patient returned the greeting and that was that. There was no need for any prolonged social chitchat or for any extended encounter.

The rule of abstinence also has implications for the handling of errors, slips, and countertransference actions generally. When the therapist makes an error, an apology should be offered to help set the matter right. The therapist should not deny that an error was made. For example, one therapist, angered by the difficulties she was having in the therapy of an adolescent boy who was coming to therapy only because of parental pressure, forgot her therapy appointment with the boy. It was appropriate for the therapist to simply apologize and not to explain why she had forgot the appointment; then the therapist had to ask herself whether she should not deal with her frustration with the therapy in a more direct way.

A friend has told us that his therapist sent him a bill for one less than the total number of scheduled sessions (the patient had missed one session because of illness and it was the therapist's practice to require payment for missed sessions even when patients are sick). When the patient paid the amount for which he had been billed rather than the larger amount he had expected to have to pay, the therapist treated this as an error on the patient's part and refused to consider whether she could have made a mistake. We consider this to be an example of the therapist's denying an error. However, where there is disagreement about who erred, and if there is no reason to suspect a countertransference response, assume that the therapist is correct.

To the rule that the therapist maintains neutrality and reserve, we advise another exception: When the patient is in great distress at the end of an hour, the therapist should allow the patient time to regain composure. It is more helpful to remind the patient a few minutes before the end of the session that time is running out and using this time for regaining composure rather than to conclude the session abruptly or permit the patient to stay beyond the scheduled time.

The Basic Rule

Free Association

The *goal* of psychoanalytic therapy is that the patient learn to understand more fully his or her own feelings, thoughts, relationships with other people, and other aspects of life. The means by which this is achieved is the patient's attempting to say, without reservation, everything that comes to mind. We call this method *free association*. Freud spoke of the instruction to the patient to say whatever comes to mind as "the basic rule" of psychoanalytic therapy.

The material that the patient produces in the course of psychotherapy consists of derivatives of her or his neurotic conflicts. A derivative is a result of an unconscious conflict, a compromise expression of that conflict which gives some discharge to the tensions of the conflict but also takes account of the realistic considerations of the current situation that the person must adapt to. Derivatives are the expression in the stream of the person's thinking and feeling of forces originating from unconscious conflicts. Because this current thinking and feeling is to a considerable degree preconscious, one may say that the derivative is a preconscious mental event that has been influenced by unconscious mental activity. It is, in other words, an over-determined mental event.

Many of the communications of the patient in free association are metaphoric. For example, a patient who told one of the authors that the air in the therapy room was smothering him was saying (metaphorically) that he wished to be, and therefore feared being, enveloped and smothered psychologically by the therapist. Another patient, who told of an incompetent physician who almost let the patient die of appendicitis before making a correct diagnosis and operating, was expressing in this way both the fear that the therapist would not appreciate the seriousness of her psychological plight and the hope that the therapist would be revealed as incompetent, which would justify the patient's holding back from participating fully in the therapy. Because so much of any patient's communication is metaphoric, it is appropriate for the therapist to seize any opportunity to demonstrate the importance of metaphoric communication: "Can you see how you used metaphors to tell me your feelings about the therapy?" The therapist can also make the point that the patient's following the free-association method made it possible for the metaphor to appear and to be understood: "You can see, then, why it is so important for you to speak whatever comes to mind."

The material that the patient communicates is both verbal and nonverbal. As we point out in chapter 5, the patient's lateness or the failure to pay the fee promptly should be considered not only to be an expression of resistance, but also to be a communication to the therapist. What the patient wears, how he or she sits in the chair or lies on the couch, and so on, may also be communications. (See Mahl's [1968, 1987] discussion of gestures and body movements in interviews.)

Facilitating Free Association

How does the therapist enable the patient to produce material through free association? The therapist does this by making direct statements or providing instructions, by giving explanations, by repeatedly expressing the expectation that the patient will free associate, and by interpreting resistance. Let us consider each of these in turn.

The therapist's instruction to the patient may be given in a long speech in an early session of the therapy, in a brief directive ("Simply tell me what comes to mind"), or in anything in-between. Although some psychoanalysts have a regular, set speech (perhaps modeled on Freud's instruction reported in his paper, "On Beginning the Treatment" [1913, pp. 134–135]) we believe that it is better to adapt one's educative interventions to the patient's needs. Thus the therapist might say at first, "Tell me what comes to mind." If the patient falters or has difficulty in free-associating, the therapist might then expand a little on the instruction: for example, "I have to know a great deal about you in order to help you. You can see, therefore, that you will do much of the talking, that your thoughts and feelings will provide the material for our learning about your living. Will you try to speak your thoughts just as they come to mind, whatever the thoughts may be."

Explanations may be given in order to show the patient the reasonableness of the free-association procedure. In the free association, as in everything connected with the therapy, we want the patient to cooperate with the therapist, as far as possible, out of an understanding of the matter rather than out of a submission to the therapist's authority. The therapist can point out that free association permits the patient's thoughts and feelings to emerge in a natural order, an order that will reveal the inner connections between these thoughts and feelings. Free association will increase the conviction of the patient that the discoveries made are truly his or hers, based on material that *he* or *she* has provided; and since what counts in the therapy is the patient's increased understanding of her or his own life, such active participation in developing the material is most in harmony with the aims of the therapy. Interrogation by the therapist might develop a good deal of information, but much that is unique for the patient might be missed. Reliance on such interrogation or reliance on material that the patient has planned out before the therapy session would make the therapy session "easier" for the patient, but at the cost of abetting the defenses against learning anything new or surprising about himself or herself. The patient is naturally afraid of surprises and fears uncovering repressed material. Such discovery is, however, necessary if he or she is to change for the better.

All of the arguments and explanations in the preceding paragraph, and more, can be used in explaining to the patient how and why free association is helpful to the therapy. Such explanations should be offered just when they are needed. For example, if a patient proposes that he or she make notes between therapy sessions and bring in these notes to read them to the therapist, the therapist will find it appropriate to point out how following such a procedure would enable the patient to avoid surprises, resulting in the patient learning nothing new.

When the patient falls silent, the therapist may at times ask, "And what comes to mind now?" If the patient responds, "Oh, it's not important," an opportunity for an explanation is presented. The therapist can point out that any thought, whether it seems important, relevant to the neurosis, or embarrassing, should be reported, otherwise the forces of censorship will dominate. When the patient makes a bare, narrative report of what happened, the therapist may wish to inquire, "And what thoughts come to mind about that?" This too is an example of what we call "prodding": the interventions by the therapist expressing the expectation that the patient will report continuously his or her stream of thought. Interventions such as these will, of course, be more frequent in the early stages of therapy.

Finally, the therapist teaches free association by interpretations of resistances. When the patient proposes to bring prepared, written notes to the therapy session, the therapist explains not only why this would be harmful to the therapy but also how such notes would serve to protect the patient from the anxiety that is bestirred when the patient risks uttering thoughts that have not been screened beforehand. When the patient falls silent after the therapist has made an interpretation that was experienced as a narcissistic affront, the therapist may interpret the silence as an indirect expression of the anger that the patient is experiencing. The therapist might say, for example, "When I pointed out to you that your wish for my advice and guidance is another expression of your very deep need for love from a parental figure, apparently you experienced my comment as a criticism. It was as though I had said, 'Stop being so childish' and you became angry at me and fell silent." Such an interpretation is aimed at bringing the unconscious elements (in this example, anger) into the open so that they may be expressed more directly, making the resistance no longer necessary for the patient.

Why Patients Learn Only Gradually to Free Associate

Though we believe that the therapist should teach free association in a variety of ways, we do not believe that the patient should be constantly badgered to free-associate. Nor do we want the therapist to present the task of free association within a framework that is coercive, involves pressure, or emphasizes a value orientation ("You should and must do as I say"). It works better if the therapist makes an appeal to the reasonable part of the patient's ego rather than to the superego. As Greenson (1967) pointed out, the therapeutic work goes best when the therapist and the patient have formed a working alliance (i.e., a relationship based on realistic considerations, aimed at forwarding the work of the therapy).

The ability to free-associate develops in the patient gradually. One expects that there will be resistances to an unhampered, open expression of thoughts and feelings, that there will be reservations on what is said and exclusions from what is reported, and that there will be falterings in the continuous production of material. Although resistance occurs throughout the whole of a psychotherapy, one may expect greater difficulty following the free-association procedure at the beginning of the therapy and less of a problem doing so later on. One may almost say that when the patient has learned to free-associate well, the end of therapy has been reached.

Some patients take to free association more readily than others. Some have a good deal of sophistication about psychotherapy. They may have read about therapy, talked with friends who were in therapy, or even have had therapy themselves previously. Such prior information may be either helpful or harmful. If what the patient has read is accurate, if a friend's experience was a good one with a competent therapist, or if the patient previously had had therapy with a competent professional, the impact is likely to be positive. These circumstances will aid the patient in carrying out his or her role as a patient.

All patients approach psychotherapy with a good deal of anxiety. Their fear of therapy interferes to some degree with their ability to carry out the free-association instruction. Afraid of what dreadful secrets about herself or himself will be discovered, a patient will become quite unable to verbalize material spontaneously. Another patient may grow deeply distrustful of the therapist (a transference reaction) and therefore unable to confide in the therapist. Other patients may expect coercion and subordination; they may have to take a combative attitude to fend off the expected domination. In general, the patient's anxiety will make it more difficult to free-associate.

Mobilizing the Patient's Understanding of Free Associating

For the patient to participate as fully as possible in the working alliance, he or she should know the principles that underlie the free-association technique. These principles are inherent in the following axiom: *Every communication of the patient during the therapeutic hour is determined by the patient's unconscious desire to participate in the therapy and is, therefore, a metaphoric, unconscious statement of mental events currently occurring in the patient's life.* Educating patients about associating, teaching them to associate, and acquainting them with the necessity for the method, all serve to impart a conviction of the truth of this axiom. Thus, when the patient knows that associations and other acts in the therapy are strictly determined and that they have unconscious, metaphoric implications, he or she is able to participate fully in the working alliance as a co-observer of the psychic processes and experiences that are the focus of study in the therapy.

The early stages of therapy accordingly provide occasions both for interpretation and for education. Indeed, the education of the patient about the principles of therapy can begin as early as the first meeting that follows the establishment of a therapeutic contract. In such an early meeting the therapist listens for a metaphoric statement of a current, specific, preconscious mental experience. (When a mental process can enter consciousness without any impediment, although for the moment it is not conscious, we speak of such a mental process as *preconscious*. See Freud, 1900, p. 541.) For example, the patient may speak of being harassed by a relative, an employer, or the drill sergeants that he or she came into contact with during military service. When the therapist understands the metaphor—in this example, an expression of concern that the therapist also will cruelly harass the patient—the therapist has an opportunity not only to interpret but also to educate.

The therapist could begin to educate by asking the patient to consider the reasons why the specific associations that had been presented were the thoughts that came to mind; she or he could have put forward any thoughts out of a very large number of possibilities. Having directed the patient's attention to how remarkable it was that *these* thoughts occurred out of all the possible thoughts, the therapist could point out the value of knowing that the patient had selected just these ideas: "As you know, we are working here to understand those hidden feelings that play a part in your experiences and reactions. Because there is only one person who knows what these feelings are (namely you, even though you are not aware of them) we have to rely on you to provide us with an indication of these hidden feelings. You have justified our faith in you because, without being aware of it, you have verbalized thoughts that came to mind while you were here in order to tell us about your hidden feelings and, at the same time, to keep yourself from becoming aware of what these feelings are. When you tell us your thoughts as they occur to you, you are expressing what you want us to know but you are doing it indirectly, in code. You and I, together, have to decipher that code."

After making such a statement the therapist can go on to demonstrate how the associations that the patient produced are metaphoric statements of current feelings in the therapy. In the example of the harassed patient, the therapist could point out how the patient's thoughts reflect concerns about therapy and about the therapist. In making this interpretation the therapist should not attempt to impose it on the patient or demand acceptance of it. Rather, the therapist should try to have the patient understand the interpretation and the reasoning that led to it. Acceptance of the interpretation can await the patient's readiness and ability to accept it.

The therapist's educative efforts do not constitute an attempt to teach the patient a complete theory of psychoanalytic psychology and psychoanalytic therapy. These efforts are not meant to invite the patient to approach the psychological processes intellectually or as abstractions. They are not an invitation to debate the unconscious implications of the patient's productions. They are not an attempt to acquaint the patient with the content of his or her unconscious. They do not provide occasions to introduce the patient to technical jargon. Their only purpose is to make the patient a knowledgeable ally in the therapeutic work.

The therapist should make use of as many opportunities as possible to carry out this educative work. This can be done through educative comments like the ones we have described and by discussing the matter after the patient has responded in a way that is opposed to the principles the therapist espouses. For example, when a patient responds with a "No!" to an interpretation, the therapist might ask how he or she knows that the interpretation is incorrect. By doing so the therapist calls the patient's attention to the fact that the validity of an interpretation cannot be judged by asking whether the patient is aware of the hidden feeling that was interpreted. To give another example: When a patient comments that she or he has been "talking about trivia," the therapist may well pose the question: "How did you happen to choose these particular items out of all of the trivia that you could have talked about?"

In making interpretations, the therapist has an opportunity to further her or his educative aims through beginning an interpretation with such words as "The thoughts that you have just reported have come to mind in order for you to tell us about. . . ." Parenthetically, we take offense at a therapist's telling a patient that what the patient *really* said was different than what the patient thought he or she was saying. The therapist, instead, should make clear that the preconscious and unconscious implications of the patient's associations are *in addition* to the patient's conscious conception of what the associations mean; in other words, the therapist does not seek to invalidate the patient's conscious experience.

Through such educative actions, the therapist creates a structure in which the patient and he or she can work effectively. Thus focusing on the preconscious and unconscious currents that lie below the surface, the patient and the therapist tacitly agree that they will not concern themselves with the realities of the patient's life; they know that the patient is able to deal with these realities, even though he or she is somewhat inhibited by neurosis. They agree that they will deal only with the preconscious mental experiences that derive from the patient's speaking of these realities in the course of therapy.

There are times that the patient, even though he or she knows the principles of therapy very well, responds to the therapist's comments as though she or he knew nothing about unconscious mental processes. The patient chooses to hear an interpretation as a comment on the realistic situation that has just been described, seeking to persuade the therapist that it was only because of the overwhelming force of these realities that thoughts about the situation came to mind. The therapist, recognizing this reaction as a resistance, takes the occasion to explain further the principles of therapy in the course of making an interpretation: "Of course, what you have been reporting really happened. Because it did happen, it serves admirably as a way for you to tell us about other feelings because you can always deny that you are telling us about hidden feelings; you need only point to this impressive actual experience that you had. We should recognize, however, that if its importance to your realistic tasks were the only reason this situation came to mind, then therapy would consist of your telling me about your experiences, to which I could comment only in terms of the realistic problems that these experiences involved. We would, therefore, have nothing to learn beyond what you already know."

To sum up: The therapist should recognize that the patient always experiences the therapist unconsciously as both an ally and an enemy. Therapists are allies because they are trying to help the patient discover the processes that are causing the patient's difficulty; therapists are the enemy for exactly the same reason, because the patient expects that encountering these processes will be very distressing (that is why the hidden feelings had to be repressed in the first place). The therapist will recognize, therefore, that all of the patient's communications in the therapy are compromises between these two responses to the therapist.

In choosing when to introduce the basic rule of free association, the therapist should bear in mind that all patients come to therapy with a good deal of anxiety, some with overwhelming anxiety. To them psychotherapy seems dreadful and dangerous. It is no violation of the general rule of abstinence for the therapist to do what she or he can to make therapy seem benign. No unnecessary threat should be introduced into the situation.

Some patients are much more sophisticated than others from the very beginning of their contact with the therapist. Some have read about therapy or have picked up a good deal of information through conversations with friends. Others are quite naive; do not know what to expect; think that psychotherapy will proceed along the same line as the medical model of advice-giving and prescription; and share with others in the group they belong to a pervasive suspicion of the "bug doctor" or "head-shrinker." If accurate knowledge is lacking, the therapist must give simple, brief explanations. Education becomes part of his or her task.

Contacts With Relatives and Associates of the Patient

For the success of the kind of psychotherapy that we are describing, it is important that the therapist *not* initiate contacts with relatives or associates of the patient. This prohibition stems from the therapist's need to maintain a posture of confidentiality and from the need to avoid real-life relationships with the patient so that the therapist can demonstrate to the patient convincingly that the patient's reactions to the therapist derive from past learning and not from current experiences with the therapist.

Such restraint from giving the patient real-life gratifications and from involving oneself in the patient's daily life through direct intervention is appropriate to the kind of therapy we are talking about. Naturally, it contrasts with what the professional person does when he or she takes a different approach to the patient's problems. Marriage counseling, for example, is by definition different from psychoanalytic therapy. Marriage counseling inevitably requires the counselor to deal directly with both husband and wife. Child therapy, because of the child's dependent status in the family, requires the therapist to become involved directly with the child's parents. It is the parents (usually) who have decided that the child needs therapy, it is they who are paying for it and otherwise supporting it, and it is they who still have such considerable power over the child that their cooperation is needed to achieve a constructive result in the treatment of the child (see A. Freud's [1946] *The Psychoanalytical Treatment of Children*). Again, family therapy with persons suffering from psychoses and their families is a different sort of approach from what we are discussing in this book. It may well be that the patient with psychosis needs to be treated as a part of the family group; we take no stand on this point. If so, the resulting therapeutic process will be different in some essential areas from therapy of the kind that we describe here.

We have recommended that the therapist not initiate contacts. Suppose the relative or associate initiates contacts with the therapist? If a relative calls the therapist, the therapist should immediately make clear to the relative that neither information about any of the patients nor confirmation or denial of a person's status as a patient will be given. (After all, the therapist cannot know for sure who the caller is.) If the therapist knows from what the patient has said and from what the caller says that the person calling already knows that the patient is in therapy, the therapist may choose to listen to what the person calling has to say. Even then, she or he will have to make clear that everything that the patient has said is confidential and that the relative will not be given any information about the patient. The therapist should further state that the patient will be told about the phone call and what the substance of the phone conversation was.

Having made these points, the therapist may feel free to learn what he or she can from the conversation with the relative. Of most interest to the therapist will be understanding why the relative is calling at this time and discovering whether this call was provoked in some way by the patient's behavior. Although the therapist will not allow herself or himself to try to get around the patient's resistance by establishing a pipeline to another source of information about the patient's behavior, the therapist will be interested in seeing how his or her understanding of the patient's real-life situation and interpersonal interactions can be deepened, extended, and somewhat corrected through making use of the information brought by the relative or associate. It is understood that the therapist does not take the statements made by the relative at face value (as though they were accurate and complete factual reports); they should be viewed in the same light as the patient's communications, as statements arising in the context of an interpersonal situation in which the communicator is involved, and as serving a number of purposes for the communicator. The therapist must ask, "Why is this person telling me this? Is this information supposed to influence me? What is this caller trying to accomplish by saying this?"

Not only does the therapist promise the relative that the patient will be told of the phone call, but the therapist actually does this at the first opportunity (i.e., at the very beginning of his next session with the patient). For example, the therapist may say, "Your spouse called last night and said . . . Of course, what you tell me is confidential, and so I said nothing about what you have told me. I also stated that I would have to tell you the substance of the conversation, both what was said to me and what I said." Such complete communication with the patient is necessary to the maintenance of the patient's trust in the therapist and of the patient's confidence that what he or she says is indeed confidential. We advise the therapist to bring this matter up immediately, because if this not done the patient may assume that the therapist is talking with the relative behind the patient's back. Such an assumption can be entirely avoided by complete and speedy communication. Even if the patient protests, "That's all right. I trust you; you don't need to tell me what you said," the therapist should insist on reporting the substance of the conversation with the relative.

If the relative says, "I'd like to have an appointment with you, doctor," the therapist should reply, "Why don't you take it up with the patient, and if it is agreeable, I can do it. But why do you want to come and talk with me?" An appointment with a relative or friend should be arranged only with the patient's permission and never at the therapist's initiation. The request for an appointment should be treated in the same way as any phone call from a relative; that is, the therapist must tell the patient that the relative called requesting an appointment, and the therapist must say to the relative, "You understand, of course, that I will tell the patient that you called asking for an appointment with me." If an appointment is granted (the patient consenting), the therapist reports to the patient the substance of the conversation with the relative. And, of course, in the interview with the relative, confidentiality of the patient's communications is maintained.

Written communications concerning the patient are shown to her or him at the earliest opportunity after they have been received by the therapist. Similarly, the therapist shows the patient any communications about the patient that are being sent out (with the patient's knowledge and consent) before they are sent.

Confidentiality

The best conditions for psychotherapy exist when the therapist can honestly say, "Whatever you tell me is absolutely confidential. I will not tell anyone anything that you say to me or give anyone any information about you." If the therapist can take this position, it is clear that she or he has a relationship with and responsibility to *only* the patient, that no other person or institution is being served, and that the patient is in charge of his or her own life and is making use of the therapist as an expert consultant.

When the therapist cannot guarantee full confidentiality, the effectiveness of the therapy is damaged to the degree that the relationship is compromised. For example, if the therapist is providing psychotherapy for patients living in an alcoholism treatment center, and if the administrators of the center insist on an exchange of information about patients between the psychotherapist and the staff of the treatment center, the psychotherapy will be compromised. The patient will expect that what is told to the therapist will be used by administrators in deciding whether to discharge or retain the patient. There will also be doubts about whether expressions of dissatisfaction with the authorities of the center will be communicated to these authorities, which could then lead to retaliation. The difficulties created by this kind of sharing of information among a staff will be brought to an irreducible minimum if the therapist makes clear to her or his patient exactly what kind and amount of communication there will be between therapist and staff. The patient can also be told, "If there are matters that you want to tell me but want me to keep to myself and not communicate to the staff, you will have to tell me explicitly what you don't want the staff to know in order to have absolute assurance of confidentiality."

We take confidentiality so seriously that some might call us inflexible. For example, one of the authors received a long-distance call from the mother of a 22-year-old man who had been a patient. She began, "You're the doctor my son was seeing, aren't you?" Because the therapist was quite sure that his former patient's mother knew this to be so, he agreed; yes, he had been the young man's therapist. (Otherwise he would have said, "My relationships with any patients are confidential, and I can't tell you whether I saw your son or not.") Then the mother continued, "Will you tell me what was wrong with him?" The therapist answered, "No." The caller continued, "But I'm his mother." The therapist replied, "I know that, but my relationship with your son is confidential, and I won't tell you *anything* that I learned about him. By the way, why are you calling?" The mother then said that her son had not been as friendly to her as she wished him to be, and she thought maybe the therapist could throw some light on this.

It is our practice, too, not to tell others whether or not a patient is still in therapy or whether he or she was ever in therapy with us. It is none of the inquirer's business to know the answers to these questions. Our relationship is with our patient and with no one else.

Chapter 7 —————————

Personal Responses of the Therapist

For the most part, discussions of the therapeutic interaction focus on the emotional involvements of the patient and neglect the personal involvements of the therapist. Yet psychotherapy is a human interaction in which we cannot neglect the humanness of either participant if we are to achieve true understanding of it.

In the psychoanalytic theory of psychotherapy, the therapist's personal involvement in the therapeutic process is discussed under the heading "countertransference." Though we owe the term to Freud ("The Future Prospects of Psycho-Analytic Therapy," 1910b), he hardly discussed this topic. Other analytic authors have written extensively on the subject; the reader may be referred to discussions by Fenichel (1941), Glover (1955), Menninger (1958), and Searles (1965). At times, analytic writers say or seem to say that countertransference embraces *any* emotional response of the therapist to the patient. In our judgment, however, such a broad definition is less useful than one that sticks to Freud's original meaning. Freud (1910b) wrote: "We have become aware of the 'counter-transference,' which arises in him [the physician] as a result of the patient's influence on his unconscious feelings, and we are almost inclined to insist that he shall recognize this countertransference in himself and overcome it" (pp. 144–145).

Thus countertransference may be defined as including:

1. Unconscious reactions in the therapist, *stimulated by the patient*, so long as these reactions remain unconscious and are not appropriately dealt with by the therapist. These reactions may be either (a) a seeking of gratifications of the therapist's needs, these gratifications being irrelevant to the therapeutic task or (b) defensive responses, sparing the therapist awareness of unconscious conflicts.
2. Reactions of the therapist, *resulting from his or her own intrapsychic processes*, which are displaced to the therapeutic situation. Such displacements include transferences of infantile conflicts to the therapeutic situation.

The therapist's displacements are, of course, not mutually exclusive from the responses of the therapist to provocations of the patient; rather, these represent extremes on a scale that ranges from little contribution from the patient to the therapist's countertransference to a large patient contribution.

Responses That Are Not Countertransference

There are other personal responses of the therapist that are not to be considered countertransference. These are (a) responses based on factors extrinsic to doing therapy with a particular patient and (b) responses intrinsic to such therapy.

Responses Extrinsic to Therapy

The therapist has feelings about herself or himself that arise because of inexperience; personal status (e.g., as a student or a professional, as a man or a woman, as a psychologist or a psychiatrist); his or her view of self-worth as a helper; the need to earn a living; or personal reputation. Any of these factors or all of them can influence the therapist's personal reactions to the patient.

Inexperience may make the therapist unsure of himself or herself. This uncertainty and lost feeling can be dealt with by either showing hesitancy or by a bravado that covers up the sense of helplessness. Among beginning therapists only one who has an unusually strong sense of self-confidence is able to act with appropriate assurance but without bravado. Such a confident person accepts his or her own limitations, knows what can realistically be offered to the patient, and finds this offering good.

Inferiority in status can, like inexperience, create a sense of helplessness in the therapist, or it can cause the therapist to feel resentment at his or her second-class citizenship and a need either to act in conformity with the externally imposed self-image or to act so as to shatter it. The therapist may *feel* second-class because he or she is a psychologist rather than a psychiatrist (especially if working in a medically oriented organization), because professional recognition among colleagues has not been achieved, because of being a certain sex or ethnicity, or, because he or she is a trainee rather than a person who has achieved full professional status. How does the therapist respond, emotionally, when the patient asks, "Are you a psychiatrist or a psychologist? What's the difference between a psychologist and a psychiatrist?" What kind of response is given when the patient asks, "Are you a student? Are you using me for a guinea pig?" Only therapists who are sure of their worth as a person and who know that they have been well taught (or if students, that they are being well supervised), will be able to accept such questions with equanimity and deal with them with poise.

We cannot assume, either, that all therapists believe in the value of psychotherapy and are persuaded that they have the capability to help troubled people. Some are inwardly disillusioned without knowing it. They have lost heart but cannot bear to acknowledge to themselves that they no longer believe in the value of their work. Some therapists, it seems to us, have never had the experience of seeing a striking therapeutic result, either in the course of their own professional training or in their work as therapists since that time. Thus they have no real conviction that psychotherapy can help people. At the same time, the therapist may be beset by critical colleagues in other fields: the clinical psychologist by skeptical and hostile academic psychologists, the psychiatrist by biologically minded fellow physicians, and the social worker by administrators and consultants who set little store by social-work psychotherapy. Pressures like these sap the therapist's self-confidence in his or her worth as a helper.

In order to be effective it is necessary for the therapist to significantly invest in the work that she or he is doing. In order to make this investment, it is necessary for the therapist to have a patient with whom to work. Accordingly, when a patient discontinues therapy, it frequently happens that the therapist experiences this as a situation in which he or she has "lost the patient." Therapists who feel that their patient has been lost experience a blow to their self-esteem, a criticism of their competence, and, sometimes, a self-confidence crisis. For therapists who respond in this way, each of their patients is as necessary to them as they are to their patients. The therapist will therefore direct a substantial part of his or her effort not toward understanding the patients and, when they quit, toward accepting their decision to terminate (whatever their reasons may be), but instead toward keeping the patient in therapy at whatever cost, regardless of how the therapy is compromised by these compromises. Such a personal reaction contrasts with the reaction of the self-confident therapist who understands the patient's decision to leave therapy in terms of the patient's unconscious motivations (especially in terms of the anxiety that is provoked when the patient anticipates confronting repressed feelings and thoughts).

The therapist's need to earn a living is another source of personal reactions to the patient. At times a therapist may accept as patients persons who are not ready for psychotherapy and cannot profit from it because she or he happens to need patients at the time; or the decision to continue therapy even though nothing is being accomplished in it may be made because the income that the therapy provides is needed. Having a sufficient demand for her or his services so that acceptance of a particular person or the continuation of a single patient will not make any appreciable difference in financial status is perhaps the best way for a therapist to guard against having decisions biased by financial needs.

Patients naturally assume that the therapist needs the money that their fees provide. Sometimes they try to put this circumstance to use in the service of resistance. A patient may accuse the therapist of greed, of exploiting patients, and of lacking any compassion for the economically less fortunate. If the therapist does not openly recognize his or her need to earn, or if this need has been allowed to bias some professional decisions, the therapist will find such an attack hard to deal with effectively. Only if the therapist is secure in the knowledge that he or she wants to earn money from his or her work, believes in the right to do so, and knows that every effort is being made to prevent this need from biasing decisions about patients' needs for therapy, can the therapist confidently face the attacking patient and say, "It is clear that you need to put me in the position of exploiter, to feel yourself to be a victim. Why is this necessary for you?"

The therapist's reputation has a demonstrable influence on her or his way of responding to the patient. In discussing reputation we can distinguish between the therapist's own view of his or her reputation and how others view him or her. A therapist who has a mediocre reputation among colleagues in the professional community of a city may be held in high repute among a smaller circle of professional persons who know her or him really well. A therapist who is held in low esteem by colleagues may, through self-deceptive mechanisms, believe herself or himself to be an outstanding practitioner. A therapist of great repute among the larger community may be held in lower esteem by close friends. Ordinarily, of course, there is a continuous interaction between the therapist's own self-evaluation and the community's evaluation; ordinarily there is a fair amount of correspondence between the two.

The therapist's reputation concern for his or her reputation may decisively influence his or her behavior in therapy when, for example, he or she is presenting a case to a consultant. A therapist who is presenting a case to the visiting, prestigious psychoanalyst may find herself or himself behaving unnaturally. In these circumstances an ordinarily loquacious therapist may become unnaturally reticent; a typically aggressive therapist may hold hostilities somewhat in check, attempting to be warm and friendly toward the patient. The presenter may fear to challenge the patient who is providing material for the continuous case conference. Any confrontation of the patient, she or he is likely to feel, will expose the presenter to the risk of not having a patient to report on, or the risk of having the consultant comment unfavorably.

Another kind of influence on the therapy grows out of the therapist's relationship to the person referring the patient. If a patient is referred by a clerical friend of the therapist, the therapist may want the patient to show progress in order to justify the friend's faith in his or her professional skill. The therapist may also have some concern about whether the patient continues to participate actively in the life of the parish. A good therapist will hold in check the tendency to avoid exploring with the patient those unconscious conflicts that may be contributing to the patient's attachment to religious institutions; but it is undeniable that the therapist may feel a twinge of concern about his or her friend's possible reaction to changes in the patient's religious practices. Or the patient may be the sibling of a professional colleague. One should not accept such a patient if the colleague is a close personal friend. Yet even when the professional relationship is more distant, the therapist cannot help worrying about the colleague's opinion of the therapy from time to time.

Responses Intrinsic to Therapy

The feeling of being responsible *to* another person, as opposed to the feeling of being responsible *for* another person, is experienced by every conscientious therapist. Therapists differ, of course, in how they respond to this responsibility. A good therapist, we believe, has a sense of commitment to the patient (see Silverman, 1963). She or he cares what happens to the patient. We also believe, however, that the therapist should not take responsibility for what should remain the patient's responsibility. The therapist should, for example, demand payment of fees without counseling the patient on ways to get the necessary funds (e.g., getting a part-time job); interpret the unconsciously determined reactions to a spouse without giving advice for or against divorce; or respond empathically to a patient's report of marital problems and encourage discussion of these matters; but she or he must not, when the patient complains of loneliness, run immediately to alleviate the distress. It is the patient's responsibility to cope with this loneliness until it can be discussed in therapy or the patient can find active ways to alleviate it.

The degree of responsibility that it is appropriate for the therapist to assume varies according to the ego-resources of the patient. A patient suffering from neurosis who is outstandingly suited to psychoanalytic therapy is expected to take responsibility for getting to the therapy sessions, for paying the fees, for dealing with crises in life, and for carrying the burden of the production of material during the therapy sessions. It is assumed that he or she has sought out the therapist with the expectation that the therapist is a skilled professional who can help solve some problems of living, but also with the expectation that he or she, the seeker of help, retains full responsibility for decisions and for outcome.

By contrast, a person with psychosis, who is unable to bear some of the frustrations that psychoanalytic therapists typically require of their patients, requires more support from the therapist to provide gratification of personal needs and requires more educative interventions to point out the way to a reconstructed way of life. One of us (as we reported in chapter 6) greeted a patient one day as she came into the office dripping wet from the rain outside. She took out a cigarette and fumbled for matches; there were none. The therapist not only provided paper towels that she could dry herself off with, he also gave her a light for her cigarette. He would not have considered making such gestures to a mentally resourceful patient with neurosis, but with this desperate, fearful, and forlorn young woman the gestures seemed right.

An implicit or explicit threat of suicide by a patient in therapy raises—as much as any occurrence in therapy—the issue of the therapist's responsibility. The therapist who feels responsible *for* a patient will likely react to the threat itself, acting to assuage whatever anxiety is aroused by the threat. These actions may include hospitalizing the patient, warning relatives, or some other extratherapeutic intervention. The therapist who feels responsible *to* a patient by contrast will recognize that the patient is free to do what she or he wishes with her or his life, that the therapist has no way, realistically, to prevent a suicide if the patient intends to kill herself or himself, and that the therapist's responsibility is to analyze the communication of the patient in the same way that other, less dramatic communications are analyzed. (We are, of course, neglecting for the moment the external coercions on the therapist from legal opinions and from threatened lawsuits; these may press the therapist to do antitherapeutic things in order to be protected from attacks based on a misunderstanding of what can be achieved by trying to coerce the patient.) Responsibility to the patient thus requires having an absolute respect for the patient's resources and requires one to allow the exercise of these resources, not overestimating or underestimating their extent. With the patient who chooses to attempt suicide or to complete it rather than to use personal resources for coping with life problems, the therapist can only respect the patient's choice. With the patient who has demonstrated a lack of the capacity for choice (e.g., she or he is in a drug-induced delusional state), the therapist would assume a degree of responsibility corresponding to an assessment of the patient's lack of resources.

Because of the threats of lawsuits in our litigious society or of other legal action, the therapist cannot always act strictly in accord with the recommendations— rational recommendations, we believe—just presented. If a patient talks about killing himself or herself, the therapist must accordingly make a written record of this in the case notes, together with a clear statement of why she or he believes there is evidence that no action by her or him is required (if there is such evidence) or an indication of what was done to prevent the suicide (if there is evidence of a real risk of the patient's killing herself or himself). The best preventive, of course, is interpretation of the motives that are provoking the suicidal thoughts, and especially of those motives that are unconscious. Karon and VandenBos (1981, pp. 262–271) provide a useful discussion of the dynamics of suicide, together with recommendations to the therapist about how to respond to threats of suicide. If these recommended actions are tried and prove to be ineffective, it is likely that nothing would have prevented the suicide. Nevertheless, when the therapist believes that she or he has not reached the patient with her or his interpretations, this concern is communicated to the patient and the patient is asked how this problem should be dealt with. In extreme situations the therapist will tell the patient that he or she feels compelled to warn responsible family members of the suicidal risk, recommend or insist on hospitalization, or to do whatever else will protect the therapist from a future lawsuit. The therapist should keep in mind, however, that the very family members who by their actions have driven a patient to suicide may deflect the blame from themselves by suing him or her for malpractice.

The responsibility for intervening in another person's life is an awesome one. A therapist is not playing games, is not spinning empty theories; what is done matters, profoundly. The therapist alone bears this responsibility. Supervision may blur the boundaries of his or her concern; theory may allow the belief that the therapist has a limited role to play; and a client-centered or passively analytic technique may shroud personal involvement with another human being. Nevertheless the therapist bears this awesome and lonely responsibility. No wonder she or he reaches out for reassurance, for technical support, and for scientific knowledge. No wonder the therapist feels, at times, so inadequate to the task.

Therapists, however, are not completely filled with feelings of inadequacy. If they have been appropriately trained, they feel a justified self-confidence in their ability to help other human beings with their problems of living. After all, they have had training in the techniques of psychotherapy and in the personality theory of which these techniques are applications and have had previous supervised experience in doing therapy. Such supervision was extremely important to their development as therapists. From it they learned to observe with some accuracy the interaction between themselves and patients, and to understand it to some degree. As therapists see their work strengthening the capacity of their patients to lead more effective and rewarding lives, as they see their apt interpretations releasing patients' capacity for self-understanding and for emotional expressiveness, they feel good about what they are doing and believe that they can help other persons as they have helped those who came to them previously.

At all times, therapists share responsibility for the treatment with their patient. For this reason, they can, when appropriate, discuss with the patient what course of action should be taken. Furthermore, therapists know that they can seek consultation as necessary and that it can help them over rough spots. They know—or should know—that there is no impugning of their own skill in availing themselves of consultation. For a therapist to insist that always and under all circumstances he or she is doing superlatively well or to insist that any difficulties that arise should be attributed to the patient, expresses a defensive attitude. That attitude betrays weakness, not strength.

The therapist's own personal therapy (we assume that he or she has experienced therapy somewhere along the way) has helped to produce a capacity to listen to the patient and to respond helpfully. It has provided a model for therapeutic action, as Ella Freeman-Sharpe (1947) pointed out. It has provided some knowledge of how the patient feels in the role of patient. Most important of all, it has produced in the therapist a conviction that unconscious mental life is real, and it has led her or him to strive to be open to what the patient is saying, whether such communication is straightforwardly in words or is allusive or is in the language of gesture and action.

It would be impossible to overstate the importance of the therapist's personality in making it possible (or impossible) to carry out the role of psychotherapist. It is not that therapists present themselves as models of good adaptation to life; it is rather that they show the kind of openness to experience and ability to accept their own and others' limitations and turbulent impulses and quaking fears, that the patient needs to strive for.

And when can therapists be open, accepting, and honest? When their own lives are not in the grip of self-deceptions and unrecognized frustrations. We believe that every therapist should at intervals throughout her or his career question whether she or he can be a therapist. The answer should be based not so much on the record of therapeutic "successes" and "failures" as on his or her estimate of himself or herself as a person. What is the balance of frustrations and satisfactions in her or his life? How much free energy is there for concerning herself or himself with others' problems of living in an undistorted, self-giving way?

Some therapists who begin their careers in a hopeful but realistic spirit, develop after a time a disillusionment with psychotherapy. They may not be aware of the disillusionment. Often the ebbing away of a hopeful spirit is covered up by a rather frantic search for new, more effective techniques. Such disillusionment happens, we believe, more often than is generally supposed.

Therapists can be influenced positively, too, by their continuing experience in therapeutic work, as Freud was. We owe his progress from hypnosis to waking suggestion, from suggestion to free association, from emphasis on content to emphasis on transference and resistance, from emphasis on analysis of impulses to analysis of the ego, etc., to Freud's ability to develop as he learned from the clinical work he was doing. Another notable example of shifting technique and enhanced understanding of the therapeutic process is given by Hellmuth Kaiser (see Fierman, 1965), who has described his odyssey from a rather impersonal technique emphasizing content interpretations to a much more personal style of therapy emphasizing free emotional communication between patient and therapist.

Finally, the therapist is influenced by the realistic gratifications gotten from doing psychotherapy. Involvement in psychotherapy enhances the therapist's ability to understand other people, a rewarding capacity. He or she feels gratification in the identification with the patient's achievement of mastery over the patient's life (i.e., it is pleasant to see the patient learn). The human contact of the therapeutic situation is in itself rewarding to a degree, even though the effective therapist cannot rely on the therapeutic relationship for any substantial part of personal needs for relatedness and mutuality. The therapist finds the sense of helping others intensely gratifying. As a rule those who chose therapy as a profession were pushed by the need to help other people, to stand toward others in a maternal role. To some degree the therapist finds in therapy pleasures derived from infantile sexual drives (voyeuristic, sadistic, maybe even masochistic), but the effective therapist finds gratification for these drives in sublimation at the highest level, the level of creative effort (Sterba, 1930).

Because the therapist is not a god, the same processes that the therapist deals with in a patient are also active in himself or herself. The therapist, like the patient, has needs, has fears of open communication, and has defensive strategies. One cannot expect the therapist to be inhumanly perfect; but one does ask that he or she be cognizant of his or her humanity.

Handling of the Therapist's Feelings: Countertransference

The therapist's personal reactions are nothing to be ashamed of, and countertransference is not a dirty word (Tower, 1956). Countertransference is not to be denied, for it is inevitable. It is, rather, to be understood.

From the technical point of view the awareness of one's own reactions provides an avenue—the most important avenue—for the understanding of the patient (A. Reich, 1951). When one is angry and when one's own neurotic needs have not contributed substantially to this anger one knows that the patient is being provocative. When one feels sexually drawn to the patient, one knows that the patient is being seductive. When one feels impelled to mother the patient, one knows that the patient is experiencing dependent longings and is sending out signals to elicit a helping response from the therapist.

When the patient's narrative is confusing and contradictory, when the verbal interchange seems to give no handhold to understanding, therapists know that their own emotional reactions can be relied on as a dependable guide to what is going on if their own psychopathology is not distorting their understanding of the situation. The need for therapists to make use of personal responses to the patient as a guide to what is happening is one of the strongest arguments in favor of their assuring themselves that they are approximately normal; sufficiently normal, at least, that they do not get a distorted reading of the therapeutic interaction.

What is prohibited to therapists is not their responding emotionally to the patient, but their acting blindly on their feelings. If, for example, a therapist is unwittingly drawn into playing the role of protector or into a bitter argument over whether it is ethical for therapists to earn so much money from their work when so many persons of modest means cannot avail themselves of psychotherapy, he or she has fallen into the trap of playing opposite the patient's transference role. As Fenichel (1941) put it, "playing the patient's game." And, as Fenichel went on to emphasize, the therapist can never analyze the transference behavior as long as she or he is playing the game; the therapist has to refuse to join in the game in order to analyze. However, the therapist's minimal response to the patient's provocations, the *tendency* to play this game, is what tells him or her what the game is.

The technical rules of psychoanalytic therapy, which advise the therapist to maintain a therapeutic neutrality, are a great help in restraining her or his tendencies to act out. They also help him or her to discover this acting out (and the feeling that prompted it) when it does occur. For example, there is a rule that one should never touch the patient after the first handshake. The impulse to touch the patient is easier to control and to understand because there is this rule. One of the authors was once confronted by an attractive young woman patient in a dramatic hysterical attack—weeping, curled up in a fetus-like position on the waiting-room sofa, apparently in a complete daze. He felt a very strong impulse to take her by the arm to lead her to the therapy room, to steady her wobbly, disoriented gait.

Because of the technical rule he restrained himself. Because of this restraint he was able to analyze his own emotional responses and his patient's in the situation. As we understand the situation, the patient through her actions communicated to the therapist her wish for succorance from him. The therapist's impulse to take her by the hand was, in part, aroused by the communication. In effect he heard her emotionally rather than cognitively. By analyzing the situation and his responses to it, the therapist was enabled not to act on the impulse. Guided by the feelings bestirred in him, he interpreted to the patient her strong wish for his care and her conviction that only by dramatically presenting herself as helpless could she achieve it.

When acting out does occur, therapists with the courage to face their own inner life can learn something from the acting out. One of the authors once completely forgot an hour with a patient; and because he had to go to this therapy office from another place to meet with this patient, the patient came to the appointment and found no therapist present. The therapist is a punctual and reliable person; this is the first and only occasion on which he missed a therapy hour through forgetting or neglect. He had to ask himself, therefore, what had motivated his negligence. It did not take him long to discover that he had become increasingly discouraged, frustrated, and angry about this particular therapy. The patient was a young man who was attending the therapy sessions only because of pressure from his wife to do so. He had come to therapy because he had been threatened with divorce if he did not "seek counseling." But he had no wish to uncover his problems, to learn about his latent resentments against his wife that were being expressed in the marital difficulties. Thus he came to the therapy sessions and passively defied the therapist (and his wife) by refusing to try to communicate openly, and verbally, with the therapist.

Having discovered the intensity of his feelings about his defiant patient, the therapist was then able to confront the patient with the patient's defiant feelings in the therapeutic interaction. The outcome was that the patient found himself still unable to cooperate in the task of uncovering his inner conflicts; and the therapist had to say to him, "Because you're only coming to get your wife off your back, this therapy can do you no good. It's wasting your money and my time. When you really want to work on your problems, come back. But for now, I'm not willing to go on." The patient left, protesting that he wanted therapy, though acknowledging that his chief feeling about it was that coming to the sessions got his wife off his back. Though it is unfortunate that this patient did not have the intrinsic motivations to support a psychotherapeutic enterprise, it was better to know this and act appropriately on this knowledge, than to persist blindly in the frustrating task of pretending to engage in therapy.

The therapist of a borderline patient, a young man who had sought therapy because he felt unable to achieve satisfying relationships with women and because he felt unslakable hostility to his mother, noticed that he wondered whether this patient was lying in wait for him, ready to stab him, after the therapy sessions. This patient was the last one the therapist saw in the evening, at a time when very few people were around in the office building. Yet, the therapist told himself, it didn't seem very likely that his patient would really attack him. The therapist's fantasy, we believe, was based upon a correct perception of the strength of the patient's hostility and also upon an unconscious evaluation of the danger of the patient's unruly impulses. The therapist, it seems, was identifying with the patient, who felt these angry impulses to be so terrifyingly dangerous that they might get completely out of hand. Having pondered the reasons for his fantasy, the therapist began to understand the associations in this new way and began to interpret to the patient the patient's angry feelings toward *him*, the patient's fear of having them burst out uncontrollably, and his expectation that the therapist would retaliate savagely.

Another therapist reports that he generally feels some sexual excitement when women patients turn to him, weeping, for his support. He made this pattern of response a matter for his own self-analysis.

One of us had occasion to observe the reactions of a beginning therapist as she had exceptional difficulty in terminating the therapy of a patient, when external circumstances made it necessary for the therapy to be brought to a close. (The supervisor was no longer able to continue the supervision, which made it necessary for the patient either to stop therapy or to transfer to another therapist in the clinic.) The supervisor repeatedly instructed the therapist to announce to the patient that therapy would have to come to an end; and the therapist frequently found herself unable to tell the patient that the therapy would end. Although the supervisor attributed the therapist's difficulty to an inability to deal with an object loss, we cannot rule out the possibility that the therapist was angry at the somewhat arbitrary way in which the supervisor insisted on termination of the case, refusing to consider carefully whether the patient might need more treatment and, if so, how it could be provided.

Those infantile wishes that, when sublimated, furnish part of the energy needed for effective professional work can, when sublimation fails, disrupt the therapist's work. There is in scientific work, as Kubie (in "Some Unsolved Problems of the Scientific Career," 1953, 1954) pointed out, an opportunity to express some aspects of voyeuristic interests. The therapist has a chance to fulfill such interests in the course of investigatory work. But at times such interests come to the fore, dominating the therapist's behavior—as one of us noticed in pursuing too forcefully with one patient an inquiry into the details of the patient's sexual life. The excessiveness of the therapist's interest was demonstrated in the lack of appropriateness of this inquiry to the current flow of material in the case.

A colleague at another university told us (taking care to conceal the identities of both the patient and the therapist) about a female graduate student who had a need to bully her woman patient through advice-giving. This bullying got completely out of control; no instruction by her supervisor had the slightest effect on it. Every supervisory comment was countered with some rationalization. The student said, for instance, that with such a poverty-stricken, uneducated person as this patient was, one had to tell her what to do.

Here, obviously, the therapist's strong needs for domination of other human beings—a need that in our opinion derived from the threat that passivity unconsciously represented for this student—distored the therapist's actions in the therapy and made it impossible for her to do effective therapeutic work. This is an example of countertransference stemming from the therapist's neurosis. It is a kind of countertransference that is likely to enter into all of the therapist's work.

The therapist usually has special difficulty in guarding against countertransference acting out when some management of the therapeutic situation is called for. By "management" we mean some nonanalytic intervention that is necessary to provide the framework for the analytic work; for example, putting the clock at a place in the therapy room where the patient cannot see it so it will be more difficult for him or her to save conflict-related communications until the last few minutes of the session or asking the patient not to prepare a list of things to talk about.

In guarding against acting out, it helps to be clear about the distinction between management and interpretation. One should not use management where interpretation is called for. If the patient comes late and then explains that she or he missed the bus, the therapist should not suggest scheduling the session 15 minutes later (a management); the therapist should, instead, inquire into the reasons for the patient's lateness (an action that prepares the way for interpretation). On the other hand, one should not interpret where management is appropriate. When the patient telephones to say his or her appointment cannot be kept because the car broke down, one doesn't attempt to analyze the resistance to the therapy over the phone. One simply agrees with the patient on the time when the next therapy session will take place. The interpretation of the role of resistance in the missed appointment should be left to that next meeting.

The necessity for management brings temptations toward acting in terms of one's own personal dispositions regardless of appropriateness to the therapeutic task. One's sadism can be expressed by the way one insists on the patient's compliance with the therapeutic structure. A therapist may say, "Well, if you can't come twice a week, you're really not very interested in clearing up these problems. Unless you can come twice rather than once a week, we'd better forget it." How much of such a response stems from a realistic evaluation of the needs of the therapeutic task, and how much from the therapist's acting out of sadistic impulses?

We recommend, therefore, that the therapist exercise a self-discipline in management of the therapeutic situation. This discipline is defined, ideally, only and ultimately by the reality of the therapeutic situation (i.e., by what is objectively necessary for setting up an effective therapeutic enterprise). Admittedly, the therapist's own personal style will exert some influence on the arrangements for the therapy. For example, the choice between handing the patient the bill at the end of the month or putting the bill in the mail matters little to some therapists, while other therapists have a fairly strong preference for one method or the other.

Just as discipline is required in management, so it is needed in making interpretations. The timing and the depth of interpretations should be objectively appropriate, not expressive of a need of the therapist to "hold the patient's feet to the fire," to demonstrate unusual skill by unusually speedy interpretations, or to prove himself or herself gentle and kind by failing to make appropriate but unwelcome interpretations.

Conclusion

To summarize now what we have said about the therapist's personal reactions in the therapy: We have defined *countertransference* as consisting of inappropriate, unconscious reactions of the therapist to the patient. We pointed out that the therapist also has many other responses to the patient, justified responses, of which the therapist is aware. We emphasized the importance to the therapist of knowing what she or he really feels toward the patient, pointing out that this information is essential for effective work in the therapy. Finally, we considered how the therapist can orient herself or himself in order to cope with personal feelings toward the patient in a way that will be more constructive.

Chapter 8

Resistance: The Ego Defends Against the Unconscious Becoming Conscious

Types of Resistances

Recognizing Resistance

Dealing With Resistance

A young woman who had been in therapy for some time and whose therapist was seeing her in the face-to-face arrangement (rather than having her use the couch) came into the therapy room one day, looked around the room, and asked the therapist who had chosen the furnishings for the office. She followed up this seemingly rhetorical question by chivying the therapist and making hostile comments about various items of furniture, the decoration of the office, and its lighting. Finally she gave her attention to the couch. In the belligerent tone that had characterized her remarks so far, she wondered out loud why it was there and what use the therapist made of it. Musing on this, she concluded that the couch must be in the room so that the therapist could sit on it with patients and "have intimate conversations." At this point the therapist made an interpretation. He proposed that the patient used her open hostility and belligerence to deny (to protect herself from knowing) that she had an unconscious fantasy that she and the therapist might share the couch for intimate activities. The therapist, having arrived at some understanding of the motivation for his patient's hostility, then wondered silently about the motivation for the sexual wish that the patient had expressed indirectly. His interest in this prompted him to listen with special attentiveness to the associations that followed this interpretation.

The associations following the interpretation, he noted, were overtly concerned with the idea that the therapist would use his patients callously, for his own purposes and gratifications. The patient then taxed him about his intent to discard his patients without a thought for their anguish or for their need for him. The therapist made the observation—out loud—that it was comforting to the patient to have the idea of an intimate relationship with the therapist. First, he said, it helped her to hide from herself how frightened she was of her desire for a dependent relationship with the therapist. Lovers, of course, have a different kind of relationship from that of parent and child. He remarked, further, that to be a lover is, to a degree, to have a closer relationship than a patient and a therapist have. Finally the therapist pointed out that being a lover would give the patient some claim on the therapist's attention and would diminish her fear of being abandoned and discarded, a fear that she was also expressing. Responding to this interpretation, the patient said, "What am I going to do while you are on vacation?" (She had been told some time before that the therapist planned to take a vacation soon.) Plaintively she said, "What if I need you while you are away?"

In this vignette we can see the dynamic interplay of the factors that are continuously active in the therapy situation: wish, defense, wish as defense, defense as wish, and both wish and defense as resistance. The hostility that the patient first presented—a hostility directed toward the therapist—was a resistance that served to defend the patient against the therapeutic process. That process, if continued, would result in her having to recognize that she had sexual wishes toward the therapist; that would entail her experiencing the anxiety that was tied to those sexual wishes. The sexual wishes were themselves, in turn, a resistance; in effect the patient preferred to derive from the therapy not an understanding of her life but intimacy and sexual gratification. At the same time, this resistance defended the patient against her fear of a dependent relationship with the therapist, a relationship that would make her vulnerable to abandonment. Our example should make clear how vital a role resistance plays in therapy as well as how necessary to the patient the resistance is.

The concept of resistance appropriately occupies a central position in the psychoanalytic theory of therapy. Yet it is a concept that is often misunderstood. We believe, therefore, that *resistance* needs to be carefully defined if the therapist is to make use of this concept effectively. For the purposes of our discussion, we define resistance as follows: It is a force within a patient that acts against the therapeutic process, against the task of uncovering and dissolving the neurotic conflict. It is a force that works to maintain repression even at the cost of the perpetuation, or even the expansion, of neurotic symptoms.

Although resistance is antitherapeutic, we should also consider it to be an attempt by the patient to adapt to the anticipated dangers that will come about through his participation in therapy. Resistance, accordingly, appears in almost every production of the patient in therapy: in associations, insofar as they are disguised, metaphoric statements rather than straightforward communications; in dreams, insofar as the latent content has been distorted and transmuted by the dream work into manifest content; in behavior, insofar as it is a manifestation of a patient's attempt to compromise the desire to reveal himself or herself with the desire to hide from himself or herself; and in symptoms, insofar as they are compromises between desires to express unconscious motives and to repress those same motives.

To put the matter more simply: Resistance results from the patient's attempt to avoid the anxiety evoked in the therapy when repressed feelings, wishes, thoughts, and experiences threaten to return to awareness. Because resistance results from an attempt to deal with anxiety, and because anxiety always occurs in response to attempts to make the unconscious conscious, anxiety and resistance will always be present throughout therapy. Their presence, therefore, is to be welcomed rather than decried. It is as important for the patient to become acquainted with the methods by which he or she protects the self from anxiety (resistances) as it is for him or her to become acquainted with what is arousing the anxiety (the repressed impulses). Furthermore, as we will soon demonstrate, in every resistance there is an indication of what is being resisted, a state of affairs that is valuable to the therapeutic work.

Let us elaborate the definition of resistance by discussing what resistance is *not*. First, resistance is not a function of the hostility of the patient toward the therapist, nor is it a battle between patient and therapist. The patient has no desire to attack and frustrate the therapist. The patient only seeks to protect herself or himself from the dangers he or she anticipates encountering as part of the therapeutic work. The therapist is not trying to force unwelcome knowledge on a reluctant patient, as one might suppose she or he would do as an ally of the patient's healthy ego (the observing, integrative functions of the ego); rather, the therapist seeks only to present observations concerning the coded messages that the patient is presenting and through doing this, to reduce anxiety and make repression unnecessary. Of course from the patient's point of view, the therapist may be perceived as an attacker of repression and, accordingly, as an exacerbator of anxiety, an enemy to be foiled. It is useful for the patient to recognize that these perceptions exist.

Resistance is not a refusal of the patient to accept the therapist's formulations or to submit to the therapist's suggestions. The question whether the therapist's formulations, observations, and interpretations are correct is not a matter to be settled by debate or struggle, notwithstanding the patient's wish (motivated by resistance) to make the resolution of this issue a matter of who is stronger. The therapist, on the contrary, has no wish to master the patient. She or he should at all times act as a commentator on the material that the patient has provided rather than as a person who knows omnisciently what is going on with the patient. Furthermore, the therapist should offer comments only for the patient's consideration, not for the patient's agreement, concurrence, or submission to the therapist's opinion.

Resistance is also not an unconscious attempt of the patient to make his or her communications incomprehensible. If the therapist has the conviction, in doing therapy, that the principle of unconscious determination is valid, then he or she has to believe that the patient can say nothing that cannot be analyzed and understood. If in providing associations the patient seems to be talking about trivia or seems to be producing nonsense, the therapist should not interpret this as an attempt to avoid talking about more relevant, sensible matters. Because the therapist knows that the unconscious will somehow be expressed in the patient's associations, he or she must approach material that is seemingly irrelevant and incomprehensible with the question, "Of all the irrelevancies that my patient could have addressed, of all the trivia that could have come to mind, of all the ways she or he could have used to appear incomprehensible or nonsensical or to avoid an important issue, why would this particular way be chosen?" Examination of the patient's associations in the light of this question will usually reveal the unconscious material that the patient is hoping, consciously, to avoid.

If the therapist comes to the conclusion that her or his failure to understand a patient derives from the patient's resistance, then, we submit, it is likely that this conclusion is an expression of countertransference. The therapist should, accordingly, examine her or his own responses to the material and pose the question "Why am I so ready to place the responsibility for my not understanding at my patient's door rather than accepting with patience the fact that although I cannot conceptualize what the patient is now presenting, I will be able to do so as soon as the patient provides more material?"

Types of Resistances

In an addendum to his monograph, *Inhibition, Symptoms, and Anxiety* (1926a), Freud listed resistances according to the structures of the mental apparatus. He enumerated the ego resistances: repression resistance, transference resistance, and gain from illness (secondary gain). Repression resistance is the manifestation of the ego's attempt to maintain the repression. Transference resistance, as Sterba (1940) has indicated, is also an attempt to maintain repression, primarily through the device of the "acting in" and "acting out" of the transference; it finds expression in the patient's demand that the therapist *be* a transference object, a demand opposed to analyzing the fantasies about the analyst as a transference object. Gain from illness is a resistance that represents an unwillingness to forgo the infantile, unconscious gratifications that are achieved through the practical results of being ill, the results that realistically entitle one to these gratifications.

The second category of resistance that Freud listed is termed, variously, "id resistance," "erotization resistance," and "resistance of the unconscious." This resistance arises from the fact that despite the insights that the patient has achieved, despite commitment to the therapy and participation in it, and despite the interpretations that the therapist has made, the repetition compulsion requires the patient to continue to protect infantile modes of perception, experience, and behavior. It is only by completing the phase of working-through that the patient achieves freedom from this resistance.

A third category (and fifth resistance) that Freud listed is superego resistance. Superego resistance stems from guilt and a need for punishment. The patient expresses superego resistance by remaining a victim of the neurotic processes and the resultant compromises.

Recognizing Resistance

Resistance appears in the therapeutic situation in the actions and the words of the patient. We understand actions to be resistant when they implicitly or explicitly abrogate the therapeutic contract. To spell this out: The patient has agreed to come to therapy, to talk, to listen to the therapist's observations, and (in most therapeutic situations) to pay for the therapy. Thus when the patient acts in such a way as to renege on these commitments, we can assume that resistance is at work. Among the things that patients do to express resistance are these: they come late to sessions, cancel appointments inappropriately, miss meetings, forget the fees, and do not remember the amount that is owed. One reason for maintaining a consistent and explicitly agreed-on structure in the therapy is to provide a neutral background against which such resistance-motivated actions of the patient can be clearly seen.

Some resistance-motivated actions of the patient are more subtle than those we have cited already. The patient may track mud into the therapist's office, may whistle or sing while the therapist makes an interpretation, may miss the ashtray when flicking cigarette ash, or may leave the door to the office open when coming in and when leaving. Other resistant acts consist of omissions, for example, not removing one's coat in the therapist's adequately heated office, failing to stay awake during the therapy, or not uncrossing one's legs or arms (which the patient keeps folded about her or his body).

More often it is through verbal behavior that the patient expresses resistance. Probably the most common resistance is silence. Though silence communicates, in an inferential way, something of the patient's experience (through the context in which it appears), nevertheless, it partially impedes the therapeutic work, which relies mainly on the patient's verbal productions for its raw material.

When the patient does speak, resistance can be expressed metaphorically. For example, a patient can use a metaphor to make clear his or her fear of the horrible consequences that participation in the therapy is expected to produce. The therapist counts such a metaphor as evidence of resistance because she or he recognizes that if this fearful expectation was valid, then the patient would have good reason to discontinue therapy and to stop seeking further knowledge of his or her unconscious functioning. Indeed, that the patient has to present unconscious thoughts and feelings metaphorically is itself evidence of resistance. The metaphor is a roundabout way of communicating about these unconscious ideas; it conceals as much as it reveals the underlying, unconscious idea.

We can conclude from the argument that we have presented that resistance is inherent in every communication of the patient and in every style of communication that he or she makes use of. In addition to the forms of resistance we have already noted, patients may: attack the therapist for no apparent reason or for reasons that the patient believes to be realistic which an objective observer would conclude not to be realistic; distort the events of the therapy by remembering them inaccurately, by perceiving them incorrectly, or by conceptualizing them tendentiously; profess themselves as unable to comprehend interpretations and act as though they misunderstood the comments of the therapist (even though they are highly intelligent); misremember what they perceived; or rework interpretations and other interventions, radically altering their implications. When patients forget what has appeared in the course of the therapy, what they forget may be an agreement they have made with the therapist, or material that they have presented and have discussed.

A common form of resistance is the patient's denying an interpretation of the therapist. In rejecting the interpretation the patient is, in effect, asserting that the validity of any interpretation depends on the patient's conscious awareness of what has been interpreted. This, manifestly, is a paradox; what was interpreted had been unconscious and was therefore not accessible to the patient's awareness. In denying an interpretation some patients are very funny; the therapist can find herself or himself laughing at the patient's incongruous remark. Such humorous presentations by the patient seem to be motivated by resistance. They express the patient's belief that a laughing therapist is less observant, and therefore safer, than one who interprets.

As the patient becomes knowledgeable about how therapy works, he or she will come to understand what is required to make the therapy go well. The patient knows, for example, that associations are needed to gain an understanding of manifest dreams and that descriptions of real events are treated, for the purposes of the therapy, as though they were fantasies. She or he knows that everything that has to be understood in the therapy will be derived from these associations. Thus when a patient does not associate to his or her dreams, insists on viewing the descriptions of life-events as realities rather than as fantasies, and tries to puzzle out psychic processes as though they were geometry problems capable of rational solution (in other words, denies what both he or she and the therapist know about the way therapy works) then resistance is being expressed.

Dealing With Resistance

The reader will recall that resistance has been defined as the expression, in and through the associations and actions of the patient, of defensive processes. The defenses serve to protect the patient from anxiety. Anxiety in psychotherapy is caused by the patient's involving herself or himself in a process of examining the unconscious and revealing the unconscious content of the moment. Because anxiety motivates resistance, it follows that the best way to reduce resistance is to reduce the anxiety that motivates it.

In reducing anxiety, the first step the therapist takes is to spotlight it. Because the anxiety that is provoked in the patient is closely tied to perceptions and expectations of the therapist, the therapist will be in the best position to reduce anxiety when she or he has taken care not to bring into the therapy anything that would seem to justify the patient's anxiety. In these circumstances the therapist can more easily show the patient that the fearful expectations about the therapist are transference. For example, if a patient consistently comes late to therapy appointments, the therapist can more effectively interpret the anxiety that motivates the lateness if the therapist himself or herself has not been late to appointments. If the therapist *has* been late the patient can assert, unconsciously, that the therapist's actions provoked her or his actions. If the therapist has made an appropriate change in the structure of the therapy and the patient uses this change as a hook on which to hang his or her resistance, this should not be allowed to obscure the more important fact that the resistance originates from the patient's anxiety provoked by his or her own fantasies, not from the structural change. In the prior example, it is not the therapist's lateness (an inappropriate change in structure) that provokes the resistance, it is the patient's fantasy (feeling rejected by the therapist) channeled through this piece of reality that provokes the resistance.

Once the anxiety and resistance have been spotlighted, the therapist can then take an interpretive approach to reducing them. The therapist should interpret, and not instruct, the patient; do not say, for example, "You have been resisting," and then admonish the patient to stop resisting. As we view these matters, the therapist cannot overpower resistance by such instruction and admonition without introducing a degree of authoritarianism into the therapy and providing thereby a reality that will produce other, more subtle resistances.

In interpreting resistance one should be very specific. Ideally, the therapist should explain to the patient not only that the patient is resisting but also what anxiety is making the resistance necessary, what specific fantasies generated the anxiety, and what determined the appearance of the resistance at the precise time that it occurred and in the particular form that it took. From such an interpretation the patient can learn both what frightens him or her and what techniques have been developed to cope with this fear.

On occasion, particularly at the beginning of therapy, the therapist can reduce resistance by using reassurance, directly and indirectly. By "direct reassurance" we do not mean telling the patient that there is no reason to be anxious or that everything will work out all right. Rather it means emphasizing that the basis of the patient's anxiety is a fantasy, not a reality. The therapist may say something like "You are telling us that you are afraid to let us know your thoughts because you *anticipate* that we will be offended by them when they are presented." An example of indirect reassurance is the therapist's failure to react with punishment or approval when the patient participates freely and openly in the therapeutic work, a response that is quite different from what the patient had expected. When the therapeutic atmosphere is genuinely nonjudgmental, anxiety and resistance are starkly revealed as products of the patient's fantasies about the therapist.

The education of the patient, so important early in therapy, should continue throughout therapy. Educative interventions can be used to help manage resistance. Through explanations and by her or his demeanor the therapist communicates to the patient the principles on which the therapy is based (see chapter 5). In doing so, the therapist helps the patient to learn about therapy and to recognize that it is a rational, objective process. Learning this, the patient can understand that his or her resistant responses are incongruent with the fundamental nature of therapy. For example: One of us had a patient who sometimes responded to an interpretation with the retort "That's *your* interpretation!" The therapist's response, "Of course it is. Isn't that what you're paying me for?" was usually helpful, permitting the patient to give up debating the interpretation, allowing him to associate to it instead.

If resistance is ignored, attacked, neglected, or avoided in the therapy, there are significant negative consequences. The least of these is a slowing or stopping of the forward movement of the therapy toward the discovery of the patient's unconscious processes. More important is the effect on the working alliance between patient and therapist. As the resistance and anxiety are overlooked and are not examined for what they are, the patient develops more anxiety and becomes more and more antagonistic to the therapeutic process. In addition, the patient is likely to conclude that the therapist has failed to deal with the resistance because the therapist is as afraid to give it up as the patient is. The end point is, of course, the patient's departure from the therapeutic scene. Thus, although the therapist can be sure that a resistance that is not examined today will be here tomorrow, she or he must recognize that a resistance that is not dealt with until next month may disappear with the patient.[1]

---

[1]Because analytic therapists are rapidly changing their conceptions about resistance, the reader can profit from consulting discussions of resistance by Brenner (1976), Greenson (1967), and Schafer (1984).

Chapter 9

Transference: The Patient Unconsciously Experiences the Therapist

"Transference" is an *unconsciously determined* reaction of the patient to the therapist stemming from the patient's previous experiences of relating to other persons that is inappropriate to the way in which the therapist has dealt with him or her. A transference reaction may be direct and obvious, such as an attack upon the therapist, or it may be indirect, such as a concern about the supposedly harmful atmosphere of the therapy room (expressing the patient's unconscious fear of being smothered by the therapist, in retaliation for the unconscious, hostile feelings toward the therapist). Though transference, viewed objectively, is inappropriate, the patient experiences it as real, current, and justified by the situation.

Finally, it is important to state that transference feelings may contribute to the rapport that the patient has with the therapist, though they are, of course, not the only source of the patient's positive attachment to the therapist. The therapist is kind and helpful; his or her realistically supportive and insight-creating actions tend to bind the patient to him or her.

Transference Is Not Simply Relationship

Transference is not a synonym for the therapeutic relationship in general. In many writings on psychotherapy transference is used loosely to designate any feelings of the patient toward the therapist. Sometimes in these writings one is exhorted to show kindness and understanding toward the patient "so that a positive transference will develop." It should be clear from our definition of transference that it is impossible, strictly speaking, to grow a transference by what one does as a therapist; the transference shows itself in the current situation, but the current situation did not create it and does not nourish it. At most, the therapist provides current cues that serve to release the readiness for response that the patient has brought to the therapeutic situation. If the therapist is attentive, interested, and helpful, she or he will surely make the patient feel more positive toward the therapist. If inattentive, out of sorts, and distracted (as all therapists are at one time or another), then the therapist will make positive feelings less likely and negative ones more likely. Such positive or negative feelings are, however, not transference reactions.

Transference Distinguished From Rapport

Nor is transference simply rapport, for (as we have said) rapport depends on what the therapist actually does. The therapist needs to do those things that will put the patient at ease. When the patient first comes to therapy, he or she is unsure that the therapist can help, expects that overwhelming tension from emerging conflicts will have to be faced, finds the therapist's way of working strange, and wonders whether he or she and the therapist will be able to work together effectively. If the therapist at this time can make the procedures of the therapy seem reasonable and if everything possible is done to take away the sense of strangeness and foreboding, the patient's anxiety will be greatly reduced. There is no need for the patient to wonder whether the therapist thinks she or he can help the patient, to be in doubt about how the therapy will proceed, or to have unanswered questions about the therapist's qualifications and training. These, at least, are anxieties that the patient can avoid.

What Is Realistic Is Not Transference

The reactions of the patient to what the therapist really is and does should not be considered transference. These reactions, of course, may be colored by transference. But if the therapist forgets an appointment and the patient is justifiably angry, the patient's reaction is not transference. If the therapist sides with the patient's spouse against the patient, and the patient feels that the therapist is not giving him or her a fair shake, this feeling is not transference. If the therapist has power over the patient's life (e.g., if he or she is a professor and the patient is a graduate student in psychology who must take courses that the therapist teaches) any tendency of the patient to please and placate the therapist can hardly be attributed solely to transference. Attempts to tell the patient that reactions that are justified by reality show transference will be at best confusing and at worst destructive of the working alliance.

Having made the point that reactions to what is realistic are not transference, we would like to introduce the idea (which we owe to Brenner, 1976) that although the conscious reactions of the patient to realistic matters are not transference, they should always be considered as indicators of transference, at least potentially. We believe that transference is always unconscious, is ubiquitous, and is expressed in everything that the patient does or says.

Theory of Transference

Positive and Negative Transference

In discussing transference, Freud (in "The Dynamics of Transference," 1912) distinguished between positive and negative aspects of transference reactions. By "positive transference" Freud meant those feelings of the patient that lead to an attachment of patient to therapist, that cause the patient to overestimate the therapist, that include all of the patient's libidinal strivings toward the therapist. By "negative transference" Freud meant all of the patient's inappropriate angry, hostile feelings. Freud pointed out that negative transference must be promptly interpreted, or else the continuation of the therapy will be jeopardized. He recommended that positive transference be left untouched except when it comprises intense, infantile erotic strivings so intense that they could motivate escape from the therapeutic situation. More moderate levels of positive transference are to be left untouched; the positive attitudes toward the therapist serve to strengthen the patient's adherence to the therapy. To put the matter in another way, the therapist is advised to leave the transference alone except when it has become a resistance; it becomes a resistance whenever it is a negative transference and whenever it is an erotic, infantile transference that is causing the patient so much tension (because of the frustration of the erotic strivings) that the patient finds it necessary to flee the therapy.

The distinction between positive and negative transference loses some of its sharpness when one sees that patients more often than not have a mixture of positive and negative feelings toward the therapist, and that frustrations of the patient's erotic strivings toward the therapist frequently produce an angry attack on the therapist. One is left with the judgment that the distinction between positive and negative transference may be of theoretical interest, but generally not of much use to the practicing therapist. This distinction does, however, enable us to see the value and necessity of interpreting transference. Reich (in his book *Character Analysis*, 1933/1945) pointed out that negative transferences must be interpreted before the patient will be free to express positive feelings toward the therapist.

Transference as Resistance

Discussing another aspect of transference, Freud (1912) pointed out that the transference often serves the purpose of resistance. The patient comes to the therapeutic situation prepared with a characteristic way of relating to other persons and driven by a set of unfulfilled longings to have another person love him or her in a particular way. In establishing a relationship with the therapist, the patient attempts to make the relationship fit her or his characteristic way of dealing with another person and to make it gratify unconscious wishes for a particular kind of love. When the therapist, by acting toward the patient simply as collaborator in the task of discovering what is going on in the patient's living, fails to play the role demanded by the patient or to offer the kind of love the patient is striving to get, the patient is intensely frustrated.

The patient's way of relating to others and demands for love are, however, largely unconscious; they are precisely what he or she needs to understand in order to overcome neurotic difficulties and is terrified of finding out. Instead of verbally telling the therapist "This is how I want to relate myself to you, and this is the kind of love I want from you," the patient simply behaves so as to demand a particular form of relationship and a particular kind of love. As Freud said ("Remembering, Repeating, and Working-Through," 1914b), action has replaced remembering. The *form* of the patient's resistance against awareness of his or her own actions and wishes is a demand upon the therapist; that is, a transference. We have, in short, a transference-resistance.

Transference Neurosis

A transference response (which we have defined as an inappropriate reaction to the therapist, stemming from previous relationships of the patient) can occur at any stage of the therapy, even at the very beginning. For example, a young man who began psychotherapy in an outpatient psychiatric clinic noticed that the therapist spoke with a foreign accent. He asked, "You're English, aren't you?" She answered, "No, Australian. But why do you ask?" He then revealed that he expected her to be around for only a few months before abandoning him and returning to the foreign country from which she had come. On the thin shred of evidence that the therapist was from a foreign country this patient hung his expectation of abandonment, a transference attitude. This episode took place in the second hour of therapy.

Such an isolated response of the patient is very different, however, from the channeling of neurotic, unconscious feelings that gradually develops in the course of psychotherapy. When such channeling focuses all of the important neurotic attitudes on the therapist, one says that a *transference neurosis* has developed.

The transference neurosis develops in proportion to the frustrations that the patient endures, as the patient brings unconscious expectations and demands to the therapy situation and strives to fulfill them in that situation. As the therapist refuses to comply with these expectations or to fulfill these demands, the childish demands are gradually expressed in a more and more direct way, until at last they are clear for all to see and, at last, yield to interpretations by the therapist.

The transference neurosis becomes more and more well defined, more and more explicit, as it develops. The development of the transference neurosis in the case of Mrs. S., a 26-year-old mother of two preschool children (a girl of 4 and a boy of 2), who went to a psychoanalyst for therapy because of depression, anger at her mother, headaches, a tremor of her right hand, and trouble in sleeping illustrates this phenomenon.

Even at the very beginning of the therapy *transference responses* were evident. As this patient came through the door into the therapy room for the first session, she said to the therapist, "Why are you looking at me? It seems like you're staring." The patient expected that the therapist would respond to her with disapproval, would consider her to be a naughty child. But this expectation was a transitory thing, it had not developed into a full-fledged focusing of feelings onto the therapist.

At the end of the initial interview it was agreed that Mrs. S. would come for psychotherapy for two 50-minute sessions each week. In the early sessions Mrs. S. dwelt on her conflicts with her parents, her problems of dealing with her children, the sense of loss she felt from the death of a son from leukemia several years before, and dissatisfactions with her marriage. Speaking of her childhood, Mrs. S. said that her parents had never got along with each other very well; her father frequently had open affairs with girlfriends. Mrs. S. recalled that her mother had once had a miscarriage or abortion and had insisted that Mrs. S. (then a teenager) accompany her on trips to the doctor's office.

After about 6 months of therapy an incident occurred that expressed, in a focused way, Mrs. S.'s intense feelings toward the therapist. The expression of these feelings had been foreshadowed, a couple of months earlier, by Mrs. S.'s bringing in two cartoons to the therapist. The first cartoon showed two stone age men in conversation. The first man said, "You have a fairly large skull, which denotes the existence of a sizable brain, housed therein." His companion, raising his hand, waved at his own head, saying, "Hi, brain." Seeing this, the first man commented, "Then again . . ." When the therapist raised the question what this joke meant, Mrs. S. replied that it just meant she wanted the therapist to die laughing. In the next session, Mrs. S. brought another cartoon, which depicted a psychiatrist's office, empty, with a sign on the door: "O.K. to slam door." As she left this session Mrs. S. asked the therapist, "Will your door slam?"

In the weeks that followed her showing the therapist these cartoons, Mrs. S. expressed in an indirect, metaphoric way many of her feelings toward the therapist. For instance, in the 40th, 41st, and 42nd sessions she metaphorically expressed her feeling of being deserted when the therapist took a brief vacation. In the 43rd session she showed her frustration at the failure of the therapist to provide direct gratifications by bringing in and presenting to the therapist a little doll made of construction paper. The doll-figure, a woman, was knitting and was holding a placard that said, "Sublimation." Despite the therapist's attempts to show her that she was expressing her own frustration and anger through the doll's actions, Mrs. S. insisted that the doll symbolized nothing except her wish to make the therapist a gift.

Again, two sessions later, the patient brought a doll. This time the doll was holding a loving cup, and the placard said, "A kind word is sufficient." Again, interpretations did not bring assent. In the next session the patient acknowledged a previously hidden motive for bringing dolls to the therapist. She said that giving the therapist a doll was like giving him a child. Her thoughts then went back to her childhood, to the occasions when her mother was pregnant. Her mother had had morning sickness throughout each of her pregnancies; the patient had concluded, at the time, that there must be a connection between eating and pregnancy.

In the 48th session—almost exactly six months after the start of therapy— Mrs. S. told of how the son who had died had discovered, quite precociously, how to use geometric configurations in his building with blocks. Mrs. S. was preoccupied with geometric figures, with colors, and with numbers, all of which seemed to come into her mind intrusively, obsessively.

At the beginning of the 49th session Mrs. S. handed the therapist another doll, saying, "I brought you another one. I need to know some things first. What's a screen image? What I was seeing in the dark [fantasies she had reported previously], was that a screen image?" The therapist made the interpretation that the fragmentary visual images were representations of some other experience that Mrs. S. had had. Mrs. S. then recalled her mother's abortion; and she talked some about her childish understanding that one became pregnant by taking vitamins and could get over pregnancy by vomiting the baby back up. She also recalled her own fear, as a child, that she would fall into the toilet and be flushed down it. Mrs. S. kept pressing the therapist to explain to her the meaning of a "screen memory," but she failed to cooperate when he attempted to elicit some specific memories of images that he could, with the patient's collaboration, explain. Near the end of the session Mrs. S. warned the therapist, "If I get halfway home and shiver and shake . . ." The therapist finished her thought, "It will be my fault."

The patient made good on her prediction: she got upset on the way home. As soon as she got home from this session, at about 1 p.m., she called the therapist in great distress, saying that she had thought of some very upsetting memories as she rode home on the bus and wanted very much to meet with the therapist right away in order to discuss these upsetting images and fantasies. The therapist agreed to meet her later that afternoon, and he did indeed meet with her for an additional 50 minutes. This second session of the day threw little light on what had proved so disturbing to Mrs. S. The images that came to mind had to do with the occasion when her mother had been hemorrhaging and had asked the patient to take her to the doctor "for an abortion." There were images of "flushing a baby down the toilet," of "taking cod-liver oil to have a baby" and retching to get rid of a baby, and of blood in connection with the expulsion of a fetus from the mother's body. Mrs. S. couldn't say whether she actually remembered her mother's attempting to abort herself, or whether she remembered her mother's having a miscarriage, or whether she had simply been asked by her mother to drive her to an abortionist. Nor could Mrs. S. say why she found these images so frightening or how the images were related to her therapy. This session, on a Monday afternoon, ended inconclusively. The patient was scheduled to come back at her regular appointment time on Friday afternoon.

On Wednesday night—or, more accurately, Thursday morning, for it was 2:30 a.m.—Mr. S. called the therapist at the therapist's home to report that his wife was terribly disturbed and to plead with the therapist to see her immediately and calm her down. The therapist asked to talk with Mrs. S. When she came to the phone he inquired what was happening and discovered that she was extremely anxious. She complained that she continued to be tormented by memories and visual images related to her mother's abortions. The therapist said that he could not see her until Thursday afternoon. He assured her that she could tolerate these thoughts and images until then.

At the agreed-on time Thursday afternoon, Mrs. S. and the therapist met at his office. Mrs. S. began the session in an accusatory tone: "Well, I think you could have given me more to work with." She complained that the therapist had not told her what "screen memories" were and how they worked. She insisted that the images that had troubled her during the night were simply the third in a series of tormenting memories. The first memory was of her mother trying to induce an abortion when the patient was only three years old; the second, of her mother on the toilet during a menstrual period; the third, of the time she had been threatened that God would strike her dead if she "told on Grandma." (Grandma's crime, according to this fantasy, was "killing babies," i.e., having an abortion.)

The therapist kept insisting throughout the therapy session that there was a reason for Mrs. S.'s choosing to call him in the middle of the night, and he kept pressing her to reflect about why she had chosen such a time. Mrs. S. kept evading his question. At length, the therapist made an interpretation: "You are re-enacting something that happened between you and your parents, when they didn't give you an answer." Then he inquired, "What were your thoughts about me, at 2 o'clock in the morning?" She replied, "You had drawn a circle and shut me out. I thought, 'I can't go through it again.' I wanted to stop it." The therapist inquired, "What did I do that you interpreted in this way?" She answered, "You said, go to Sinai Hospital, didn't you?" The therapist acknowledged that he'd indicated that she could go to the emergency room at Sinai Hospital if she felt she *must* talk to someone immediately and couldn't wait until the therapist could see her. But, he pointed out, this was after she'd called the therapist. What had she felt before she called him?

The therapist insisted that there was a reason why the patient called at 2:30 a.m. He then proposed that Mrs. S. was acting as though she were a four-year-old experiencing a night terror. He continued, "This had to happen just the way it did, to demonstrate that when you needed me, I would shut you out. You wanted to show I was heartless and would *not* respond to your need. It's a protection against facing any friendly feelings you have toward me."

Mrs. S. said, "I felt I'd been a baby-killer. I felt I would have a baby if *they* [her mother and her grandmother] wouldn't." Again the therapist asked why Mrs. S. had had to call at 2:30 a.m. She answered, "I wanted you to get me a drink of water and a pill, probably a vitamin pill." The therapist pointed out, "Instead of having it as a thought and saying it, you sort of acted it all out: 'I'm sick, give me something to calm me down.'"

The patient commented, "I got you out of bed with your wife, didn't I? Does everybody do this?" Recognizing her actions of the previous night as expressing feelings she had had toward her parents, Mrs. S. then said: "A pill, a glass of water, you have to go to the bathroom. My parents were most displeased when I was sick to my stomach or the opposite, when I would have a bowel movement."

The therapist said, "You showed me in action instead of in words that you would like me to give you a pill and a glass of water, and that you wanted me to get out of bed so that I wouldn't be in bed with my wife. What you did expressed these two wishes. You had to tell me in this way, you were protecting yourself against thinking the thoughts directly." The patient volunteered, "I would want Daddy to get in bed with me, but he wouldn't, you'd draw a circle and shut me out."

We have reported this 51st session in detail so that the reader can have the material that we had access to when we concluded that Mrs. S. relived in and around the therapy some important emotional experiences from her childhood. We believe that this patient wanted, unconsciously, to live out a wish she had to have a very special, sexual relationship with her father. We believe that there is considerable evidence that she understood the sexual relationship in oral-incorporative terms, that is, that she had the fantasy that a woman becomes pregnant by taking a substance from the father into the mouth, that the woman can abort the child by retching, and that the baby is born through the anus. We believe that there is strong evidence that intense sexual longings for her father and rivalry with her mother were transferred to the therapist and his wife; and that when these feelings reached a certain intensity they were expressed through the sleep-disturbing phone call of 2:30 a.m. We believe that one can trace the development of these intense transference feelings through the sessions in the weeks immediately preceding the dramatic early morning phone call.

This example illustrates a significant fact about the experiences that are relived in the transference neurosis. What were originally experienced in childhood and are now relived are fantasies charged with strong emotions, including such feelings as anxiety, sexual excitement, rage at frustration, anger, intense longing, jealousy, the full gamut of affective reactions. Furthermore, because of the incompletely developed ego of the child at the time of the original experiences, the pressures of the affective arousal, and the situation in which the experiences occur (at night, in isolation, or in half-sleep) these fantasies are fragmented, confused, incoherent, and sometimes incapable of articulation in words. Infantile experiences relived in the transference are therefore never presented in the form of elegant, schematized constructs as in textbooks.

Therapeutic Use of the Transference

As we can see from this example, then, patients use the therapist as a past object: that is, they express the same wishes, longings, and fears that they are driven to express toward internal objects, showing in their current behavior what kind of relationship they had established formerly with another person. Because the behavior toward the therapist is a reenactment of the earlier object relationship, the therapist can learn about that earlier relationship from the patient's current behavior. Sometimes the reliving is dramatic.

For example, a man who had been a combat Marine in Viet Nam and who came to therapy because he found his marriage to be in deep trouble, had been prepared for this alienation from his wife—so we were told by the colleague who worked therapeutically with this patient—by his own early experience of abandonment. The patient's father had died in World War II, and the patient had never seen him; the patient's mother had remarried, and her husband had adopted the patient. The patient, having very little interaction with his biological father's family, felt quite cut off from them and from his biological father.

This patient transferred the feeling of abandonment to his wife, expecting always that she would abandon him emotionally, as his own father had in his fantasy. He also transferred the feeling of abandonment to his therapist and similarly held back from emotional involvement.

One day the therapy session went this way: The patient spoke of attending a Gambler's Anonymous meeting (he had had a slight gambling problem with the state lottery) and of finding out that the leader of the group would not be there at that meeting. The patient then spoke of a brother-in-law, a born-again Christian, who was intent on converting the patient to fundamentalist Christianity (which the patient found unacceptable). In an earlier session, the patient had expressed concern that the therapist could not tolerate hearing about the patient's marital problems because the therapist's wife had died two weeks previously. The therapist understood all of these communications to be expressions of the theme "I can expect to be abandoned." The therapist believed that the patient experienced abandonment by the Gamblers Anonymous leader, by his brother-in-law (and God), and by the therapist. Believing that these feelings of abandonment were real (i.e., currently experienced feelings), the therapist pointed out: "There's a theme running through what you've said today. You felt abandoned by the group leader, you felt condemned by your brother-in-law, and deserted by God."

In the next session, the patient reported that he had rented a video recording of a movie about the Viet Nam war. As he was watching it, he began to weep; it brought back memories of his own painful experiences during the war. When his wife returned from a meeting she had been attending, the patient felt ashamed of his crying and tried to bring it under control. The patient then mentioned that his faith in God had been shaken by the carnage and the suffering that he saw in Viet Nam. The therapist said, "You must feel, 'If God is good, how could this be permitted to happen?' And so you feel that God has abandoned you."

The patient then went on to relive his painful experiences in Viet Nam, when, as a support person, he had to recover the bodies of dead buddies and put them in body bags. He wept as he recalled these painful experiences. He remarked to the therapist, "Since this happened to me, I've never talked about it to anybody."

We see clearly in this example how the patient transfers an expectation of abandonment from his father to his wife and to his therapist; how this expectation causes him to avoid involvement and communication with his wife and his therapist; and how appropriate interpretation allows him to experience formerly warded off feelings and to establish contact emotionally with the therapist (and, as it turned out, with his wife).

To give another example: One woman patient, lying on the couch for the first time after about 3 months in therapy in which she sat facing the therapist, implored her therapist: "You wouldn't leave me, would you?" A few sessions later she imagined what it would be like for the therapist to hold her tightly in his arms, as her father had held her when she was a little girl. Both her fear of abandonment and her wish for body contact were a reliving of the earlier object relationship, her relationship with her father.

We see, therefore, that patients use the therapist as an object with whom past object relations can be relived (that have been internalized). This enables the patient to bring these object relations directly into the therapeutic sessions. They become live, current experiences; the emotions are present and real.

Psychoanalytic therapy, therefore, attends primarily (and as exclusively as possible) to the patient's reactions to the therapist, who is, in Fenichel's terms (Fenichel, 1941, p. 72), a "mirror" and can therefore become a figure upon whom the transference neurosis is focused. This view contrasts with the type of psychodynamic therapy that deals with the patient's psychological processes as they are expressed in the patient's interpersonal relationships. In such a *transactional* therapeutic approach, the therapist relies on the patient's report of interpersonal encounters rather than on the direct evidence of the patient's interpersonal experience within the therapeutic dyad. Furthermore, psychoanalytic therapy can be contrasted with Sullivan's approach: In psychoanalytic therapy the therapist is not "real" to the patient (see Tarachow, 1963); he or she is primarily a fantasy object. In Sullivan's style of therapy the therapist is seen to function as a "real object:" The therapist communicates to the patient personal experiences in the therapy and focuses on the interpersonal processes that underlie both her or his experiences in the therapy and the patient's.

For example, a patient might begin the therapy session complaining of an excruciating headache that developed during a conversation with an employer. During this conversation the employer refused to give the patient a raise in salary. The transactional therapist would focus on the headache as a manifestation of the rage that the patient experienced when rejected by the employer. The Sullivanian therapist might report his or her own feeling of desiring strongly to provide some relief to the patient, calling the patient's attention (by this confession) to the way in which the patient provoked this reaction. The psychoanalytic therapist, understanding the patient's reference to the employer as a metaphor, would emphasize in the therapy the patient's report as a communication of the patient's experience at the moment of reporting, as a communication of the patient's rage at the therapist (a transference object who is perceived as ungiving). The interpretation of this transference phenomenon would elicit, we expect, associations showing the origin of this reaction of the patient.

As the neurotic conflicts increasingly become channeled into transference responses, the patient slowly gives up the channeling of these conflicts into daily living. Expression of the neurotic conflicts toward the therapist drains off a good deal of the tensions created by the conflicts, making it much less necessary for such tension to be discharged toward spouse, children, boss, fellow workers, and friends. The more realistic behavior that results makes it seem that considerable progress has been made toward a solution of the neurotic difficulties. We know, however, that the improvement is temporary. It depends entirely on the draining off of tension through the relationship to the therapist. Such temporary improvement is called a "transference cure."

Nevertheless, the turning of the energies from expression toward others in daily life to expression toward the therapist is an important and valuable development in the therapy. This shift puts the neurotic conflict into a setting in which the therapist and the patient together can study it intensively and come to understand it thoroughly.

As the patient channels neurotic conflicts into the therapeutic situation, perceptions of the therapist become distorted by transferences. One patient, intensely reliving the relationship to his mother while lying on the couch, spoke of the strong sexual feelings he had for the therapist. He said he wanted her to hold him tightly in her arms. He said she even *looked* very much like his mother. He reported that he was very much afraid the therapist would hit him on the head; and he turned to plead, "You won't leave me, will you?" It hardly needs to be said that the therapist had done nothing to provoke these sexual feelings, had not menaced him so that he had reason to fear a blow to the head, and had done nothing to justify the expectation that she would leave him. In reliving earlier experiences with his mother, the patient felt the sexual passion he had felt as a child, expected the rough treatment he had received then, and anticipated that his experiencing sexual feelings toward a woman would lead now—as he thought it had then—to a disruption of the relationship.

A young patient who was very afraid of aggressive impulses would sometimes voice the fear that the air in the therapy room was harmful and suffocating. In experiencing an expectation that the therapist would cause harm, the patient was, of course, projecting onto the therapist aggressive impulses, which were felt to be terribly dangerous.

A therapist who has been the model of tact and caution may be accused by a frightened patient of "pushing" him or her to look at turbulent, unconscious feelings before he or she is ready to do so. A therapist who has been unusually insistent that a patient take initiative and responsibility may be accused of coercing the patient into coming to therapy and of holding him or her prisoner in the therapy. Examples like these show what we mean when we say that the patient forms a "distorted" perception of the therapist.

That the transferences expressed in the transference neurosis are repetitions of past experiences, perceptions, and fantasies has been evident in several of our examples. For instance, the patient who expected the therapist to hit him on the head and to leave him, the patient who called the therapist at 2:30 a.m. as she relived what she had experienced as a little girl who wanted her daddy to bring her a drink of water—these are repetitions. A patient has been known to curl up in a chair in the posture she had assumed as a little girl; another patient, when she lay on the couch, kept one knee protectively elevated, just as she had done when her father was attempting to seduce her many years before. Each of these repetitive actions or attitudes tells us a great deal about the experiences and the fantasies that shaped the patient's development.

Indeed, we find that the patient lives out the infantile neurosis directly in the transference. The patient's repetition is a very real, current act. A 30-year-old man who is clinging to the position that he is weak and helpless—out of the unconscious wish to be cared for as he would be cared for by a mother taking care of an infant, and out of the need to fend off the attack he expects to provoke should he behave assertively—presents himself to the therapist as weak and helpless. He expresses the demand that the therapist *give* him treatment, free of charge, simply because it would gratify his need to be cared for. He reports the fantasy that the therapist, during the previous 4 years of the therapy, has been setting aside all of the patient's payments, and will now return them to the patient so that he will have most of the money he would need to buy a $15,000 sailboat. Then the patient directly attacks the therapist, saying, "With all the money I've given you, one would think you could buy a better table lamp for the office, one that stood up straight." From this example it should be clear that the transference is a live, current experience of the patient and one in which he makes the therapist, too, experience feelings, as the therapist becomes a target of the patient's demands and expectations.

The foregoing conceptualization of transference and transference neurosis imposes two requirements on the therapy and therapist. The first of these is that therapy take place against a background of consistent structure, so that there is as little as possible of reality to fit with the transference fantasies. Those variations in structure that do occur will very often be seized on as hooks upon which the patient hangs unconscious transference fantasies. By doing so the patient can protect herself or himself, implicitly protesting that this reaction has nothing to do with her or him; this reaction, she or he asserts, has only to do with the reality of the change in structure.

The second requirement is that the therapist respond only with interpretation to transference manifestations. To do otherwise (e.g., to respond as though the transference distortions were realities) is to reinforce the resistance of the patient, thereby defeating the therapeutic goals.

Interpretation of Transference

Writers on psychoanalytic technique are agreed that interpretation of transference should have priority over interpretations of content. It is obvious that interpretations of resistance have the highest priority, for if the motives that led to the resistance are not exposed and dealt with, the therapy will be disrupted, perhaps defeated altogether. Resistances are frequently in the form of transference resistance. It follows that this kind of transference response just has to be interpreted, as swiftly and as effectively as possible.

Other transferences, which are not resistance, also are strategic for interpretation, because when the patient is talking about material that expresses transference, he or she is then and there experiencing affects (longings and fears) that are real, intense, and (above all) immediate. The patient knows what she or he has been experiencing. He or she may not, before the interpretation, recognize its significance or label it accurately, but in a way is aware what has been happening inwardly.

The therapist, too, has been a participant in the situation that provoked or released the patient's experience, and, mostly through empathy, knows what the patient is experiencing. Both the patient and the therapist know what the actual transactions between them have been, and they know to what degree these transactions have justified what the patient is experiencing and to what degree this experience is determined by readinesses to perceive the situation in some unrealistic way. These readinesses were established in earlier experiences of the patient with important persons in her or his life. Because therapist and patient alike have such full information about the therapy situation and about their participation in it, it is an ideal situation for demonstrating to the patient how he or she characteristically deals with the therapist and, most likely, with other people, and how this characteristic style is determined not by current stimuli but by readinesses from the past.

Interpretations of transference may bring out clearly the origin of the current reactions in past object relations. Nevertheless, transference interpretations need not be so ambitious. For example, a young man who was soon to leave on an exciting trip to Bermuda with his girlfriend—which would separate him both from his parents, to whom he was much attached, and from the therapist—asked the therapist, "Won't you miss me? How can you stand having me that far away for a whole week?" The therapist simply replied, "Isn't it really the other way around, you're wondering how you'll stand being away from me?" At this, the patient laughed, and the therapist joined in the laughter. The therapist had interpreted the patient's current feeling toward the therapist, while leaving uninterpreted the origin of this feeling in the psychological development of the patient. The therapist, of course, paid close attention to the associations that followed in the expectation that they would provide clues to the historical antecedents of the patient's reaction.

Acting Out of Transference

Ideally, transference feelings are experienced, talked about, and clarified in the therapy session. Their inappropriateness to the current situation is noted, and their origin in some other, past object relationship is discovered. But the patient, at times, must defend herself or himself against experiencing transference feelings consciously and talking about them with the therapist. Because the patient fears this direct way of dealing with transference feelings, these affects are expressed outside of the transference, toward other persons.

For example, a 35-year-old married man, who had come to psychotherapy because of his alcoholism and his marriage problems, became very angry with the therapist when the therapy continued for many months without the therapist's granting him the dependent gratifications he unconsciously was seeking from the therapy. One night, after a session that the patient found especially frustrating, he left the therapy with a great deal of unexpressed rage toward the therapist. Leaving the therapy session, the patient walked to a nearby bar. Somehow he managed to get into a heated argument with the waitress there, giving her a piece of his mind. Then, full of angry feelings, he got into his car to drive the 45 miles to his home. Despite thorough knowledge of vehicle dynamics and the principles of safe driving, the patient tailgated another car at 40 miles an hour through a built-up area. The car he was following made a turn unexpectedly, without proper signalling, and the patient's car plowed right into it. There was extensive damage to both cars (for which the patient was legally liable) and the patient was rather badly cut and bruised on the face and chest. We understand this whole sequence of events as an acting out by the patient of his angry feelings toward the therapist. Defending himself against becoming aware of the hostile transference feelings, he expressed them instead by actions against the waitress and against the driver of the car ahead of him.

Actions in therapy, too, can express transference feelings. Such *acting in* (in the therapy, that is) differs somewhat from *acting out*. In acting out, the patient presents a report of a fait accompli, an action that has taken place without an opportunity for the patient and the therapist to analyze it. In acting in, on the other hand, the patient acts in the presence of himself or herself and the therapist. The action is resistant in that it is nonverbal, but it is easily accessible to interpretation. As an act it expresses indirectly and in action what the patient did not want unconsciously to put into words.

A colleague has described to us an episode in his treatment of a young man who felt great ambivalence about cooperating in psychotherapy, because to him such cooperation seemed a submission to the therapist. The patient had been sitting on the couch, which he preferred over sitting in the chair facing the therapist. (We will not discuss at this point the pros and cons of agreeing to such a request by a patient for a somewhat unusual seating arrangement.) As the patient began to express some rather critical thoughts about the therapist, he suddenly lay down. The therapist insisted on focusing the patient's attention on why he had lain down at just that moment. The patient replied, "I just feel more comfortable lying down." The therapist proposed that the lying down may have expressed a submissive attitude, which the patient felt necessary to assume after his aggressive outburst. After hearing this interpretation the patient sat up and began to discuss straightforwardly his ambivalent feelings of submissive dependence and rebellion toward the therapist.

Acting in should be distinguished from nonverbal communication of never-verbalized (i.e., preverbal) experiences. One of us observed a patient who, seeking to communicate her hunger for visual contact (as she had experienced that hunger during infancy), turned over on the couch to look the therapist in the eye. We believe that in doing this she was repeating some aspects of an experience that occurred before she could talk. We would not consider this nonverbal communication to be a resistance, because it was not that the patient did not want to put the action into words, it was that this experience had never been verbalized.

Transference Cure

In his paper "On Beginning the Treatment" Freud (1913) pointed out that the transference is able to remove symptoms, but only for a while—only for as long as the transference lasts. Such an improvement in the patient is a "transference cure." If the patient seizes on such an improvement as evidence of recovery from neurotic difficulties, overemphasizing the degree of improvement and its significance, we see a use of the transference cure in the service of resistance. There is a part of the patient that welcomes a respite from the work and anxiety of the therapy and is willing to settle for whatever improvement there has been in the patient's happiness, short-lived though such improvement may be.

Mistakes by the therapist can contribute to this kind of resistance. An interpretation that is partly correct but inexact—missing some important aspect of the current flow of material—will provide relief of anxiety and some impulse-gratification to the patient, thereby reducing her or his motivation for continued exploration of her or his living. Because such inexact interpretation derives its effectiveness from the authority of the therapist rather than from a rationally supported explanation, we consider it to be an effect of transference. Any amelioration of symptoms that stems from inexact interpretation is, therefore, a kind of transference cure.

We can see how the therapist's influence was used to alleviate symptoms, but at the expense of a more radical improvement, in the following example of therapeutic work with a 35-year-old business executive. This executive, who had serious difficulties in controlling his drinking and severe characterological problems that threatened both his marriage and his career, sought therapy from a psychologist. Within 6 weeks the therapist had commanded the patient to stop drinking, had told him that he was overdependent on his wife, and had explained that the patient's problems originated with his mother's not showing him enough love when he was a child. Feeling considerable relief as a result of these interventions of the therapist, the patient then had little motivation to continue exploring his mental and emotional life. In particular, he was enabled to build up a fence around one important area of his living, his relationships with his father and with other men, being aided in this defensive strategy by the therapist's assurances that all of his problems could be traced back to an unloving mother. An inexact, premature interpretation thus cut off a whole area of the patient's life from further exploration.

At the same time, the interpretation that this man was "too dependent" on his wife served, paradoxically, to cover up the whole issue of *why* he needed to be so dependent on her. He simply attempted to act less dependent, expressing his dependence, therefore, in more subtle ways, while buttressing his defenses against looking at his fears of performing in an adult, masculine role. Thus many of the symptoms of dependence disappeared, but at the expense of making these symptoms unavailable for analysis and unavailable as routes for the discovery of the unconscious conflicts that had determined them. Glover, in his paper on inexact interpretation (1931), discussed the way in which an inexact interpretation strengthens some repressions, offers relief of anxiety, and cuts off the exploration of deeper problems. He pointed out that inexact interpretations have such effects because they rely on suggestion rather than on analytic understanding.

How can one discriminate between a feeling better that is superficial and not likely to be lasting, and a deeper, more solid improvement? If the patient reports feeling better, but he or she and the therapist cannot really understand the reasons for this improvement, one should look at the change with skepticism. Solid changes for the better are likely to follow upon decisive changes in the patient's emotional understanding of himself or herself. When a change is solid, the patient will have a sense of inner freedom. He or she will not feel compelled to act in a characteristic way (compelled, for instance, to be combative when challenged or to feel bereft when rebuffed or to feel unworthy when slighted) but will have a sense that the direction of life lies in his or her own hands. There will be a sense that she or he "does not have to" act as she or he always acted in the past.

The patient whose therapist can understand the inner psychic changes that are producing the improved adaptation, the patient who has been freed from the sense of being compelled to repeat old patterns of thinking, feeling, and acting—such a patient has achieved a lasting change rather than a transference cure.

A further clue to differentiating transference cure from structural change in the personality, is the suddenness of change. Transference cures are typically sudden and dramatic; structural changes often are noticed only by the less frequent reporting of symptoms by the patient. For example, during a substantial segment of therapy a patient would report, in the session following an interpretation, that the dynamic that had been interpreted had been resolved. On one occasion, when the patient's reports of work inhibitions had been interpreted as expressing a wish for the therapist's encouragement and urging, she came to the therapy at the next session reporting that she was working full-steam. When the therapist inquired into the reasons for this change, the patient responded that the interpretation of last session had altered her motivational pattern. When, however, the therapist commented that the patient seemed to be trying to say that the demand on the therapist for encouragement no longer existed and therefore did not need to be explored further, the patient plaintively asked, "Isn't there anything I can do that will please you? Why can't you ever say anything nice?"

For illustrative purposes we have distinguished sharply between transference cure and structural change. In practice, however, one sees a mixture of the two. Even upon a successful completion of analysis, residuals of transference continue, if only in the form of the patient's being pleased that the therapist is pleased with the way the therapy has gone. Conversely, in situations where transference has been the primary motive for a patient's declaring herself or himself cured and for departing from therapy, there is likely to be some structural change. Thus, although it is more probable that transference cures will not last as well, it frequently happens that a transference cure produces lasting gains.

Chapter 10

Understanding Communications From the Unconscious

Unconscious Determination

In psychoanalytic therapy the therapist cannot know directly the nature and function of the patient's unconscious processes and contents. Therefore he or she has to rely entirely on the patient to provide that information. Patients, however, are unaware of their unconscious. Furthermore, patients cannot present unconscious thoughts and feelings straightforwardly. The paradox that these facts create can be resolved if both patient and therapist realize that, granting that unconscious phenomena cannot be known by direct observation, they must be approached by more roundabout routes.

Unconscious Determination

To follow these routes the therapist must be totally committed to the principle of unconscious determination of all of the patient's behaviors in the therapy. In essence this principle asserts that the patient's desire to participate in the therapeutic process, as evidenced by his or her presence in the consulting room, mobilizes what may be called "the therapeutically cooperative functions of the ego." These functions ensure that all of the patient's verbal and nonverbal behaviors in therapy occur during therapy for the purpose of communicating, indirectly, whatever the patient's ego has selected as important at that moment. In other words, one takes as a given that *everything* a patient says or does is a disguised communication from the unconscious, no matter how superficial it seems.

The principle of the unconscious determination of behavior in therapy can be better understood if we discuss its facets. First, this principle applies at all times and to all behaviors and statements of the patient. It is never correct to assume that a patient is talking about alpha in order to avoid omega, is talking about trivia rather than substance, or is acting to avoid talking or associating. Although the patient may hope unconsciously to accomplish these defensive aims, unconsciously the alpha is precisely selected, specific trivia are chosen to come to mind, and the actions reveal what they are intended to hide.

A second facet of the principle of unconscious determination is that resistances have embedded in them the very psychic process that generates the resistance. A patient who refused to keep track of his therapy appointments and therefore had to ask the therapist how many times they had met in the past month, became angry when the therapist refused to tell him. The therapist then suggested that they examine the patient's motivation for failing to keep track, making use of the patient's associations to make this examination. The patient expressed his anger through silence and through sullen recriminations about the amount of time that was being "wasted" over this trivial issue, a waste that the patient attributed to the therapist's "arbitrary" stance. Inherent in this resistance was the patient's unconscious wish to have the therapist assume responsibility for the patient's participation in the therapy. This wish was a specific manifestation of a more general, characteristic desire of the patient to achieve passive, masochistic gratification by receiving instruction on how to live. Contrary to the way the patient saw it, the therapist in refusing to tell the patient how many times they had met during the previous month was serving as an agent of reality; that is, the therapist, perceiving (correctly) that the patient was an adult, expected the patient to keep track of the meetings, if for no other reason, because the therapist might make a mistake. The therapist therefore could not comply with the patient's demand without confirming by such compliance the patient's view of himself—determined by neurotic and unconscious motives—as an incapable person who needed direction.

The third facet is the most frequently observed type of association in therapy, the patient's description of a realistic situation occurring in the recent past (usually since the last therapy session). The patient, as an experiencer in the therapy (rather than as observer), thinks of this recital as nothing more than the telling of a critical real-life incident. The therapist, however, looks on the matter differently, regarding the report of the incident as significant only as a metaphor that gives expression to an unconscious reaction that is occurring now in the patient. For the therapist, the telling of the incident is an action unconsciously chosen in order to present the hidden reaction in a disguised form, which enables patient and therapist to observe it. From the therapist's point of view, this so-called realistic situation is no different from any other account of the patient's experiences; it can be considered, for the purposes of the therapy, as equivalent to a fantasy. One likens it to a fantasy because, as is true of daydreams, night dreams, and other experiences reported by the patient and recognized by him or her as having no basis in fact, the presentation of this material can be understood without reference to what really happened. Accordingly the therapist treats the report of what happened as though it were a daydream recollected by the patient during the therapeutic hour in order for the patient to communicate an unconscious experience of the moment.

The following case is an example of metaphoric communication. A patient described a recent visit to an internist. While describing the visit, the patient complained of the doctor's coldness, an attitude of indifference towards his symptoms, and lack of solicitude for his well-being. The therapist of course did not know whether this description was accurate; indeed, she had no way of knowing whether the visit actually took place. Nor does the therapist have to know, because she should be concerned only with the metaphoric communication that the association represented: The patient was telling the therapist that he felt that she was cold, uncaring, and uninvolved. The patient *knew* that the therapist was interested and concerned, but he *wanted*, unconsciously, to feel that she was not, so as to justify his anxiety about participating in the therapy. Furthermore, the patient through these associations communicated the wish for the therapist to be nurturant to him.

Why can't the therapist first respond to the realistic event that the patient is describing, possibly with sympathy and reassurance, and then look to the unconscious implications of the association? This cannot be done because responding to the associations as though the patient were presenting a realistic matter that should be dealt with as a fact is contradictory to the therapist's basic approach, which assumes that the associations express unconscious fantasy. If the therapist later tries to deal with the association as a fantasy, his or her position has already been undermined. The patient would be able to assert a resistance along these lines, for example: "If I had a fantasy about your being cold and uncaring, why did you go along with my belief that I was only talking about an external reality?"

Although what we have just said makes clear that the therapist must always be aware that all of the patient's communications have unconscious implications, the therapist should not always act on this awareness. After all, therapy is a human endeavor to which the participants bring a reasonable degree of their humanness. Thus the therapist responds to a patient's greeting with an appropriate greeting. When the patient says, "Good evening," the therapist doesn't respond with a question, "What comes to mind about that?" This realistically human quality of the therapy prevents the process from becoming cold, mechanical, and stereotyped. If therapy were too sterile, no therapy would happen. Few patients can develop transference feelings toward a machine.

In summary, the principle of unconscious determinism requires the therapist (a) to be aware that unconscious determination of behavior is an ever-present reality, (b) to understand that both wish and defense can be expressed as metaphor, (c) to hear realities as fantasies, and (d) to ignore—appropriately so—the principle when the good of the therapy requires ignoring it.

The Unconscious Reflected in Transference

Understanding the implications of the concept transference aids the therapist substantially in the understanding of communications from the unconscious. We cannot, for the most part, view psychoanalytic therapy as a situation in which the patient has come to tell the therapist about her or his life and to analyze the psychic forces that lay behind the reactions that are described. Rather, we can view analytic therapy as a situation to which the patient comes to live life (revealing this life in words, in tones, in gestures for 45 to 50 minutes at a time) while she or he and the therapist interrupt this flow, from time to time, to observe it. In such a living of life, the patient perceives the therapist in a variety of ways that, because the therapist provides no basis in reality for the perceptions, are projections onto the therapist of the patient's unconscious attitudes, wishes, fears, conceptions, misconceptions, and emotions. These ways of construing the therapist derive from internal images that the patient has of herself or himself and of others.

For example, when a patient describes in detail an argument with the boss, which is described as ending in his or her submitting to the boss's wishes, the therapist can hypothesize:
1. The story is a metaphor giving expression to unconscious processes of the patient.
2. The boss in the story represents the therapist.
3. The patient fears being forced to submit to the therapist.
4. A wish to submit underlies this fear.

5. The experience of the patient with the therapist is a reliving of a perceived or fantasied occurrence at an earlier time that has emotional significance for the patient.
6. The further associations of the patient will confirm, modify, or disprove the therapist's hypotheses.

Thus the therapist always must ask of the patient's associations: What feelings and fantasies about the therapist and about the therapy is the patient expressing through the associations as she or he lives life in the therapy? Although the answers to the question are always exquisitely specific, some general guidelines can be offered.

The associations of the patient often reflect the stage of therapy that the patient is in at the time. At the beginning of therapy the therapist is a stranger to the patient. In consequence, the patient's associations at this stage frequently express conscious and preconscious expectations and questions of the patient that the patient is constrained from asking directly. The patient is so constrained because he or she does not know—indeed, cannot believe—that the therapist is neutral and nonjudgmental. The patient expresses fears, therefore, in associations: fears about being criticized, punished, seduced, overwhelmed by impulses and emotions, and made crazy by the treatment.

As the patient comes to understand the therapeutic process, having heard the therapist's interpretations and educative statements and having observed his or her therapeutic demeanor, the patient can ally himself or herself with the therapist. (The therapist's reassurances and protestations of goodwill have little impact; what counts is the therapist's actual nonjudgmental behavior.) With the development of this alliance the patient can begin to present associations that express unconscious perceptions of how he or she is related to the therapist. For instance, the associations often indicate longings for care by a magically powerful, totally benevolent being, a person who will make all things right for the patient without the need for the patient to make any effort. Accompanying these fantasies there may be corollary fears of rejection, abandonment, and separation. As the therapist interprets the resistance aspects of these unconscious experiences of the patient, the patient develops a positive attachment to the therapist, of which an essential ingredient is trust. This trust is based both on the realistic perception that the therapist is trustworthy (which we speak of as the *working alliance*) and on the misperception of the therapist as a good parent to the patient-child (called *positive transference*).

With the development of this attachment, the patient can present, via associations, those unconscious constellations of experience as they are lived in the patient, with the patient as subject and the therapist as object. Examples of such unconscious phenomena include the patient's wish for and fear of: having an affair with the therapist, merging with the therapist, fighting with the therapist, and having the therapist's child.

As the therapy progresses the patient becomes more and more able to act out neuroses with the therapist, to relive in the present those past, infantile misperceptions and misconceptions that produced various aspects of the infantile neurosis. The childhood origin of the transference neurosis (the repeating with the therapist of the various aspects of the infantile neurosis) is attested by the primitive nature of the unconscious fantasies expressed in the patient's associations. There are cannibalistic wishes, defecatory urges, murderous wishes, and fears of castration. The analysis of the transference neurosis, and with it, of the infantile neurosis, is the final goal of the therapy. Although these stages of the therapy are never as systematically or as sequentially presented as we have outlined them here, it does help the therapist to keep in mind what stage of the therapy the patient is in.

The associations that the patient presents are always, we assume, the product of an unconscious wish of the patient, of the anxiety that is aroused by that wish, and of the unconscious defense erected against the anxiety. To understand any series of associations fully, the therapist needs to look for all three parts of this wish-anxiety-defense triad. In looking for the elements of the triad one does well to remember that the patient experiences every wish, anxiety, or defense in specific terms with specific images. Patients do not live their unconscious experiences in concepts, they live them through concrete representations. Concepts such as anger, love, fear, desire, and rage are helpful abstractions. They enable the therapist and the patient, as observers, to formulate and theorize about the concrete, unconscious experience. Yet in order to arrive at this understanding the therapist must look always for the concrete and specific wish, anxiety, or defense.

The patient who wishes to be loved by the therapist experiences a specific urge that reflects the specific aim and object of the wish. Contrast (for example) the great difference between a wish to be loved that is experienced as a desire to be held in the therapist's lap and suckled at a breast and a wish to be loved that is experienced as a desire to be penetrated by the therapist's penis and made pregnant (pregnancy being understood as having a part of the penis left inside the body, then swollen into a large, space-occupying thing) and therefore "fat." It is concrete wishes and fantasies such as these that constitute the stuff of the transference, based on unconscious, infantile experiences that provide its prototype.

Until the moment in the therapy when the anxiety has been reduced sufficiently and the defenses analyzed sufficiently, the patient cannot experience the concrete, infantile wish, desire, or urge consciously and cannot become aware of the accompanying affect and excitement. Most often the therapist learns about these contents through the patient's metaphors, allusions, symbols, slips, and dreams; those are observed in the associations that the patient offers. To understand the communications from the unconscious, therefore, the therapist has to decipher the coded messages.

We should point out, too, that these coded messages are never transmitted all at once. They are, rather, sent by the patient piecemeal, over periods of weeks or months. They are transmitted first as mere hints, only later becoming more direct statements of the concrete fantasy and of the fantasies connected to it. Indeed, it may well be weeks or months later that the patient becomes able to experience fully all of the aspects of the constellation of the fantasy and its derivatives. It follows from what we have said that in order to understand the material of any particular therapy session the therapist has to know the context; the themes of preceding hours; the present, active themes in the transference; and the transference neurosis. The therapist, of course, will not simply make use of past knowledge to figure out what is going on; she or he will also revise formulations of the case by making use of the material of the current hour. These revised formulations will be used to confirm, modify, elaborate, or abandon the hypotheses that have been brought to the current hour.

Why Look for Unconscious Meaning?

Now we must confront the challenge that patients (and, sometimes, beginning therapists) frequently make: "Why can't you simply take the patient's associations and other manifest communications at face value? Why must one always look for an additional, unconscious meaning?" The answer to these questions is integral to the psychoanalytic conception of mental processes. According to this conception, behavior is a compromise between wish (impulse, drive, instinct) and defense. To the extent that a wish generates anxiety, it must be modified or disguised before it can be expressed. Wishes seek expression, excitations push toward discharge, instincts aim for satisfaction; these forces find expression in words if not in actions. It follows that the patient who is sitting in a chair or lying on a couch in the therapist's office experiences this psychic process unconsciously; because she or he does, we must expect his or her productions to be the outcome of that process. The therapist accordingly assumes, and at appropriate times tells the patient, that it is not what the patient knows consciously that creates psychic difficulty, it is what is "known" *unconsciously* that creates the problem and needs to be understood. Indeed, the therapy in broad outline consists of an attempt to elucidate these hidden contents.

Because the therapy orients itself to the study of the contents of the patient's unconscious, the therapist needs a knowledge of unconscious processes in order to do therapy properly. As Freud discussed psychic contents early in his career as a psychoanalyst, he conceived of certain areas of psychic contents, defined by whether these contents were accessible to consciousness. In this "topographic" model he distinguished the preconscious (what one can easily become aware of) from the unconscious (what one can learn about only with difficulty). In his paper "The Unconscious," Freud (1915c) listed the special characteristics of unconscious processes: Unconscious thoughts are exempt from mutual contradiction; they are subject to the primary process (in particular, to displacement and condensation); they pay little regard to time and reality; and they are subject to the pleasure principle. The qualities of unconscious processes are sometimes directly evident in the patient's associations. Whether they are evident or not, they are at all times active in the processes that shape associations.

Here is an illustration of how the characteristics of the unconscious mode of thinking plays a part in associations. A male patient in speaking about his forthcoming marriage alternated between detailing the plans he was making and describing his fiancee as a person who displeased him in almost every way. The patient was quite unaware of the contradictions in this presentation.

In every metaphor that a patient presents there is a displacement from the therapist to the figure in the metaphor that represents the therapist. Thus doctors, teachers, bosses, police, etc., in the patient's associations can be hypothesized to represent the therapist.

Any particular psychic presentation (e.g., a symptomatic response) may have several different meanings condensed in it. For example, one patient who would play with her keys during therapy sessions used this action to communicate about masturbation, about possession of a penis, about her desire to lock the therapist into or out of her life, and so on. Indeed, Katan (personal communication, June 1956) cautioned against interpreting such symptomatic actions in the therapy prematurely, lest when one interprets one meaning of the action one causes the action to disappear, and with it, the other meanings of the action.

The phenomena of transference illustrate timelessness, illustrating as well the repetition compulsion. Patients experience the therapist and themselves as though they were in another era during the therapy hour. Without recognizing that they are doing it, patients bring the past into the present in their words, in their gestures, and even in their omissions. The therapist as a parent in the transference, therefore, is a parent of a time past and is perceived as belonging to a past time and responded to as though in that past time. The omnipotence that patients often attribute to their therapists is the omnipotence that the patients attributed to their parents when they were children.

For the patient, and sometimes for the therapist, it is difficult to accept that everything the patient does, thinks, feels, and says is to some extent in the service of the pleasure principle. That is, every response does the patient some good unconsciously, serves some unconscious purpose, fulfills some unconscious wish. Realizing this is especially difficult when the matter concerns some conscious manifestation that is unpleasant on the surface. The patient who has been lamenting that nothing has been accomplished in the therapy, that the process will go on for 20 years, is startled when the therapist responds, "Those are comforting thoughts; they help you to reassure yourself that you are still safe from the unpleasant experiences that you expect will arise when you confront your unconscious feelings." This lament expresses, too, the wish that the patient can put off dealing with the feelings he is having now until 20 years from now.

As unconscious processes are examined in the therapy the patient comes to see that they stand in a constant relationship to what is conscious. The associations are compromises between the patient's desire to express unconscious feelings and the desire to hide them. In other words, what appears consciously is the product of the patient's wishes and defensive distortions, modifications, and alternations of these wishes. The patient's associations, in short, are products of defense. To understand communications from the unconscious, the therapist tries to recognize what defense has been called into play and has worked on the content of what the patient unconsciously wants to express. Knowledge of the mechanisms of defense, accordingly, assists the therapist in her or his work.

Patients who are in treatment have symptoms. They have these symptoms because there has been a threatened failure of repression, a threatened return of the repressed. As a result of this threat there has been a regression, resulting in an attempt—using primitive processes—to reestablish the repression. The symptoms are the result of these primitive, regressive efforts. It is, therefore, not surprising that when a patient comes to therapy he or she is in some sense asking (without saying so in our technical jargon) for the therapy to help reestablish the repression as it was before. Even though it may not be shown on the surface, the patient reacts with anxiety to the psychoanalytic therapist's proposal that instead of reestablishing the status quo, the patient further lift the repression, permitting still more unconscious material to appear. Thus no matter how cooperative, how hardworking the patient may be, she or he necessarily views the therapist as an enemy: an enemy of repression, one who proposes that the patient acquaint herself or himself with the feelings that the patient anticipates will be dangerous. This anticipation leads the patient to show in all of his or her associations an attempt to maintain the repression of unconscious contents. Fortunately the therapy does not founder on this resistance; if the patient comes, talks, and listens, he or she will tell the therapist of unconscious reactions despite intentions not to do so.

Unconscious reactions, whether defensive or expressive of instinctual drives, always have an aim, an object, and a subject. By altering one or more of these aspects of the content the patient can achieve a means of expressing the unconscious reaction in a disguised way. The examples that follow illustrate how alterations in the aim of the unconscious reaction result in disguised, conscious associations.

The patient who speaks at length, gratuitously, about liking somebody (e.g., the therapist) may lead the therapist to conclude, "The lady doth protest too much, methinks." He or she would understand this overevaluation as a kind of *reaction formation*. The therapist infers that the patient dislikes the therapist and asks himself or herself, "What specifically is bringing out this negative reaction?" Indeed, sometimes one can point out to the patient that the overevaluation betrays an underlying dislike, then ask the patient what the basis for the dislike is, and be rewarded with either a straightforward answer or an allusion that leads to an answer.

At times every patient, no matter how sophisticated, denies that she or he has an unconscious. This denial may assume humorous, irrational proportions. For example, one patient who knew a good deal about therapy and about communications from the unconscious spent the first part of a session speaking vehemently, indignantly about a recent event reported in the news. When the therapist asked him to consider why he was focusing on this topic he replied, "Would you believe it is because I just read about it in one of the magazines in your waiting room?" After the therapist responded that he did not believe that, the patient acknowledged, "I don't either," and went on to provide associations that revealed the unconscious significance of the thoughts that he had reported.

In understanding communications from the unconscious, the therapist *listens* and *formulates*. In listening, the therapist goes into each therapy session with an "empty mind," totally without any preconceptions, expectations, recollections of other sessions, or formulations about the therapy. The therapist tries to have his or her mind function as an empty receptacle. It is into this receptacle that the therapist receives the patient's associations and other manifestations of unconscious activity. Also into this receptacle will flow the therapist's associations to what the patient is presenting. As the passive recipient of this inflow of material, the therapist makes no effort to think about it; it's simply allowed to fill his or her mind.

Sooner or later the therapist will experience that the material in his or her mind seems to be organizing itself. Certain associations will have a common element or theme; certain double entendres will point to the hidden implications of the patient's conscious verbalizations; certain words will connect associatively to elements of a reported dream. When the appearance of such organized compositions are noticed, the therapist shifts the mode of functioning from passive listening to active thinking. Recognizing that such preconscious compositions are compromises, he or she then goes back into the associative material to seek answers to the questions: (a) What defenses are operating in this compromise-formation? (b) What dangers and anxieties necessitate the formation of the defense? and (c) What specific, concrete unconscious wishes are connected with the danger, are being defended against, and are finding partial expression in the compromise-formation? In this manner the therapist obtains a psychodynamic formulation from the material the patient presents.

Having arrived at a formulation, the therapist then checks it against other associations that did not originally play a part in arriving at the formulation. With each confirmatory comparison, the therapist's level of certainty about her or his formulation increases. When the therapist is absolutely certain that the formulation has been heard from the patient, the therapist is ready to interpret and the patient is ready to receive the interpretation.

To work as we have just described, the therapist must trust the associative method; she or he must trust the patient to choose associations that best communicate the message from the unconscious and trust himself or herself to hear, eventually, the message for which she or he has been listening.

Chapter 11

Interpretation: The Therapist and Patient Bring the Unconscious Conflict to Light

Interpretation is, by definition, an intervention of the therapist by which she or he attempts to make conscious to the patient what has been unconscious. What has been unconscious is, usually, repressed. Accordingly we need to consider what repression is, how it comes about, and what its consequences are, before proceeding with a discussion of interpretation.

Repression

We say that an idea, or a representation of a feeling, or a representation of a wish, is repressed if the patient is not aware of it, though it was once experienced consciously. What kind of material gets repressed? In general what is repressed are conceptions about the nature of the world and about oneself to which strong affects are attached.

Why repression? We answer that repression is necessary as a means of managing anxiety—which we define as the affect that accompanies excessive stimulus input—or as a means of controlling affective buildup (because inner stimuli as well as outer ones are sources of anxiety).

What are the consequences of repression? The most obvious consequence is the inhibition of the expression of infantile wishes. The little boy who longs for sexual union with his mother, experiencing a threat of castration gives up his direct strivings for this sexual gratification without being aware that he is doing so. Thereafter he does not know that he has sexual desires for his mother, and he does not pursue these desires.

But repression also results in the gratification of infantile wishes through derivative wish-fulfillment. For example, such oedipal wishes as we have just described can be gratified derivatively in marriage, which through allowing a relationship with a substitute object gives a partial gratification of the original wishes; the wife is a substitute for the mother. We view this acceptance of an appropriate substitute as a constructive solution to the original conflict. As Freud said (see Freud, 1925, and Murdock's [1949, pp. 289–300] discussion), the normal resolution of the oedipal conflict involves a giving up of direct sexual strivings toward the mother and a turning of the boy toward an object outside the nuclear family.

If a repression is so strong and so far-reaching that it inhibits not only the expression of the original, infantile wishes but also inhibits many derivative gratifications that society would consider entirely acceptable, the person having this kind of repression will experience a continual buildup of drive tension. At some point this tension will become so great that the repressed infantile wishes will find expression in symptomatic and regressive forms. Such a state of affairs occurs in the *return of the repressed*, as we explained in our discussion of the psychoanalytic theory of neurosis (see chapter 2).

Whether a repression is mostly inhibiting the expression of drives or is mostly allowing indirect expression of them, whether it has led to the formation of symptoms or not, it has the effect of preventing infantile conceptions about the world and the self from being altered by later-acquired conceptions. As Waelder (1960, p. 213) pointed out, repression "has cut the inner communications," it separates the repressed drives from the tendencies of the rest of the personality. The processes of which we are conscious can be influenced by appeals to reason, by argument and exhortation, by success and failure, and by rewards and punishments; the processes that are unconscious cannot be so influenced (Kubie, 1950). To the extent that behavior is driven by unconscious forces, it cannot be influenced by experience. A person dominated by unconscious conflicts is doomed to strive for unknown goals that can never be attained, with cravings that are unrealistic and insatiable. This behavior is repeated endlessly, with errors recurring as frequently as successful responses, regardless of the happiness or unhappiness that results.

Freud himself used a striking analogy to express this difference between conscious and unconscious material. In explaining to the "Rat Man" how uncovering the unconscious could be helpful, Freud (1909) offered an explanation that he reported as follows: "I then made some short observations upon *the psychological differences between the conscious and the unconscious*, and upon the fact that everything conscious was subject to a process of wearing-away, while what was unconscious was relatively unchangeable; and I illustrated my remarks by pointing to the antiques standing about in my room. They were, in fact, I said, only objects found in a tomb, and their burial had been their preservation: the destruction of Pompeii was only beginning now that it had been dug up" (p. 176). When the once-buried objects of Pompeii were at last uncovered, they were exposed to the ravages of sunlight, air, wind, and rain; they began to be changed. So it is with unconscious and conscious mental contents: The unconscious contents are changed not at all by the person's experience, only the conscious ones can be influenced by current experience.

Because unconscious tendencies are not changed by current experience, the person with strong unconscious conflicts is fated to repeat the same strivings over and over again. Such a *repetition compulsion* is characteristic of neurosis, as Kubie eloquently pointed out in his classic paper, "The Repetitive Core of the Neurosis" (1941). What maintains these repetitive action-patterns? The symptom-compromises that are repeated are maintained by (a) need gratification—a partial gratification, to be sure, but still a gratification, and (b) the gratification of anxiety-reduction, through the partial expression of defensive forces in the symptom. The reader may be reminded here that every symptom is a compromise between drive forces and defensive forces; the symptom, therefore, drains off tension (both drive tension and anxiety) sufficiently to reinforce the symptom and to allow the incomplete repression to continue.

The Therapist's Role

We turn now to the question, "How does the therapist aid the undoing of repression?" First, the therapist acts as a person who can be used by the patient as a transference object; he or she allows himself or herself to be the target of the patient's transference fantasies and transference demands; and he or she does not respond unthinkingly to these demands (i.e., does not reinforce them). The demands, therefore, grow more intense, becoming expressed more and more directly as the therapist continues to frustrate the patient's attempts to gratify them. Then, second, the therapist labels the infantile wish that is provoking the transference demands. By this labeling the therapist reduces the patient's anxiety, thereby lessening the patient's need for repression. The mechanism by which interpretation reduces anxiety is incompletely understood. We know that at times labeling makes discriminations possible (as Dollard and Miller [1950] pointed out); discriminations between infantile weakness and jeopardy to danger and current strengths and conditions of safety can be made, with the help of labeling. The labeling of infantile fantasies as fantasy permits the person to judge that the world is not as it was imagined to be, taking away the terror of these fantasies; fantasies in which the patient had imagined herself or himself and her or his wishes to be powerful, dangerously destructive, and ungovernable. Finally we note that labeling makes possible an explicit comparison of infantile fantasy with the reality of the therapeutic situation in which the transference occurs. The patient is enabled to compare personal transference perceptions with the therapist's actual behavior. Sometimes, indeed, the therapist spells this out for the patient, saying, "You have imagined that I would respond thus-and-so, but in fact you know, and I know, that I have acted quite otherwise." Every interpretation of a transference reaction carries this message implicitly even if the lesson is not made explicit.

Interpretation, so to speak, opens a window, transiently, in the repression barrier. This enables the patient to make a conscious comparison of repressed ideation and affect with later-acquired knowledge. This kind of comparison, repeated with every interpretation, makes possible the decathexis—the withdrawal of emotional investment—of the unconscious conflict. The bit-by-bit decathexis of the elements of the unconscious conflict constitutes an important curative effect of the treatment. Insight that the patient obtains through interpretations results, not in the patient's taking corrective action against the symptoms, but in experiencing an unconscious "withering away" of the symptoms, as the underlying conflict becomes less important emotionally.

The Context of Interpretation

Therapy occurs in an obvious interpersonal situation. Not so obvious is the nature of the dyadic relationship between therapist and patient. This relationship can be one of dominance and submission, of exploitation and offering oneself to be a victim, of helper and the helped, or of cooperation in the task of increasing the patient's self-understanding and capacity for observing personal feelings and intentions. We now indicate some of the actions and attitudes of the therapist that facilitate the development of this last kind of relationship between patient and therapist. Such a cooperative relationship we call (following Greenson, 1967) the working alliance.

In a good working alliance the therapist has allied himself or herself with the patient's cooperative ego. Therefore the therapist does not attack the patient by labeling some aspect of the patient's behavior as "pathological" or "bad." For example, if the patient comes late, the therapist's inquiry is not pursued in the spirit of reprimanding the patient for a breach of the rules and finding out why she or he is resistant ("bad"), but rather it is directed to understanding what is happening in the patient's inner life that makes it necessary for him or her to come late. Arriving late is against what the patient, in that part of his or her functioning that is committed to the resolution of neurotic difficulties, wants, namely, a maximal opportunity to profit from the interchange with the therapist.

Another example of interpreting with respect for the working alliance is as follows. A young man, whose young wife was murdered by a vagrant intruder into the house (when the wife was alone), finds himself unable to mourn his wife's death. He is, however, tormented by the memories of her that are stirred up by the house in which he and his wife lived together. The young man, still living in this house— though he could move into his parents' house if he chose—talks bitterly of this house that has brought him so much sorrow. Then he announces his intention to tear the house down, though he still has an unpaid mortgage on the house and cannot afford to build a new house for himself.

The therapist judges this man's plan to be totally unrealistic, yet expressive of the widower's need to attempt to destroy, symbolically, his ties to his wife. The therapist appreciates that she cannot get her patient to address himself to his deeply ambivalent attitudes toward his wife so long as his plan for action (tearing down the house) crowds out contemplation of these feelings. Yet if the therapist should say, "That's a ridiculous idea, to tear down your house. Isn't that concealing from you some inner conflicts about your wife?" the patient would be put in the position of having to defend his plans (to tear down the house) and his thinking (that he would relieve his suffering by destroying the structure that reminds him of his beloved wife).

Instead of attacking his patient's reasoning, the therapist can say, "You feel yourself to be in a real bind, because on the one hand you find it so painful to live in a house that reminds you of your wife, and on the other hand you know that it just isn't practical to get rid of the house. And even though you know it isn't practical, your feelings about the house are so strong that you can hardly keep from tearing it up a board at a time. It sounds like your intense feelings about the house are expressing some other feelings that you find it hard to think about in a more direct way." Such an interpretation does not attack the patient's position, does not make it necessary for him to defend a position against the therapist; rather, it offers the suggestion that the patient himself is in conflict between his reasonable judgment about the folly of tearing down the house and the fantasies associated with these intensely angry feelings toward the house. Emphasizing that this is a conflict within the patient, the therapist allows the patient to observe his own thinking and feeling processes while working with the therapist. Such a joining together in observing the patient is an example of the working alliance.

We have so far defined the relationship of interpretation to the working alliance negatively; we have said that the therapist should *not* attack the patient by labeling her or his behavior, thinking, or feeling as pathological. Now we turn to a positive characterization. First, the therapist recognizes, by means of empathy with the patient, the patient's sense of disharmony within herself or himself. For example, a young man who was struggling to free himself of an irrational dependence on his ex-wife (with whom he was repeating the ambivalent relationship he had had with his mother) started his therapy session one morning by announcing that he felt the need to act in the outside world rather than to talk, talk, talk in the therapy. He expressed a deep discouragement about therapy. In effect he was threatening to quit. The therapist could have said, "You're running away from your conflicts about dependence on your ex-wife" and by saying that, attack a "resistance." She chose, however, to try to feel her way into what the patient was then experiencing that had made it necessary for him to propose a disruption of the therapy. As the hour continued, the patient spoke of his need for a dependent relationship and of his struggle to break out of it. At length the therapist said, "I have the sense that you feel there is no one in the whole world who really gives a damn about you, who really cares what happens to you. It's awful hard to act autonomously, to break away from this dependence, when you feel nobody really cares about you."

Such a comment, we believe, recognizes the patient's inner sense of disharmony and communicates some appreciation of this disharmony. This approach is likely to build the working alliance; an approach that considers the patient's struggles from a distance, without emotion, is not likely to build it. We did not fail to consider how the patient's complaint about his inability to free himself from dependence is also, indirectly, an indication that he wanted to be dependent on the therapist yet also feared allowing himself to feel that dependence. Our comment is not intended to advocate a neglect of that aspect of the interaction; our focus at this point is, however, on another issue.

When interpreting effectively the therapist communicates to the patient her or his passionate desire to understand the phenomena of the patient's living. Did the patient have a wretched, miserable weekend? The therapist wants to know what thoughts and feelings of emotional import caused the misery. Did the patient forget the name of an author who had been mentioned during the previous session? The therapist invites the patient to consider, with him or her, what the forgetting means. Did the patient feel a disinclination to come to the therapy session? The therapist wants to hear about the thoughts and feelings that are related to this disinclination.

The therapist's conviction that the patient's thinking and feeling processes are important, deserving of serious scrutiny, is also communicated through the intensity with which the therapist offers an interpretation. When the therapist says to a young patient with great earnestness, "You must have had many questions—unanswered questions—that you wanted to ask your parents, just as you do now as you're so full of questions that you are putting to me," the patient cannot help being impressed that the therapist is serious about understanding and is not playing games with her or his life. The therapist is not idly speculating about the origins of pathological behavior. Patients sometimes tell the therapist, "You really do believe what you're saying, don't you?" In such a comment they express their surprise that the therapist really cares about truth and is committed to it.

Although there are times during a long course of psychotherapy that the work may tire the therapist, generally the therapist as a student of human psychology finds much that is fascinating in how the patient communicates unconscious thinking and feeling processes. The therapist may well articulate some of this fascination to the patient, inviting the patient to view the patient's psychological problems with the same interest that the therapist has in the patient's—and his or her own—psychodynamics.

At the same time, for all of the devotion to the therapeutic task, the therapist grants to the patient the right to disengage temporarily from the therapeutic endeavor. The therapy cannot be considered a duty or an obligation to which the patient is bound; rather it is a work that the patient has freely chosen to undertake, to which he or she feels a commitment—a commitment that is continuously renewed without a need for coercion by the therapist or by anyone else. Viewing the therapy in this way, the therapist refrains from acting like a taskmaster.

Instead, the therapist accepts completely the necessity for the patient's current psychodynamic functioning. Resistances are necessary. They have been helpful to the patient. Their service must be acknowledged. Transferences are necessary. Because they represent a way by which she or he has come to terms with other people, they can be relinquished only when the patient can avail herself or himself of a more satisfactory way of relating to others. Accepting in this spirit the patient's functioning, the therapist's goal is not to change the patient's behavior. The therapist knows, of course, that some of the patient's behavior that once served him or her well, is now ineffective; and that the patient when given the opportunity to examine this behavior and to consider the reasons for it, will often decide to give it up. Yet the therapist sees his or her role as only the facilitating of the patient's examining and considering the behavior; he or she does not play the role of advocate of one or another course of action.

In particular, the therapist does not expect that the patient must immediately give up each resistance that the therapist becomes aware of and interprets. With resistances as with all of the patient's responses, the therapist accepts completely the necessity for the patient's current psychodynamic functioning. The therapist implicitly encourages the patient to adopt the same acceptance of the patient's psychological functioning.

Accordingly, in interpreting resistance the therapist does not tell (accuse) the patient that the patient is "avoiding," or "escaping," or "defending." Rather, the patient is asked to observe how she or he "protects" herself or himself from the anticipated dangers and from the anxiety that accompanies them.

Qualities of the Patient That Aid the Working Alliance

So far we have considered the therapist's actions that contribute to a strong working alliance. What characteristics of the patient facilitate the work of therapy? First, it is important that the patient have the ability to relate to another human being. In collaborating with the therapist, he or she must take a trusting attitude and have the willingness to follow the therapist's instructions, even though he or she cannot know that following them will bring about the results that are wished for.

Second, the patient must have the capacity for a therapeutic ego-split. As Sterba (1929) pointed out, in effective psychoanalytic therapy the patient is required to experience affects and memory images and to observe them. If the patient is too afraid of experiencing affects and cannot allow himself or herself that regressive activity, the work of therapy cannot be adequately performed. Simply taking an intellectual attitude toward personal mental activity is insufficient. On the other hand, if the patient cannot allow himself or herself to reflect on his or her experience or conceptualize what is happening, he or she will not be able to perform the work of the therapy adequately. These two ego functions need to be combined. It is likely that in combining these functions the patient will oscillate from one function to the other.

Third, the patient needs the ability to accept the premise that *understanding* leads to the resolution of problems of living. By "understanding" we mean a process of cognitive *and* emotional apprehension of one's own living, not an intellectual, bloodless explanation. To accept this premise the patient has to have some capacity for delaying immediate gratifications and for bearing frustrations. The lonely, 40-year-old woman who is hopelessly in love with her boss clamors for the therapist to tell her how to win the boss's (or the therapist's) love, or how to renounce it. She wants the therapist's advice to still an intense, immediate hunger for love. If she cannot be put off and cannot settle for the more indirect route of solving her problems through understanding, a sturdy therapeutic alliance cannot be established.

Fourth, the patient needs the ability to understand and accept the assumption that she or he communicates—in words and actions—*unconsciously, in a psychically determined way*, and *metaphorically*. Accepting this assumption, the patient is willing to join with the therapist in trying to discover what was unconscious, to learn by what forces the communications were determined, and to appreciate what idea lay behind the metaphor.

Finally, the patient needs the ability to come to a realization, as a result of experience in the therapy, that the therapist has no wish to violate the patient's integrity, either benevolently or malevolently; that the therapist is willing for the patient to choose her or his own path. Where this point may be in doubt, the patient is willing to trust the therapist's impartiality on the basis of past experience. The therapist's past trustworthiness is money in the bank.

Readiness for Interpretation

According to psychoanalytic thinking, for an interpretation to be effective it must be both *correct* and *timely*. Incorrect or partially correct ("inexact") interpretations either disrupt and confuse the therapy or, at best, enable the patient to arrive at a partial but incomplete resolution of real-life problems. Premature interpretations at best slide off the patient's back, apparently without effect (though they may plant a seed of understanding). At worst they frighten the patient so much that the topic of the interpretation or even the therapy itself is avoided for a long time.

It is important, therefore, that the therapist's interpretations be both accurate and well timed. Elsewhere, particularly in the chapter on understanding the unconscious (chapter 10), we try to provide the reader help in understanding the patient's communications, to the end that he can, as a therapist, make accurate interpretations. In the present section we discuss how the therapist can decide whether an interpretation would be timely.

The therapist needs to consider, first of all, the accessibility of psychic derivatives to the patient's conscious awareness. Such an appraisal is made for each specific kind of expression of the root conflict because several layers of derivatives, each of them stemming from this same conflict, may be discernible in the pattern of the patient's communications. Fenichel (1945) recommended that the therapist interpret what is preconscious or about to become so. Other authors speak of staying with "the current flow of material."

To illustrate staying with the current flow of material: A young woman who had yet to resolve her conflicts about activity and passivity, who clung to an unconscious fantasy that her body had been damaged—which had made her a girl—reported a dream at the start of a therapy session. In the dream, one man was chasing another. The man who was being chased had asked the other man for help; the second man had taken out a knife and had begun to chase the first one. The man who was being chased had paper strips around his neck, streaming out behind him; the man with the knife was trying to cut them off. If he succeeded in cutting them off, the first man would die. The therapist, of course, asked for associations to the various elements of the dream report. In arriving at an understanding of the dream the therapist made use not only of these associations but also of all that was known about the patient from other sessions and from other communications in the current session. One of the associations had to do with an examination that the patient would have to undergo soon to check for possible cervical or uterine cancer. If it turned out that she had a malignancy, she would have to have an operation—an event she greatly feared.

One may speculate that the dream derives in part from deeply repressed, unconscious conflicts. For instance, it may derive from the patient's assumption that she was born with a penis that later had been cut off, a mutilation of her body. One may also speculate that she wants, unconsciously, to be brutally attacked by a man. (Of course, she would also greatly fear such an attack.) But these conflicts, though possibly symbolized in the dream, are not what is most accessible to the patient's preconscious thinking.

If one asks, "Why is the therapist told about this dream *at this time?*" one can make a tentative formulation of what is dominant in the patient's preconscious thoughts. We notice that the man who attacks with the knife is described as a helper. We know that the patient has sought help from the therapist who is a man. The therapist tells us that the patient found it very difficult at times to cooperate with him in the therapeutic work. He reports, too, that she was dependently demanding on him, pressing him for assurance that he would help her, reproaching him for not talking more, and prodding him to give his opinion.

In this context the therapist concluded that the dream expressed a wish of the patient to have the therapist pursue her and press her, and a fear of the consequences of such an attack. At a deep level (we believe) she wishes and fears a brutal sexual attack; but at the point of the current flow of material, she wishes and fears to be guided, pushed, and coerced by the therapist. The therapist's interpretation, therefore, should be in these terms, should speak of the patient's wish to be guided and pushed and of her expectation that this would be both exciting and dangerous.

A second major consideration involved in decisions about timeliness of an interpretation, is how critical the interpretation is to the progress of the therapy. If the patient's associations hint at an important conflict but no strong feelings are currently invested in the present derivative of that conflict, the therapist can easily

decide to wait until the associations provide more convincing material for the interpretations. On the other hand, even when the patient offers only hints of the conflict,
if the feelings connected with the conflict are now intense, if these feelings infuse
the transference, and if their intensity will make it necessary for the patient to
disrupt the therapy unless there is some relief of the tensions, the therapist had
better make an interpretation.

That is to say, any threat to the continuation of the therapy requires an interpretation. The therapist labels what for the patient has been an unconsciously sensed
danger. That enables the patient to compare the fantasied danger with the real
risks. For example, the therapist shows how the patient is repeating a rebellion
against a coercive parent; as a result, the patient refrains from a rebellious departure
from the therapist. More abstractly: This is an example of a needed interpretation
of resistance that prevents a premature termination of therapy.

In judging the patient's readiness for an interpretation the therapist should
also take into account the patient's stage in therapy. At the beginning the patient
usually has little understanding of the principles of therapeutic work. Understanding of these principles grows partly as a result of the educative interventions that
the therapist makes as therapy proceeds. The attachment of the patient to the
therapist—the "transference," as it is usually called—also grows as the therapy
continues. Repeated evidences of the therapist's trustworthiness, interest in helping
the patient, and neutrality of judgment, continually strengthen this attachment.
When such an understanding of the therapeutic process and such an attachment to
the therapist have developed, the therapist can dare to make interpretations that
she or he would not risk making at the start of therapy.

Relatively late in the therapy, the therapist will be in a position to make
constructions, that is, comprehensive interpretations that explain whole patterns
of the patient's living. Before such constructions can be assimilated, the patient
must be thoroughly familiar with the task of psychological understanding, must be
trusting of the therapist's good intentions, and must have accepted many prior
interpretations upon which the construction builds.

It hardly needs to be said that an interpretation should be consistent with the
theme of the patient's unconscious, almost-preconscious, current preoccupations. It
should be at the growing edge of the patient's understanding of himself or herself.
On a day when the patient feels that other people are always doing something to
her or him (she or he is the victim of assaults) the interpretations should focus on
this theme. The therapist should urge the patient to consider how she or he *expects*
to be victimized. In a session when the patient is telling the therapist (and herself
or himself) metaphorically about feeling like a victim, the therapist is in a position
to underline this feeling, to bring it into sharp relief, to show how all-pervasive it
is. The therapist is *not* at that point able to demonstrate how the patient invites
attack and victimization, though some groundwork can be laid for making such an
interpretation in a later session.

Finally, assessment of the state of resistance to interpretation enables the
therapist to judge whether the patient is ready for an interpretation. For example,
if the therapist in questioning what it means that the patient, a 50-year-old man,
has a great aversion to "oral sex" (as he calls it; he means cunnilingus) with his
wife, is met by an angry assertion, "She doesn't keep herself clean, and I think

anyone would feel disgust at that!" the therapist may well judge that he has touched an issue that is too hot for the patient right now. His patient is surely far from able to accept the idea that his own wish for oral gratification is involved in his intense aversion.

Steps in the Interpretive Process

As our previous examples have suggested, we do not consider interpretation to be an isolated act of the therapist, a single speech in which the therapist connects formerly unconnected events or makes an unconscious feeling conscious. Interpretation is, instead, a process in which one may mark out several stages. Though, as with any process, the division into stages is somewhat artificial, one can mark off (a) a preparatory period during which the therapist refuses to join in the neurotic interaction that the patient is demanding; and (b) five stages of interpretive intervention by the therapist: confrontation, clarification, interpretation, construction, and working through.

Fenichel (1941, pp. 52–53) described this sequence in slightly different language. He wrote that, first, what is to be interpreted is *isolated* from the experiencing part of the ego. Second, patients' attention is drawn to their own *activity*: they themselves have been bringing about what they believed they were experiencing passively. Third, they learn that they have motives for this activity that previously they did not know about. Fourth, patients come to see that at some other point, they too harbor something similar or something that is associatively connected. Fifth, with the help of these observations they become able to produce less-distorted derivatives, and gradually by this means the origin of their symptomatic behavior becomes clear.

The preparatory period occurs as the therapist refuses to participate as a complementary actor in the neurotic interaction that the patient is striving to create. The patient attempts to elicit the therapist's response to provide gratification of the patient's resistance needs or transference wishes. The therapist's frustrating these attempts makes the resistance or the wish stand out against the neutral background, thereby bringing the resistance or the wish closer to consciousness.

Confrontation is the first step in presenting to the patient the more-than-preconscious. It is simply a calling of attention to an action or an utterance. For example, a young woman who in many ways was manifesting a resistance to revealing herself to the therapist, in particular a resistance to letting herself and the therapist see that she was experiencing intense sexual feelings toward the therapist, was sitting with her large purse placed on her lap, concealing her body from the therapist. As a beginning step in the interpretive process the therapist said, "Have you noticed how you are holding your purse on your lap in front of you? Perhaps this is expressing some feelings that you are having. What are they?"

The therapist's calling the symbolic action to the patient's attention is a confrontation. He followed up this confrontation by noting other ways, as well, in which the patient was finding it necessary to protect herself from the direct scrutiny of the therapist. Citing all of these instances of self-protection constituted a clarification. The explanation proffered by the therapist, "You're finding it necessary to protect yourself from scrutiny because you expect it would be terribly painful to have both of us know just how you feel and what you want," is an interpretation.

Clarification consists of a description of the basis on which the therapist perceives the operation of an unconscious process. If a therapist says, "What common theme do you see in what you've said?" and the patient answers, "I've been speaking of ways that I feel I've been hurt," we have the start of a clarification. When the therapist continues, "Your frozen hand, your mistreatment by a spouse, your inability to make acquaintances at your new apartment—they're all ways in which you feel you've been hurt. And I have the sense that you're reaching out to me to fix the hurt. For instance, you've practically asked me to advise you what to do for your frozen hand and to explain to you why your chest hurts when you cough." When the therapist says this, she or he is making a clarification. She or he is drawing together the pattern of evidence from which an interpretation of the patient's dependent wishes can be made.

Interpretation is an intervention that makes what was unconscious conscious. What is made conscious may be a feeling, a wish, a fear, an intention, or the connection between two thoughts. In short, interpretation is the labeling of a wish-defense complex in any of its aspects or layers.

Interpretation is so named because it gives meaning to events that previously had no meaning. An accurate interpretation is not arbitrary or a way of seeing events that happens to please the therapist; rather, it is a serious attempt to understand, deriving an explanation that fits the available evidence. Though an interpretation is offered seriously, it cannot be considered infallible. Therefore the therapist offers it to the patient for the patient's consideration in the spirit, "Here is how I understand what you've told me. Consider my understanding and make use of it as you see fit." The therapist should not attempt to impose this understanding of the patient on the patient; observations and responses should be offered as material that will aid in the collaborative task of achieving greater understanding of the patient's living. Nor should the therapist succumb to the temptation to argue for or to justify these interpretations.

We speak of interpretation as "labeling" because what is vital in distinguishing primary-process functioning (the mode of functioning of the mind when it is functioning unconsciously) from secondary-process functioning is the use of words to designate mental representations. Freud first called attention to this characteristic of secondary process in *The Interpretation of Dreams* (1900); he elaborated on it in his paper "The Unconscious" (1915c). Dollard and Miller (1950) provided a behavioristic rationale for the importance of verbalization in secondary-process functioning, then explained interpretation as the therapist's providing labels to the patient, labels for emotional conflicts.

A *construction* is a pattern of interpretations, extending over time and meetings, having to do with a segment of the infantile neurosis. It is, in other words, a coherent set of explanations about a realm of the patient's behavior. One interpretation builds on another in the development of a construction. Our definition parallels Freud's usage (Freud, 1937a) but gives less emphasis to the historical aspects of the system of explanation (i.e., to "genetic" interpretations). A classical example of construction is Freud's (1918) thorough explanation of the determination of the Wolf-Man's remarkable dream of the six or seven wolves sitting on the bare branches of a walnut tree. A construction attempts to answer the question in the therapist's mind, "What kind of prototypical experiences in the patient's psychic life could have led to the unconscious dynamic I have just interpreted?" By "unconscious dynamic" we mean the organization of compromise-formation, defense, anxiety, danger, and unconscious wish. Finally, we remark that during the therapist's presentation of a construction the patient frequently recollects formerly repressed experiences.

Working through is achieved by the interpretation of each aspect of a segment of the infantile neurosis. The patient comes to recognize the impact of the neurotic conflict in many areas of her or his life and in relationships with people. He or she becomes increasingly familiar with this unconscious conflict as a theme that has penetrated much of his or her behavior, becoming gradually less afraid of acknowledging the wishes and feelings connected with the conflict.

Techniques of Interpreting

How to Confront

In effect, when the therapist makes a confrontation he or she is seeking to grab the patient's attention. A confrontation is, ideally, an invitation to the patient to observe with him or her an interesting phenomenon that the patient has presented.

When the therapist makes a sophisticated reflection on the preconscious theme of a session, not necessarily following up with a clarification or an interpretation, we can appropriately speak of a confrontation. For example, when a patient throughout the session constantly pressed the therapist to explain things and to provide information and assurances that the therapy would be helpful, the therapist pointed out that the patient was clamoring for some kind of reassuring response. This was a confrontation. Another patient described how she relied on her 21-year-old son for companionship. The therapist remarked, "You have a very close relationship with him." Again, this was a confrontation. Often the patient's associations are a tangled knot. Confrontation invites the patient's attention to a manifest production of the patient that is a loose end—a thread that if pulled will unravel the tangle.

Sometimes an insistent confrontation presents the patient with a direct statement of the reality implications of overdetermined behavior. The therapist makes such an insistent confrontation when the patient's defenses against self-observation force the patient to not recognize the consequences of her or his behavior and to miss its overdetermined quality. For instance, a young male patient announced one day that he had decided to get married and had set the wedding date for a couple of months hence. In the rest of the session and in several subsequent sessions the patient presented one way after another in which he found his fiancee to be totally unsuited to be his wife. Yet he kept speaking of the coming marriage as an inevitable event. Finally the therapist commented on the discrepancy between the patient's misgivings about his fiancee and his unquestioning execution of the marriage plans. The patient immediately responded, "Maybe I shouldn't get married to her after all, when I have so many unexplained doubts about whether it's a good idea." The therapist's comment was a confrontation.

Another example: A young man was consistently 10 minutes late for every therapy session, for a dozen sessions. Gentle probing, "Does your lateness express some feeling about the therapy?" elicited no self-reflective activity. At length the therapist decided to insist that this repetitive pattern had a meaning. "After all," she told the patient, "You now know exactly how long it takes you to get here, and you know that we always end on time. You know that you are only hurting yourself by taking away the time available for therapy. Yet you are consistently 10 minutes late." The patient attempted to dismiss the matter as of no importance, saying, "I'm late for everything! I'm late for work too. Is it all that important that I'm on time for therapy?" The therapist insisted that the patient take his own behavior seriously. It turned out, when the patient considered the meaning of the tardiness, that the consistent lateness indeed had a meaning. It was intended to communicate to the therapist, "I'm in control; I don't have to submit to you."

Another patient, who had recently been divorced from his wife, missed a therapy hour when his son fell and hurt himself badly and the patient's ex-wife asked the patient to take the 4-year-old boy to the hospital emergency room. The boy was living with the ex-wife, and his care was, of course, primarily her responsibility. Yet the patient without question accepted responsibility for taking the child to the hospital, despite the impact of this on his work and his therapy.

In confronting the patient with the significance of his action the therapist pointed out that the patient now was no longer responsible for the boy, because the ex-wife had custody of the child. The accident was not so serious that the boy was in real danger, nor were there difficulties that the ex-wife could not cope with. Yet the patient behaved as though he were still married to his ex-wife and still had full responsibility for the boy's care. The therapist raised the question, Why?

In the face of the reluctance of the patient to consider the meaning of this behavior, the therapist forcefully insisted on his examining it. At length the therapist made the interpretation that the acting as though he was still married to his ex-wife expressed the wish that he were still married to her and that she loved him.

We warn the beginning therapist that the patient will experience any confrontation that is not followed up by clarification or interpretation as a criticism. For instance, if the therapist of the example just given had only pointed out that it seemed inappropriate for the patient to take his son to the hospital, without offering an interpretation of the patient's motives for doing so, his confrontation would have been simply a criticism. [We recognize that there are realistic and appropriate elements in the patient's wish to care for his son; we are not considering at this point the balancing of these concerns with the patient's realistic need to work at his job and to attend the therapy session.] As another example: A therapist pointed out to a patient that the patient did not consider the therapist's comments thoughtfully, instead tended to brush them aside. The therapist offered no interpretation of why the patient found it necessary to do this. Taking the therapist's comments as a criticism, the patient could only answer, "I'm sorry. I'll try to do better."

How to Clarify

How does one clarify—that is, delineate the topography of the experience that the patient is reporting in the therapy? One's goal as one makes a clarification is to present the material of the patient's associations to her or him with the defensive elements modified so as to create a new gestalt. Whereas interpretation involves making an unconscious mental event conscious, clarification involves the bringing together of preconscious mental events into a new pattern.

During one therapy session a businessman complained that his employees lacked the dedication to getting their work done that he wished they had. They all left at 4:30 rather than staying until the work was finished. He then complained that his son, who had agreed to cut the lawn, had not done so but still expected to have the use of one of the family cars. The patient also felt that his wife was unreasonable in not having made dinner reservations at a restaurant for some entertainment that he and his wife were doing on the weekend. Instead, she had asked the patient to make the reservations. The patient then fell silent for several minutes. He broke the silence by saying that he would be able to catch up on his work on Monday (the Memorial Day holiday) because he would have the office to himself and would be without interruptions from the telephone.

At this point the therapist intervened with a clarification—an intervention that drew together the threads of a common theme that ran through much of the material that the patient had presented. The therapist pointed out that the patient seemed to be speaking in various ways of people who let him down by not doing for him what he hoped they would do: his employees, his son, his wife, even the therapist (for the therapist was not meeting with the patient on Memorial Day, even though Monday was the day of a regular therapy appointment and the patient had hinted that *he*, at least, would be willing to meet that day). And, the therapist continued, the patient felt a sense of outrage that all of these people were failing to meet his needs; indeed, he felt exploited by them.

This observation by the therapist is counted as a clarification, an intervention that draws attention to the common theme of a series of communications. It cannot be considered an interpretation because no explanation is offered, no hidden motive is adduced, and no purpose served by the behavior is proposed. The clarification, therefore, stays with the preconscious; it does not probe unconscious dynamics.

A clarification may sometimes make use of information known to the patient but not presented by the patient as material in the current session. For example, a young woman in the twenty-sixth hour of her therapy, during a phase when she was preoccupied with her passive, feminine strivings, started the session saying that the therapeutic situation made her uncomfortable. She felt uncomfortable, somehow, sitting in the chair; she would be more at ease sitting on the couch. At that point the patient got up from the chair and moved to the couch, where she sat, leaning back against the wall beside the couch (sitting approximately parallel to the therapist and about 4 feet away). She continued to speak of what made her uncomfortable about the therapy. It was, she said, that the therapist's office was so impersonal; it was a professional office.

The therapist pointed out that in fact this office, to which the patient had just started to come after several months during which she had met with the therapist at a mental health clinic, expressed the therapist's individuality more fully than the office at the clinic had. The pictures on the walls had been personally chosen and reflected the therapist's individuality; there had been no pictures on the walls of the clinic office. The furniture in the private office had been chosen by the therapist and expressed personal tastes; the furniture at the clinic had been chosen by someone else, on behalf of the clinic. The therapist reminded the patient, further, that she had complained about the clinic office because it was far from soundproof (one could hear conversations from the adjoining room) which made it less possible for her to feel free to be as expressive as she at times wanted to be. The new meeting place *was* private and so invited her to be more expressive but also frightened her because it allowed her to be more expressive.

The therapist's citing of all of these considerations might be called clarification. The patient was shown how all of these elements in the situation in fact were stirring up in her the temptation to be more expressive to the therapist, to attempt to become more personally involved. After making these points the therapist added, "Maybe you need to believe that this situation is more impersonal because you're fighting to keep in check your wishes for a deeper involvement with me." Such a comment is, of course, an interpretation.

In making clarifications the therapist needs to exercise therapeutic tact. By "tact" we mean the choice of the correct time to make a clarification or an interpretation and the choice of the correct aspect of the conflict to bring to the patient's attention. The current presentation by the patient is at some point along a continuum of displacement, it is at some distance from the original instinctual conflict. That original conflict is still active in the patient, but it is manifested in *derivatives* rather than in its original form. A clarification is intended to move the patient's articulation of the conflict back one displacement-step nearer the original, instinctual conflict.

The therapist generally makes a clarification by calling the patient's attention to certain associations as specific instances of a theme, or as variations of or elaborations on a theme. The theme is a preconscious representation of some original, instinctual conflict.

Those associations that are most closely connected to the early childhood conflict deal with images and with representations and memories of concrete events, rather than with concepts, explanations, and conclusions. We believe, therefore, that the most helpful verbalizations of the patient are concrete rather than abstract. The therapist's interventions accordingly should be directed toward encouraging such concrete associations.

How to Interpret

As we see it, interpretation ought to be expressive of the experience of the therapist in the treatment. Interpretations should be personalized, not artificial, stilted, or mechanical. Effective interpretations are made out of personal conviction rather than from a theoretical conception that the therapist holds to because someone stated that it is so or because it has been published. The interpretations are a natural outgrowth of the therapist's observations and understandings.

What is interpreted is a *mental symptom* (that is, a part of the stream of associations) in its defensive and its wish-expressive aspects. The mental symptom, like any symptom, is always a compromise. Wish leads to anxiety, which in turn leads to defense. The symptom is a product of this total process, necessarily giving expression to both the defensive and the wish-expressive forces.

In making interpretations the therapist does best to deal first with the defensive side of the conflict. The reason for this rule is straightforward: The patient will be unable to think about the wish-impulse component until the strength of defensive forces has been somewhat reduced. The patient anticipates a dangerous situation to arise from acting on a wish, even from thinking about it. This anticipation of danger makes it necessary for the patient, as a self-protection, to avoid stirring up within himself or herself the cues associated with the wish. The therapist's first order of business, then, is to call the patient's attention to the avoidance of communication, raising the question whether the patient's self-protective avoidance is really needed. While granting that the avoidance has served the patient well (it has protected him or her against anxiety), the therapist expresses doubt that allowing the impulse-related material to come to mind will have such dire consequences as the patient supposes. Encouraged by such a prompting, the patient may then risk communicating some of the impulse-related material.

What should be interpreted? In general, the therapist should interpret (a) the transference as resistance, (b) the transference as current wish, and (c) the transference as a repetition of an infantile object relationship. The order in which we listed the content of interpretations is also the priority that should be given to these contents. Resistance must always be interpreted before anything else is dealt with; if it is not interpreted, nothing else can be achieved. If there is no appreciable resistance then the therapist becomes able to deal with what the patient is currently striving for. The therapist's interventions sharpen the patient's awareness of this striving, enable the patient to experience longings more intensely, and naturally lead to the question: Where do these intense longings come from?

The interpretation of the origin of these longings can only be done with profit when the longings have been experienced very intensely and with great specificity, because otherwise any discussion of the patient's wishes would have an abstract and lifeless quality. Thus genetic interpretations, in which the therapist demonstrates that current object relationships (including the object relationship with the therapist) are new editions of early childhood object relationships, must await the full development of the patient's experiencing of the current wishes.

Feelings toward the therapist, which can be directly experienced in the therapy session, are the feelings that can be talked about with most profit. Because these feelings are immediately present, they can be labelled with precision. The anxiety evoked by them is currently active; it can be extinguished when the patient observes that no dire consequences ensue upon his or her experiencing the feelings and holding them in conscious awareness.

We offer an example taken from a therapy session of the intertwining of the three aspects of transference. The patient is a young woman who has been involved in therapy, meeting with the therapist twice a week, for more than 3 years. She is married and has one child, a daughter about 9 years old. She works as a professional in a field that is allied with psychology.

On this particular evening the patient began the session by saying she had been thinking, as she sat in the waiting room, about the institution for which she works and about the therapist. She quickly dropped that line of thought except to say that the interpretation made by the therapist in the previous session, to the effect that the patient was unconsciously taking a derogatory attitude toward herself, was certainly true.

There was some apparently aimless, and rather abstract, conversation about how the patient derogates herself, all of this presented in psychological jargon. Then, without transition, the patient recalled that she had been taken into her father's confidence about his business affairs. Her father had employed her in his business during the summers between her high school years. Although the work she did was clerical, she believes that she was far better informed about the business than her mother was. In other ways, too, she seemed to be closer to her father than her mother was; she used to cut her father's hair, and while she was doing it they talked about many very personal things.

She then recounted how she had taken her daughter on a Girl Scout camping weekend, speaking of her slight concern when she learned that everybody would be sleeping in cabins that would not be locked up at night. She felt uneasy that all the girls and women would be unprotected; yet the doors had to be kept unlocked so that any of the girls who had to go to the toilet during the night could go out to the wash house (in a separate building) and return to the sleeping cabin without bothering anyone else.

Without providing further material from the session, let us simply illustrate the three aspects of transference. First, we note the patient's holding her feelings at arm's length during the earliest minutes of the session. While she is talking in this abstract way, avoiding any conscious experiencing of feeling, she is at the same time involved in an identification with the therapist. Indeed, we believe that she is using this identification with him as a professional person as a defense (i.e., in the service of resistance). If she put her experience into words, she would say here, "I'm a psychologist just as you are."

The patient's associations then turned to the relationship that she had had with her father during her adolescence. She had identified with *him*, too; *she* was a good businessperson, while her mother couldn't understand business matters. But at this point a further theme emerges: the patient pictures herself as being favored by her father, as being preferred by him to her mother. In our opinion the patient is presenting here the *wish* that she could triumph over her mother in the competition for the father's love. The identification with the therapist is, we believe, a *repetition* of the earlier object relationship of the patient with her father. Not that the patient necessarily was, in fact, favored by her father over her mother; she wanted to be so favored, and she wants now to believe that she was favored, and she is reexperiencing all of this toward the therapist.

Finally, we notice the intrusion of this conflict—this wish to win out over mother and to have father for her own, and the fears that the patient experiences as she allows herself to begin to become aware of this wish—into the patient's current life. Her fear that a man would break into the cabin at Girl Scout camp and attack her sexually exemplifies the intrusion of an early-childhood conflict into a patient's current living. Unconsciously, she wants to be taken sexually. Specifically she wants the therapist to take her; yet she also fears this. The receptiveness and passivity that are so fascinating to her also seem terribly dangerous.

We recommend that interpretations be made in the sequence: resistance interpretation, current transference interpretation, genetic (historical origins) interpretation. In the session that we have just discussed, a resistance interpretation might be along these lines: "You find it necessary to emphasize how skilled you are in understanding your living, and how much allied with me in professional work you are, in order to keep from experiencing your feelings in a very direct way. You are afraid that if you communicate these feelings to me, you'll be overwhelmed or I'll reject you for having such thoughts."

An interpretation of current wish would be along the line, "Your fantasy that a man might break into the cabin and attack you sexually is connected with the feelings that you've been experiencing during the session. You've talked about how close you were to your father, sharing his interests in the business; and you've emphasized how you share my skills in psychological analysis. This points to a wish to win my love, to be my favorite, and probably to be loved sexually, too."

A genetic interpretation would be premature in this session. It would be timely only after the patient was familiar with the current feelings, only after she knew in many ramifications the feelings she was experiencing toward the therapist. At that point the therapist could say, "You want me to prefer you to my wife; you want to share my professional life; you imagine that I'm already doing so and that you must defend yourself against my attacking you sexually. At the same time, you know that I've given you no grounds for expecting all these things. So the expectation must come from your previous experience, from fantasies and events in your earlier life, from the relationships with your mother and father."

A good interpretation combines both cognitive and affective elements. Without the cognitive aspect, there would at best be a catharsis having no lasting effect. But without the affective element, the interpretation would be an empty shell. There are two sources of this affect: (a) the unconscious affect that the *patient* is experiencing, which she or he comes to experience consciously, and (b) the affective experience of the *therapist*, as he or she lives through the therapeutic process with the patient. It can be appreciated, therefore, that an effective interpretation cannot be an intellectual game; it must be the stuff of real life.

To show how the cognitive and the emotional aspects are combined, we offer an example from the therapy of a 43-year-old man, who had been married and divorced four times. This man had great difficulty trusting any woman, yet felt a great need for a loving relationship with a woman. During the therapy it became clear that as he developed greater closeness with a woman—for instance, with his current woman friend—he became frightened and irrationally suspicious of her. He even had fantasies that this friend was "bisexual," that because of this she wanted him to become bisexual.

The therapist recalled many previous discussions in the therapy in which this man had recalled his mother's intrusive, dominating, emasculating actions toward him (or what, in his fantasies about his relationship with his mother, he believed to be such actions). The therapist recognized his patient's loneliness and longing for affection, and had some feeling for it. The therapist reasoned that the patient would not be so frightened of closeness with a woman and have such strong anticipations of being attacked by a woman, if it were not for an intense longing for attachment; a longing that probably was largely frustrated during his early childhood, even though his mother at times may have been kind and giving.

The therapist said, "When you were a boy, you very much wanted your mother's love, and yet sometimes when you turned to her for love, she so overpowered you, and (it seemed to you) so attacked your masculinity that you became very frightened. That's why you're now so suspicious of women." The patient responded, "I feel like crying. That must mean you've hit a sore spot."

A merely intellectual discussion of the dynamics of the patient's suspiciousness would not, we believe, produce any therapeutic effect. We believe that an intellectual understanding of the dynamics coupled with a real feeling for this man's experience, as a boy, of longing for his mother's love can be therapeutically effective.

How to Work Through

Working through is not an interpretation. It is, rather, a process that results from a series of interpretations made over a period of time that focus on a particular area of the infantile neurosis. These several interpretations are related to each other as elaborations, extensions, clarifying comments, and complementations. They are all elements of a network of ideas that provide a detailed understanding of the dynamic area.

One technique promoting the working through is to follow up a specific interpretation of the material of a session with a comment that shows the relationship of that interpretation to the sessions and the interpretations that have preceded. We suggest that the therapist continue to deal with all of the many facets of a particular area of the patient's life until a new area opens up in the material that the patient is presenting.

Responses to Interpretations

The first response of a patient to an interpretation may be a commentary on or evaluation of the interpretation. For example, the patient may say, "You're absolutely right. How brilliant you are!" or "That's absolutely wrong; I couldn't think anything like that!" or "That doesn't make a bit of sense." Whatever reactions the patient makes to the interpretations, the therapist should resist the temptation to hear these reactions as anything other than thoughts that came to mind (i.e., as associations). After all, if the patient cannot consciously know her or his unconscious, she or he is in no position to comment validly on the merit or lack of merit of an interpretation. Such comments therefore have to be understood as associations to the interpretation, and when they are understood this way the comments prove to be valuable additions to the formulation being offered. They may even be confirmations of the interpretation.

Consider the following interchange:

> *Therapist*: So we can see that you have been telling us that you respond angrily in situations where you are frightened of your affectionate feelings, in order to protect yourself by denying that you have affectionate feelings.
> *Patient*:   That's bullshit!
> *Therapist*: Precisely!

Intervening via the Working Alliance

Finally, we draw the reader's attention to a valuable technical guideline: "Intervene via the working alliance." We can best show what we mean by this through an example. A very capable professional man, during a session that fell on February 16, told of his work experiences during the preceding week, all of which were reasonably successful and some of them brilliantly successful when viewed objectively, but all tinged with a feeling of defeat and dissatisfaction as he recounted the week's events. Then he told of coming home from a business trip on the evening of February 14, finding his wife sick with flu and depressed because it was the anniversary of her mother's death; she was in general mentally groggy. The patient had felt quite disturbed at finding his wife so down.

Now the therapist could have intervened by pointing out that the work successes of the week hardly justified the patient's gloomy mood. The therapist might have continued, "Isn't it true that your gloomy mood stems from another source—from the bleak reception you felt you got from your wife on Friday night?" An interpretation along these lines would probably be accurate. It would, however, put the therapist in the position of an outside observer who receives the patient's reports, finds a contradiction, and points out the contradiction, the lapse of logic.

Better that the therapist should say, "You know, your feeling about the week is very gloomy, and yet you recognize, I think, that it wasn't all that unsuccessful a week. The picture I get from what you've been telling us is of a pretty successful week; in fact, of one that was brilliant at points. *You* know that, and yet gloom is the predominant mood. Shouldn't we assume there's some other aspect of the week that you experience as a failure, perhaps the encounter with your wife on Friday night?"

Notice that the suggested interpretation does not disqualify what the patient actually experienced (gloom). It does not suggest that he has no right to be downhearted. Furthermore, this interpretation poses the problem as an internal problem of the patient: *He* knows that he's been successful, yet *he* experiences depression, and *he* knows that this is a contradiction. (Rather than: "You dumb son of a bitch, don't you see that you've contradicted yourself.") The patient and the therapist are viewed as allies in discovering how the patient functions mentally, in working toward discovering the cause of the depression. The therapist has in mind, of course, that February 14 was Valentine's Day and has speculated that the inability of this man and his wife to express love to each other may have been especially obvious on this holiday, probably contributing to the patient's depression. Such a surmise may be brilliant. But, as Freud said, it is not the therapist's job to show how smart she or he is, but to help the patient. The therapist helps a patient best by intervening via the working alliance.

Chapter 12

Support and Relationship in Psychoanalytic Therapy

People who have heard or read about psychoanalytic therapy but don't know it firsthand, often get the impression that therapists are passive, uninvolved technicians; that they stand back, watch their patients squirm, plead, weep while being untouched by it all. Although there may be therapists who call themselves psychoanalysts who are stiff and distant, as the stereotype stamps them, we have observed that the psychoanalysts whom we respect are not at all like that. The therapists we respect enter into the therapy as human beings.

In our opinion there is no therapy that does not require the therapist to enter into it as a human being rather than simply as a fantasy object. The purpose of this chapter is to set forth the principles that the therapist should abide by in order to participate humanly in the therapy. The reader should know by now that we do not believe that the therapist can do whatever feels right, without reflecting on the reasons for certain behaviors, and still have a constructive impact on the patient. Our discussion of countertransference in chapter 6 points out the dangers of that course.

To state our view about support and relationship succinctly: The therapist's involvement in the therapy as a human being is both a necessity of the therapy and a danger for the therapy.

The Necessity of Involvement

R. Sterba (personal communication, 1962) has offered a striking analogy to explain why a distant and uninvolved therapist can't touch the life of a patient: Electric current cannot easily pass through distilled water. There must be impurities— minute impurities, but impurities—if the current is to flow. Another physical analogy comes to mind: A chip of silicon or germanium can't function as a transistor unless there are very slight impurities in it. Thus unless the therapist does more than behave purely as an analyst, as one who seeks an intellectual understanding of the patient's life and makes interpretations, no therapy will take place.

Nor can the therapist be completely heedless of the social amenities and of social reality, or totally inhuman. As we pointed out in the chapter on structure of the therapy (chapter 5), no patient could tolerate confiding in a therapist who was such a monster.

Furthermore, the protection of the patient requires of the therapist an alertness to the patient's interests when there is a real danger that the patient will in some way harm himself or herself, physically or interpersonally. In these circumstances the analytic therapist, believing deeply in the patient's autonomy, intervenes in such a way as to preserve the patient's autonomy. If the patient is thinking seriously about suicide, the therapist attempts to expose the motivations that lie behind these fantasies (desires for revenge, anger at others' neglect, fantasies of reunion with a dead parent, and the like) so that the patient will be in a position to consider, consciously, whether committing suicide would in fact get him or her what he or she wants.

In the extreme, a patient may through anxiety and troubled behavior communicate to the therapist that she or he wants to be put into a mental hospital so that controls against impulsive actions can be supported by the milieu in which she or he is living. If the therapist becomes aware of this message, it would be appropriate to assist in getting the patient hospitalized. We believe that a therapist will rarely encounter this situation if (a) the therapist genuinely believes that one can, in therapy, think anything one pleases, so long as one does not act on impulses that one judges to be destructive, (b) the therapist conveys this conviction to the patient, and (c) there is sufficient opportunity—as by frequent therapy sessions—for the patient to talk with the therapist about the fantasies that disturb her or him so much. Karon and VandenBos's (1981) discussion of when to hospitalize patients suffering from schizophrenia presents the issues that we think ought to be considered.

The Risks of Involvement

As we said, the therapist's personal involvement with the patient constitutes a disturbance of the therapy. As we understand the therapeutic process, one should expect the patient to constantly try to bring about the therapist's direct involvement in his or her life. With some patients and at some times this happens subtly; with other patients and at other times, it is more direct. Every transference response is, in effect, a demand upon the therapist: "Be involved with me so as to gratify my need."

Accordingly, as the therapist decides how to respond to the patient a judgment about whether and when and how to intervene should be made. Unless the decision is made consciously, it is very likely that in responding the therapist will fit into the transference demands. If the therapist does this, the patient learns nothing that he or she does not already know too well.

How Does One Intervene?

When the patient expresses conflicts in action, by acting out a transference or by living out an inner conflict, it must mean that anxiety has grown beyond manageable limits. When this happens, the therapist should intervene.

The first principle of intervening is: Do it with as little element of suggestion (i.e., the use of authority) as possible. For example, a young man may propose that the solution to his life problems is a divorce from his wife; another man may suppose that his life will be fulfilled by his buying a house and getting married; a young woman argues that quitting her job and taking another one in a distant part of the country will rescue her from loneliness. If we assume that these are decisions for the patients to make, not for the therapist to advise for or against, then the question becomes: How can the therapist aid the patient to probe more deeply into the sources of the fantasy—the fantasy that taking the proposed action will be a solution to the patient's life problems? The therapist can, first of all, formulate the unconscious dynamics associated with the imminent action, presenting that formulation to the patient. Then on the grounds that the action is linked to unconscious dynamics, the therapist can suggest a restraint of action until the patient understands, somewhat more fully, what has provoked the plan of action. Not that the therapist would take it upon herself or himself to forbid the action; rather, she or he would say, "This is an important decision in your life, which will have long-lasting consequences. Don't you think you should try to understand your thoughts and feelings about it as fully as you can, before you act on this plan?"

Beyond this, the therapist can (if he or she and the patient agree that it is appropriate) try to present what is presumably a more objective view of the matter, based on the information that the patient has provided. For example, the therapist might say, "As I understand it, the advantages of your taking a job in Colorado are that high-technology industries are better developed there than in Michigan, that you would be closer to winter recreation areas that appeal to you, and that your prospective employer seems to have more opportunities for advancement than your employer here offers. The disadvantages are that you would have to sell your house— which you haven't been able to do yet—that you wouldn't make very much more money but would have considerably higher living expenses, and that you'd leave some friends you've made here over the years. It isn't quite clear why you're so eager to go." By the last statement, the therapist points to the unacknowledged, unconscious elements in the decision to move to Colorado.

The therapist may provide information if he or she thinks he or she knows something that the patient doesn't. By and large the therapist avoids doing this, because the therapist assumes that the patient should be allowed to run his or her own life and to obtain the needed information. For example, it would probably be a mistake for the therapist to recommend to a patient her or his own dentist (a superb professional and technician, who is very concerned about the welfare of patients) or own dermatologist. On the other hand, it might be appropriate for the therapist to make sure the patient understands that the effects of Valium® and of alcohol are very much alike, with the result that it can be dangerous to take both at the same time. How does this differ from providing information about a good dentist and a good dermatologist? The therapist is in fact an expert about behavioral science, and within the role as therapist has acted as provider of information on the effects of Valium and alcohol to the patient; the therapist has made no such contract with respect to providing information about the ordinary tasks of life.

The Therapist May Make a Direct Prohibition of Action

Psychoanalysts commonly tell their patients at the beginning of an analysis, "You must agree to try, for the duration of the treatment, not to make any basic changes in your life until the actual and immediate necessity for the change and its unconscious meanings have been thoroughly explored. This applies to such matters as changing houses, jobs, occupations, schools, or marital status." As Kubie (1950) explained, there are two reasons for this limitation on a patient's freedom during an analysis. One is to protect the patient's own interests, the other is to make sure that the conflicts are expressed in thought rather than in action. As Kubie said, many human beings find it less disturbing to act than to think. The therapist does what is possible to encourage thinking rather than acting. The therapist may point out how a particular action may prove damaging to the therapy; for example, how drinking four to six beers immediately before each therapy session can make it impossible for the patient to address hidden fears such as desperate loneliness and the fear of death.

The therapist does make a direct prohibition when the patient violates the agreed-on structure of the therapy. For example, when the patient picks up the ash tray on the table beside his or her chair and threatens to throw it at the therapist, the therapist warns, "You may be angry at me, but you're not permitted to act on those feelings; you must *tell* me how you feel."

Reassurance and Support

When to use reassurance? Briefly, whenever affect threatens to become unmanageable. The principle is: Keep affect at a manageable level.

Examples of Reassurance

The most effective reassurance is achieved through dealing appropriately with the dynamics of the patient's behavior, sometimes by making interpretations. The following interpretive and quasi-interpretive actions are examples of effective intervention.

Example 1: Discriminating Between Thinking and Acting

To a 45-year-old woman whose fate in life throughout the past 25 years had been to bring up eight children, mostly by herself—her husband was alcoholic, and after years in a miserable marriage she had divorced him—her intense longings to be taken care of, to have someone else do for her what she'd been compelled to do for others for so long, constituted a dangerous temptation. She feared the intensity of these longings, thinking she would be so overwhelmed by them that she would dissolve into a helpless inertness. Her therapist was able to reassure her, "You can allow yourself to know you'd like to be taken care of, and to think about it, without becoming completely inactive, without collapsing into helplessness."

A 26-year-old man had grown up in poverty after his father, who had been a foreman working for a large industrial company, died of a heart condition when the patient was about 6 years old. The patient felt strong anger at his father for abandoning him in this way and at his mother for providing for his needs so inadequately. When the therapist pointed out that the patient's hostile wishes towards his mother could in no way damage her so long as he did not act on them, and that his becoming more fully aware of these feelings would be helpful to his therapy, the patient was greatly relieved.

Example 2: Discrimination Between Past and Present

A therapist pointed out to a 40-year-old, twice-divorced man: "When you were a kid, you were the second boy, neglected in your family while most of the attention went to your older brother. You resented that but felt helpless to do anything about it. Now, when you feel neglected and feel you're not getting enough attention, there *is* something you can do about it. You're not helpless now as you were then." Such a discrimination, by making the patient aware of his present-day resources, can counter the patient's feelings of helplessness and despair.

Example 3: Making Clear the Patient's Resources

A young woman who very much wanted to have a child but believed that her husband didn't want one and feared that if she expressed her wish to have a child he would abandon her, needed to be reminded of her own strengths and to be encouraged to ask for what she wanted for her own satisfaction. The therapist pointed out to her that if she insisted on having a child and her husband refused, she could divorce this husband and marry a man whose values matched hers. She could support herself if she had to separate from her husband; she could also find a new husband if she so desired. The therapist also compared the patient's previous situation, when she was living with her husband before they had got married, had become pregnant, and had—under pressure from him—had an abortion she didn't really want, with her current situation in which she is married and in a much better position to take care of a child if she has one. The therapist pointed out that at the previous time she received no support from her family in her wish to have the baby and active opposition from her live-in boyfriend and his friends; but now her family would support her desire to have a child, and her husband might be more inclined to accept it than he had been under the previous conditions. This intervention is, of course, a discrimination between past and present. (See Dollard and Miller, 1950, pp. 305–320.)

When the therapist says, "Yes, that's what *you're* frightened of," it is implied that the patient's fear is excessive and that the patient's resources are greater than the patient has realized. When the therapist says, "Your fear is worse than the material that's coming out," again the therapist is implying that the patient's resources are greater than the patient has supposed they are.

Example 4: The Value of Verbalization

Patients usually expect that their impulses will be terribly destructive, and it comes as a surprise to them to learn that allowing impulses to come into awareness will increase rather than diminish their control over these impulses. (See Dollard and Miller, 1950, pp. 321–328.)

Example 5: Making Clear the Origin and Function of Behavior

To make clear to patients the origin and function of their behavior increases their control over the behavior, thereby reducing markedly their concern about possible destructive and socially disruptive effects. For example, a male patient asks, "Am I a homosexual?"[1]

The therapist responded, "There was a time when you felt that the only way to be loved by a man was to be a woman." In this interpretation, the therapist reminded the patient of the patient's earlier longing for love from a man (from his father, in this example) and exposed to the patient his assumption that he would have to take a woman's role—understood by the patient to be a submissive role—toward the man in order to receive the longed-for love. When this assumption was put into words, the patient could appreciate that friendship with a man doesn't always require submission of a weak person to a stronger one. He also came to understand that the desire to play a submissive role grew out of his earlier, desperate search for love. His current, less desperate need for love eliciting a tendency to submit could now be understood in terms of the origin of the behavior. Because the patient now knows that he *can* now get love without demeaning himself, the understanding of the origin of his wish to be submissive serves to reassure him that he need not act submissively.

Aspects of the Therapy That Reassure the Patient

Some aspects of the very structure of the therapy have a reassuring effect. First, *the therapist's lack of fear is reassuring.* The therapist is not afraid to talk about impulses: anger, sexual passion, and longings to be cared for by another. The therapist talks about these impulses with genuine feeling but with a calm confidence that impulses can be channeled to effective expression or reliable renunciation. The therapist deals directly with the material, calling a spade a spade. To a considerable degree the patient identifies with the therapist's attitude toward the impulses, taking courage from the therapist's confident approach.

Second, *the patient feels relief when discovering that the therapist doesn't challenge his or her report or greet it with disbelief.* In short, the therapist doesn't tell the patient whether she or he is observing life accurately.

When the patient uses psychotic mechanisms to deal with conflicts, the therapist's interventions sometimes challenge the patient's understanding of the external world—if the therapist is doing therapy in the spirit of the approach recommended by Karon and VandenBos (1981). But even with the patient suffering from psychosis,

---

[1]We want to make clear to the reader that this patient is in fact—according to his reports to the therapist—a practicing heterosexual. We also point out that we believe that the therapist's intervention, which we are about to describe, was appropriate for *this patient* because of the facts of this patient's life and behavior. We are not trying to state a theory of why people in general might be afraid that they are homosexual, let alone state a theory of the origins of homosexuality.

Furthermore, we explicitly disclaim believing that every homosexual relationship involves domination and submission; that generalization is no more true than the belief that every heterosexual relationship must involve domination and submission. Our point is that *this* patient held such an erroneous belief, and that the interpretation exposed it.

one gives full respect to the patient's autonomy of judgment. As Karon and VandenBos (1981) point out, "When a patient reports something that sounds frightening and unrealistic, this does not necessarily mean it is a delusion. The therapist always addresses what the evidence is, and what the data are" (p. 185).

If the therapist violates the principle we are advocating, the patient is bound to feel that the therapist doesn't understand him or her. The patient's distorted appraisal of the external world is, after all, made necessary by the experience of intense needs and by the anticipation that dangerous things will happen to her or him. These experiences and anticipations are real enough, even though the projections on the external world are not. For the therapist to say, "This isn't real," has to be experienced by the patient as a disqualification of what has been experienced.

Taking the experience seriously as experience, focusing on it as a communication about psychological events, ignoring as much as one can whether it corresponds to something that really happened; this approach has much to recommend it. The therapist taking this approach can demonstrate time and again that she or he is committed to understanding the patient's experience, and can show how valuable it is to the patient to deepen her or his understanding of this experience.

Third, *the continuity of the therapy is reassuring*. The regularity of the therapy sessions contributes to an atmosphere of reassurance; the patient knows that within a few days he or she will meet again with the therapist. Anticipation that there will soon be another session is reassuring because the patient has experienced relief of anxiety during previous sessions. Besides the specific therapeutic interventions that reduced his or her anxiety, there was the reward of the therapist's attention and of the opportunity to have someone to talk to—someone who would listen attentively, without becoming distracted. Langs (1973, p. 252) speaks of a therapeutic *hold*, that is, a framework of consistent caring for the patient in which the patient is free to develop psychologically. Langs took over this term from Winnicott, who in 1960 described a phase of *holding* as the first of three stages in the mother–infant relationship.

How important the therapist's attentiveness is to the patient is demonstrated whenever the therapist shows that she or he remembers what the patient said in some previous session. In our experience, the patient is always surprised—and pleased—that the therapist has remembered.

There are other ways, as well, for the therapist to demonstrate that he or she is attentive and in touch with what the patient is trying to communicate. The therapist can find something in the session to comment on, mainly for the purpose of showing that the patient's discourse is being paid attention to. R. Sterba has recommended that the therapist do this in every initial interview, to demonstrate at the very beginning that he does understand the patient.

Fourth, *the patient finds it reassuring to discover that the therapist cannot be conned or taken in*. For example, when a woman who was beginning to face anxiety-provoking material in her therapy proposed to cut back from four sessions a week to two, for reasons that didn't make any sense, the therapist refused to agree with her specious reasoning.

Coming into a therapy session with a ready-made interpretation is frequently an attempt to con the therapist, to get him or her off the scent of the patient's deeper problems. A woman who was struggling with her intense need to be taken care of, to allow herself to gratify her dependent wishes, came in one day and said to the therapist, "Yes, it's really true, as you pointed out last time, that I want to compete with Bill (her husband) at work by outshining him, but am afraid to do so." She proceeded to adduce other evidence that she was avoiding competition and thereby depriving herself of success. The therapist was genuinely puzzled at the interpretation ascribed to him (he couldn't remember having said that); and he found it hard to make sense, emotionally, that fear of competition with men was an overriding, current issue for this patient. He kept in mind the patient's fear of passivity— so clear in the previous session—and seized every opportunity to confront the patient with how she had a need to avoid coming to grips with this fear. In short, he refused to be conned. In general, the patient also finds it reassuring when she or he cannot elicit inappropriate activity from the therapist.

Fifth, *when the patient is upset, but the therapist isn't (and shouldn't be), it is reassuring.* For instance, the patient reports a dream in which he kills his mother. He is terribly upset that he has had such a monstrous fantasy. The therapist takes it all very calmly, knowing (from what she learned about the patient in the previous session) that this is not a person who acts impulsively on his fantasies. The therapist's calm helped the patient to calm down.

Sixth and finally, *the therapist's accurate reflection of feeling makes the patient feel understood.* Knowing that the therapist understands is reassuring. When the therapist summarizes, Rogerian-style, what the patient has been saying, the patient knows that she or he has been alert to the emotional aspects of the communication. "It's very frustrating to you, isn't it, when your wife doesn't get any pleasure from sexual intercourse. You feel, 'I can't be much of a man if she never has an orgasm,' and it makes you angry." Such a reflection of feeling indicates not only understanding but also acceptance. In this example the therapist is implying that anyone would be expected to feel frustrated, to feel a loss of self-esteem, and to feel anger, and that these emotions are acceptable.

How to Reassure

In intervening to reassure the patient, the therapist should—we believe—follow a strategy derived from an understanding of the transference. If the therapist rather than approaching the task from such a reasoned set of principles simply responds as her or his feelings dictate, she or he will necessarily respond on the basis of countertransference. When this happens, some responses will be inappropriate. Countertransference feelings are not to be viewed as horrible. Acting upon these feelings unreflectively and destructively *is* horrible.

If the therapist keeps in mind that reassurances have to be understood in the context of the transference, he or she will understand that encouragement to the patient to talk about the patient's wishes and to think more freely about them, will sometimes be experienced as an invitation to act on them. We describe this state of affairs as a *seduction.*

As an illustration of these points we present to the reader a young woman, divorced and the mother of two children, who was struggling to disengage herself from an unhappy love affair. The therapist sensed that the patient was bearing a great deal of sexual frustration, and he felt inclined to urge her to bring these sexual tensions into the open by talking about them freely. He realized, however, that if he prodded the patient to talk about sex at a time when she had not explicitly raised sexual frustration as a problem, his prodding would be viewed by her as a seduction, as an invitation that she consider him as someone who would in some way fulfill these needs. Because this young woman had talked about her loneliness and about the burden of taking care of her children in a new neighborhood, the therapist did believe that he could reasonably raise the issue, "What do you find lacking in your life, the lack of which is making you so miserable now?" Pursuing this approach seriously and persistently, he elicited from his patient the confession that indeed she felt sexually frustrated and had felt that way during the previous nine months.

The therapist's style of intervention avoided the kind of prodding that would be experienced as a seduction, while at the same time it also showed an openness to talking about whatever frustrations the patient was experiencing. To have shied away from any discussion of the patient's sex life would have been a mistake as serious as forcing such a discussion on her; it would have expressed the therapist's doubt that he could openly and objectively discuss sex with the patient without becoming somehow sexually involved with her. We say "somehow" because there can be a psychological involvement with a patient through a mutual talking about sex even if there is never any overt sexual activity.

Whenever the therapist makes an interpretation, the interpretation can have reassuring or frustrating effects. We have already given examples of reassurance through interpretation. Interpretations that call the patient's attention to wishes that he or she is trying to gratify while making it clear that the therapist will not cooperate in helping the patient to gratify these wishes are necessarily frustrating. Telling a young woman that her rage at the therapist stems from her longing that he nurture her as she has always hoped a parent would, but as never happened in her experience, would—we hope—enlarge her understanding of a major source of her continual, smoldering dissatisfaction with her life. It might do that; it surely would be experienced as a frustration, for it is clear that the therapist will not and cannot provide the parental care she longs for.

The therapist doesn't comment on reality.   Ordinarily the therapist doesn't comment on the patient's reality situation. There is no need to belabor the point. As we said before, the therapist doesn't view it as his or her task to explain to the patient what is going on in the world. Nor does the therapist have any special knowledge of the world outside the therapy room.

There are exceptions to this rule. When a patient reports the conditions of his or her life, the therapist (as would any human being) responds humanly. For example, when a patient tells the therapist that everyone in the family is sick or that a daughter has run away from home, it is appropriate for the therapist to say, "That's too bad."

How Support Fits Into the Therapy

It is basic to our understanding of therapy that strands of impulse-expression, of resistance, and of interpretation are intertwined throughout the course of the therapy. No single thread can be taken in isolation as defining the therapy or as predominating. All three threads are important at all times. Therefore interpretation, though essential, is not sufficient to psychoanalytic therapy. Motivating and re-assuring interventions, which have their impact in relation to the impulsive and defensive strands of the therapeutic braid, are as necessary as interpretations.

A Comment on Parameters

Eissler (1953) adopted the word *parameter* to refer to therapeutically appropriate departures from classical psychoanalytic technique. Langs (1973) considers all non-interpretive interventions to be parameters, except for those that are expressions of human concern. And yet noninterpretive interventions are essential aspects of the therapeutic process. In the first place, the patient needs the therapist as a real object, if only to develop a transference. We cannot imagine deep transference feel-ings developing toward a cold and aloof therapist. But the need for a therapist to offer herself or himself as a target for transference is not the only reason that a therapist needs to be human. If therapy is to be effective, the therapist must have the desire to help, and in some way the patient must sense this desire. We do not advocate an excessive therapeutic zeal or a need to nurture that would cause the therapist to dominate the patient and deprive him or her of autonomy. We simply mean that the therapist is committed to helping, so committed that the patient can sense it. Therefore the therapist need not be overconcerned about remaining "pure" in her or his analytic technique.

The Realities of the Patient's Life

The realities of the patient's life (i.e., job, marriage, children, financial affairs, etc.) are of considerable importance to the therapy and they have generally been ne-glected in psychoanalytic writings. Psychoanalysts of the so-called cultural school, including Horney and Fromm, have gone farther than others toward giving an appropriate place to the realities of the patient's life. Dollard and Miller (1950), who created an amalgam of psychoanalysis and behavior theory, took for granted that the new insights and more effective behavior developing out of analytic therapy would not be sustained long if the patient's world failed to provide rewards for the healthier conceptions and for the more adaptive behavior. Finally, A. Freud (1946), in discussing child analysis, made clear that the external situation of the child had to be taken into account in child analysis.

Contrasting with the attitude of these authors is the all-too-frequent attitude of some psychoanalytic clinicians, who take for granted that they will intuitively understand the circumstances of their patients' lives. For example, although they grew up in upper-middle-class households, and their social interactions occur within the compass of particular ethnic groups, many therapists take for granted that they will understand the very different circumstances of the lives of their patients.

We believe that this is a mistake. The therapist would do well to be alert to the ways in which his or her own background and experience have been different from those of the patient. When she or he becomes aware of these differences, the therapist will often be able to respond to the patient with empathy, rather than in a way that the patient will experience as showing misunderstanding and lack of empathy.

Chapter 13

Theory and Strategy of Dream Interpretation

Orientation

In his classic book on the interpretation of dreams S. Freud (1900) wrote, "The interpretation of dreams is the royal road to a knowledge of the unconscious activities of the mind" (p. 608). Because Freud also taught us that everyday actions and, indeed, all of our thoughts and feelings as well as our actions, are determined by a number of other thoughts, feelings, wishes, fears, and actions, one may wonder whether the dream is peculiarly valuable as a key to the hidden determinants of thought, feeling, and action. Is the dream a more royal road to the unconscious than other roads?

We answer: Yes, it is. A dream reported in a therapy hour gives focus to the whole hour; subsequent associations are relevant to the affective states underlying the dream. The dream occurred under circumstances that produced less need for defense because the dreamer was asleep. One might say that on the sandy beach of the dream, the high tide of the unconscious rolls in, unimpeded by rocky necessities for defense. The resistances—those needed defenses that we observe in the therapeutic situation—will come forward strongly as the therapist sets out to work on interpreting the dream through the patient's associations to the dream elements.

The Psychoanalytic Theory of Dreaming

Before we can recommend to the reader how to handle dreams within the therapeutic situation, we need to sketch the psychoanalytic theory of dreaming. The reader who is familiar with this theory only in the most general way, should strengthen her or his grasp on it by reading such expositions as Brenner's (chapter 7 of his *Elementary Textbook of Psychoanalysis*, 1973) and Freud's (*The Interpretation of Dreams*, 1900).

We have said that the dream gives expression to unconscious forces in a much more direct way than other mental contents do. We commented that this is possible because the dreamer is asleep. Let us start our discussion of dreaming with this fact. A dream occurs only when one is asleep. Sleeping consists of the withdrawal of interest and attention from the stimuli of the world outside our bodies. Sleeping also involves a stopping of actions directed toward the outside world. Under these conditions, thoughts and feelings can be allowed to come into the mind much more freely because one will not go into action, and inner processes will play a proportionately larger role in these thoughts and feelings because outer stimuli are not being attended to.

Among the inner processes that feed the dreaming are memories of events of waking life (usually experiences of the day preceding the dream) and conflicts continuing from early childhood—conflicts that are repressed, therefore unconscious, even in sleep. The unconscious conflicts are constituted of wishes striving for expression and their opposing defenses. At times, outer stimuli that occur during sleep also provide material for the formation of a dream; but such nocturnal stimuli are not essential for a dream.

The unconscious, early-childhood conflicts, the preconscious day-residues, and the preconscious nocturnal stimuli (when present) are, however, not simply represented in the dreamer's consciousness as ideas or thoughts or memories. In order to enter into the dreamer's consciousness they must first be translated into visual images; then they enter into the dream, represented by a series of images. The dreamer remembers and reports verbally this series of images. We call this report "the manifest dream." We call the psychological structure from which the manifest dream was developed "the latent dream."

According to Freud the manifest dream is a distorted version of the latent dream, not only because thoughts and feelings had to be translated into visual imagery but also because repressive forces of the personality were active and brought about a disguising and censoring transformation of the material. One who wants to interpret the dream, to recover as fully as possible the latent dream-thoughts, can best approach this aim, said Freud, by getting the dreamer to give associations to each element of the manifest dream.

Strategy of Dream Interpretation

With this outline of Freud's theory of dreaming as a background we are now ready to consider how the therapist can best deal with a patient's reporting of a dream. We offer the following general guidelines:
1. Consider the material of the dream-report in the same way you consider any other material that the patient provides.
2. Get associations from the patient as the basis of dream interpretation if at all possible.

Commenting on the first guideline, we remind the reader that the dream-report is a compromise between expressive and defensive tendencies. Therefore in dealing with the dream the therapist cannot afford to neglect the resistant aspects of this production. With the dream, as with every other production of the patient, the therapist must judge what is ripe for interpretation and what is not, what aspects of the derivatives of unconscious conflict can now be dealt with and what aspects must be left untouched for the present. Furthermore, she or he has as much need with dream material as with other material for the rule, "Interpret from the ego side; interpret defense before interpreting content."

The sensitive therapist knows, too, that the dream-report can be (and usually is) a communication of how the patient feels about the therapist and the therapy. The patient makes the dream report at the time that he or she makes it for a purpose. It may be that he or she is making a gift to the therapist, silently telling the therapist, "I know that you want dreams, so here's a dream for you." At other times the presentation of a dream can mean, "See what senseless and confusing material is in my mind; I dare you to make any sense of it." At still other times it can mean, "See how frightened I am about my turbulent impulse-life. You can't really mean for me to explore that, can you?" It is clear that the therapist would do well to pay at least as much attention to the reason why the dream has been reported as to its ostensible content.

Turning to the second guideline, which advises the therapist to get associations, we remind the reader that the latent content of a dream is to be discovered through the dreamer's associations. If the therapist fails to elicit the patient's associations he or she will run a serious risk of unknowingly using personal associations to interpret the dream. To be sure, there are some symbols that can be counted on (95 times out of 100) to have the meaning that is assigned to them by psychoanalytic lore. For example, climbing a stairway means a rising sexual excitement, and cutting off one's finger represents fear of castration. Yet, as Freud said, there are times when a church steeple in a dream is to be understood as a church steeple rather than a phallic symbol.

In the context of therapy it is also true that what the patient has said before reporting the dream gives clues, through associative links, to the latent content of the dream. The therapist knows a good deal about the patient and has a reasonably good idea of what the current preoccupations of the patient are. Therefore the therapist has less need for directly obtained associations than a person who knew nothing of the dreamer's life would have. But why should the therapist handicap herself or himself by failing to get associations to a dream, if it can easily be done?

From what has just been said it follows that a very appropriate way to deal with a dream is simply to ask the patient to associate to each element of the dream-report, taking these in the order of their occurrence in the report. Alternatively, one can take these elements in some other order. A particular element may, for various reasons, seem to the therapist to be especially striking or to offer opportunity for exploration of currently active unconscious conflicts. On the other hand, the mood or emotional quality of the dream may impress the therapist. The dreamer may have reported intense anxiety, strong anger, or intense sexual feelings. Such an affect can be taken as the first element for associations.

The overall pattern of a dream may impress the therapist, and he or she may wish to ask for associations to this. As a general rule, however, the therapist is better advised to deal with the manifest dream element-by-element, because the work of disguise usually has produced a change of pattern as well as a coding of elements. Therefore it is usually more effective to decode each element then to attempt to discern a pattern in the decoded elements or to attempt to deal with the pattern of elements in the manifest dream. Another approach to eliciting associations is to inquire about the events of the previous day that have contributed to the formation of the dream.

Finally, the therapist may choose simply to consider all that follows in the therapy hour to constitute associations to the dream. With wit enough, how this subsequent material is related to the dream-report and where these latent dream-thoughts came from can be discovered.

Ideally the associations to the manifest dream, obtained in a systematic way, would tell the therapist what the dream means. Practically it is not always so. If the therapist asks for associations to each element, the patient may attempt to produce them, but resistant forces can be so strong that associations are sparse or almost totally absent. In such an instance the therapist may then have to confront the patient with the patient's need for defense. It may even occur that the therapist decides not to ask for associations to the elements of the dream; she or he may believe that the reasons for the patient's having reported the dream in the first place are far more important to deal with than the content of the dream; that these reasons have overwhelming priority in the immediate therapeutic situation and that they must be interpreted.

There are even times when the therapist avoids asking for associations because to get these associations would be equivalent to making an interpretation—the patient would have been forced to focus his or her attention on the meaning of the dream—and the therapist feels that it would not be timely to pursue such interpretive work.

Other Comments on Dream Interpretation

Sometimes a patient forgets part of a dream, not recalling that piece of it until later in the therapy session. Such a forgotten part of a dream is likely to be of special importance, and it may well be taken as the focus of interpretive work. The therapist would be well advised, therefore, to begin the inquiry by asking for associations to the forgotten element.

If the patient at first reports a dream and then, later in the session, repeats the dream (perhaps because the therapist has requested it, saying, "Would you tell me again the dream you told me about earlier"), a comparison of what is included in both versions and a consideration of what is different can be most instructive. Nuances in the narrative on the two occasions may make the therapist aware of the point at which the patient has a special need for defensive operations, and of how the patient satisfies this need for defense in different ways at different times.

What should the therapist do if she or he has not gotten all the associations to a dream during the session in which the dream was reported, has not fully interpreted the dream, or has not dealt with all of the dreams that were reported in a session and time has run out? Should the therapist bring up the dream next time and continue the work of interpretation? We recommend against such a practice. We believe that one should do what one can with the material of a session in that session and, next time, consider the total situation of the new session on its merits (making use of the current material and responding to the *current flow of material*). The only exception that we would make to this advice is to recommend that when there are urgent, unresolved issues involving the vital structure of the therapy, the therapist should take an initiative at the beginning of a session in bringing up these issues. But a dream is not such an issue (though it might express such an issue), and the therapist should not bring up dream material from a previous session.

Cautions on Dream Interpretation

As a final commentary we caution the reader against some errors that beginners in dream interpretation are likely to make. The novice may be so struck by the apparent theme of a dream-report or so taken by its symbolism that she or he fails to get the dreamer's associations. As we pointed out above, by failing to get the patient's associations the therapist substitutes her or his own. To do this is bad therapy; the price is inexact, perhaps inaccurate interpretations.

The beginner may also be inclined to try to interpret every element in every dream. If the therapist does indeed interpret everything in sight, this would be a virtuoso performance, but not of much help to the patient in the patient's self-understanding. Nor should the therapist interpret the meaning of a dream that the patient is not yet ready to deal with. The aim of dream interpretation, like the aim of all therapeutic technique, is to advance the patient's understanding of those issues that are currently alive in the therapy. Unless the interpretation illuminates some active impulse-defense conflict, some transference attitude, or some resistant position, the interpretation should not be made.

So it follows that the therapist should interpret not out of personal need to interpret or because of the belief that an interpretation of the dream is expected from him or her, but because the interpretation serves a therapeutic purpose. If the therapist, at the moment, lacks sufficient understanding of the immediate therapeutic situation to see how the dream is related to that situation, it is best to say nothing.

If the therapist makes an interpretation and the patient disputes it, it is wise for the therapist not to enter into a defense of the interpretation. Assent can never be coerced; if the patient can't believe the interpretation, the therapist's offering other examples and going to great lengths to justify the interpretation is not likely to convince the patient. To be sure, there are times when the therapist can point to clear lines of converging evidence that support the therapist's view of the matter and do so succinctly. If the resistance is not too strong, such an appeal to a pattern of evidence may be useful. More frequently, however, it is useless to argue for an interpretation, as we discuss at greater length in our chapter on interpretation (chapter 11).

Dreams in the Context of Therapy

A man who had been in once-a-week therapy for about 7 months reported the following dream at the beginning of a session:

> I had a very unusual dream last Saturday night. [The session was on a Tuesday.] In fact, I woke up screaming. My yelling disturbed Mary, and she woke up and asked me what was wrong. In the dream I was at Bill and Ann's house with Gordie and Kathy. They went next door where there was a graveyard that nuns were buried in. Gordie lifted a stone and went down some stairs. Gordie released some evil spirit by going down the stairs, and Kathy and I ran back to the house. Where was Gordie? I was in bed with Kathy. Gordie came in. He was different; he was possessed. There was a doctor there. He gave Kathy and me instruments—like large syringes—to defend ourselves with. I threw one of the instruments at Gordie and hit him in the head. He fell down. The doctor pushed one of the instruments in the back of a girl's head, and she died. I wondered who the bad guys and who the good guys really were. Then a nun came toward me in her white habit.

> She was wearing a cross, which got larger and larger. I was very
> frightened. I wondered what side I was on, the bad guys' or the good
> guys'.

The therapist probed for associations, first inquiring about the remark that the patient's yelling had awakened his wife. The patient replied, "I didn't tell her the dream immediately. I was afraid she would think I was silly and would laugh at me." He had been depressed all day Monday and had barely spoken to Mary. The therapist inquired what had occurred to the patient about "Bill and Ann's house." The patient explained that Bill and Ann's house was where he'd been at a poker game on Saturday evening—the evening before the dream—with Gordie and Kathy. The therapist probed about "Gordie and Kathy"; the patient said that Kathy had taken him to the hospital when he'd cracked his rib in a soccer game. Her husband, Gordie, had stayed with the patient's children so that Mary could go to the hospital to be with the patient. Similarly the therapist asked for associations to other elements of the dream-report: the graveyard in which nuns were buried, Gordie's going down the stairs, the evil spirit, the patient's being in bed with Kathy, Gordie's being possessed, and the doctor's pushing an instrument into a girl's head.

Most of the inquiries led to associations that shed no light on the latent dream-thoughts; in essence, the patient simply repeated each element as it had appeared in the dream-report. The therapist abandoned probing.

As the patient continued talking, he reported that during the past few days he has experienced a burning sensation in his legs, as though his body would burst into flame from "spontaneous combustion." He then remarked that at times he feels like saying, "Fuck it all."

The therapist observed, "That's very apt language you're using. You have been experiencing sexual tension—as is clear from some of the images in your dream and from your reporting the burning sensation—and this sexual tension is causing you a lot of suffering." (The therapist relied on a very competent internist who was working with the patient concurrently to evaluate and to treat the patient's physical illnesses.) This interpretation focused the patient's attention on his sexual wishes; he then began to talk about his dissatisfactions with his sex life.

What can we learn from examining this dream-report and from considering how the therapist dealt with it? We are struck, of course, at how difficult the therapist found it to make use of the copious, complex dream material therapeutically. A dream-report that was long and full of symbols still did not carry with it the key to its interpretation; and its length was no proof that resistant forces had been overcome. In making an interpretation the therapist made use of all of the knowledge that was at hand about this patient; about the patient's most important adaptational problems and what was learned from the dreamer's associations. The therapist focused on what was then believed to be the patient's most important conflict, a conflict between intense sexual wishes and a fear of expressing such wishes. In the interpretation the therapist made reference to the patient's choice of words ("That's very apt language"), to an association in the previous minute of the session ("your reporting the burning sensation"), and to an aspect of the manifest dream ("some of the images of your dream"). The interpretation did not take account of the defensive aspect of the dream. We cannot doubt that the defense was as important as the impulse; after all, the fear of the impulses was so strong that the patient had awakened up in terror.

Another man after 2 years of therapy brought the following dream-report:

> I was crossing a bridge. I got partway across and was afraid to go
> farther. I clung desperately to a pole on the bridge. Then I woke up.

When the therapist asked for associations to the various elements of the dream-report, the patient emphasized how dangerous he had felt his situation in the dream to be and how frightened he was. Nothing occurred to him in connection with the "pole," except that he had held on to it in desperation to avoid being plunged into the river below. The therapist abandoned, for the moment, the task of interpreting the dream. In the free associations that followed, the patient spoke of concerns about damage to himself and about defeat in tasks that he might undertake. The therapist understood these statements to be allusions to a fear of castration.

Knowing that a week before this therapy session the patient had entered a hospital for a hernia operation and that the patient had returned to work only the previous day, the therapist commented, "The operation was more upsetting than you realized." In response the patient acknowledged his fear that something would go wrong, that the stitches would not hold or that an infection would set in. He expressed his pleasure that his wife had looked at the scar from the incision to assure herself (and him) that the wound was healing properly. He then mentioned "a cute, young nurse" on the afternoon shift, who came into his room from time to time to check on him. "I would have liked to take her to bed," he said. Then the patient acknowledged a burden of guilt that he could think of being unfaithful to his wife, who had been so supportive of him, though she was a less-than-enthusiastic sexual partner.

We can speculate that the hernia operation, like any operation, bestirred fears of bodily damage; we assume that such fears are linked associatively to fears of castration. Castration (or, more accurately, cutting off the genitals) is the punishment that the patient expects for illicit sexual behavior, or even for a wish to engage in illicit sexual behavior. The patient soon revealed to the therapist such an illicit wish—the wish to go to bed with the cute, young nurse.

In retrospect we can interpret the danger of the dream as the danger that the patient would act on his illicit sexual wishes—toward the expression of which, as he experienced it, he had already moved halfway—and that he would suffer the consequences of having these forbidden wishes. The therapist interpreted the dream not by making direct, detailed use of associations to dream elements, but by linking the predominant affect of the dream (a sense of danger) with a significant event in the patient's life. The therapist knew very well, of course, that an operation is bound to provoke fears of bodily damage and that castration fear arises whenever someone is tempted to perform forbidden sexual acts. The therapist used this general knowledge as a guide when commenting on what the patient was saying. Because of theoretical knowledge, the therapist was able to interpret the dream (or, at least, some aspects of it) despite the lack of useful associations. Finally, the reader should notice that the aim of the interpretive process is to make the patient more aware of the unconscious conflict provoked by sexual frustration, kept unconscious by the burden of guilt over sexual wishes; and this aim was furthered even though the dream could not be fully interpreted.

We do not offer these examples of dream interpretation within psychotherapy as models of good practice but rather as illustrations of the kind of difficulties the therapist often faces in making use of dream-reports therapeutically. The therapists who were kind enough to provide us with these examples did not handle the dream interpretation perfectly. But their difficulties and their struggles may nevertheless be instructive.

Chapter 14

The Changes Produced by Therapy

Patients come to therapy to relieve their psychological suffering. When the therapist is competent their suffering is nearly always reduced. Sometimes the relief of the patient's suffering brings behavioral changes that other people (friends, spouse, employer, parents) do not want. At times, too, the patient and the therapist must choose between relatively quick but limited improvement in the patient's psychological functioning and a more radical, more helpful change that requires much more time and effort. Often the patient comes to therapy hoping to alleviate a few troublesome symptoms but winds up changing the way he or she lives. It is clear, therefore, that in considering the changes that occur as a result of therapy we cannot avoid a consideration of the value-systems of patient, of therapist, of friends and relatives of the patient, of insurance companies (if they are paying for the therapy), of government agencies (if they are paying for it), and of society in general.

What Does the Patient Want?

By our definition of psychotherapy, the therapist–patient relationship does not qualify as psychotherapy unless the patient voluntarily chose to involve himself or herself in the "therapeutic" process. Where there is less than a minimum degree of self-determination in the patient's involvement in the therapy, we propose to call the interaction "persuasion," "intimidation," "argumentation," "pleading," or whatever other term may be more accurate than "psychotherapy." We want to reserve psychotherapy for instances where there is a substantial voluntary element in the patient's participation.

When a patient comes to therapy voluntarily, she or he wants (a) relief from ego-alien symptoms and (b) relief of subjective distress (i.e., of anxiety, depression, and general dissatisfaction with what life has to offer). According to psychoanalytic theory, patients will achieve relief from symptoms and from neurotic anxiety and depression when personal conflicts are resolved through their permitting themselves a more direct gratification of some of their wishes while establishing a firmer repression of other wishes. (Psychoanalytic theory also tells of other ways to achieving relief of symptoms; because these other ways are not psychoanalytic therapy, we ignore them in this context.) Therefore improved adaptation is expected to accompany the symptom reduction achieved through resolving a conflict. Patients appreciate, too, that their inhibitions interfere with their functioning effectively, thereby robbing them of many satisfactions they could get from mastery of their environment (as in work-life) and from interpersonal transactions (as in love relationships).

What Do Others Wish for the Patient?

Other people who know the patient (family, friends, employer, physician) know that his or her behavior is troublesome and that he or she is suffering. They want the patient to achieve better adaptation, that is, to have a more effective interaction with other people and to make a greater contribution to society. The others who know the patient may also wish that he or she would treat them better and would conform better to social codes. Although the therapist joins with these people in wishing for the patient to be relieved of suffering, he or she should refuse to accept their goals that the patient achieve better adaptation (as they define adaptation) or that the patient conform better or accommodate their desires.

What Does the Therapist Want?

Therapists want, first of all, to relieve patients' suffering. Having presented themselves to the world as professionals whose task it is to relieve mental suffering, they strive to keep this promise. Therapists want to exercise their skill in relieving psychological distress and to make money doing it.

Do therapists set any limits on the conditions under which they will relieve a patient's suffering? Suppose Adolf Hitler had come to a therapist in 1921 asking for alleviation of the tendency he had to clash with his co-workers in the National Socialist Party. Would a clinician who believed that she or he could alleviate this difficulty but would not be able to change Hitler's hatred of foreigners and of Jews or his passionate, destructive tendencies, have been willing to devote herself or himself to the relief of Hitler's suffering? We believe that a therapist would not wish to relieve a patient's suffering if doing so would seriously jeopardize things that the therapist personally values.

The dilemma a therapist is put in when a patient wants something from the therapy that violates the therapist's standards is illustrated by an incident reported to us by a colleague. (We believe that our colleague did not breach confidentiality because she described the circumstances of this episode to us in only the most general terms.) Her prospective patient had had an automobile accident which caused him a great deal of pain and some serious medical problems. The medical problems had, he asserted, made it impossible for him to work at his supervisory job in an insurance company. He wanted the therapist to support his contention that he had been disabled by the accident and to become involved in documenting his claim against the person at fault in the accident or against the Social Security Administration (should the accident claim fail, which would lead the patient to claim that he needed Social Security disability compensation).

As the therapist learned more about the patient's life, she came to believe that the patient was in fact physically able to perform the work of his job at the insurance company. It seemed to her that he found the job detestable because it required him to work with others in the office whom he intensely disliked, and because he had built up, over the years, a seething lake of resentment against his employer for allowing these distressing circumstances in the office environment to continue. Moreover, she learned that the patient was conducting a sideline tax-consultation business at his home—an activity that was more physically demanding than anything he was required to do at work.

When the therapist expressed her misgivings about supporting the patient's legal position, the patient implored her to continue to "do therapy with me," by which the patient meant, "continue to give me an opportunity to persuade you to intervene in my legal affairs and in other aspects of my life." But he had not even the slightest interest in learning about the psychological contributions to his suffering (i.e., in really doing therapeutic work). When she could not budge her patient from this position, the therapist, with sadness, had to refuse to continue to offer her professional services to him.

A psychoanalytic therapist believes that an enlargement of the patient's self-understanding, that is, a structural change, is what is most likely to produce permanent improvement. She or he believes that where there is neurotic conflict, the patient's suffering can be relieved in such a way as to assure there will be no recurrence of the neurosis, only if there are intrapsychic changes: the undoing of repression, the making conscious of unconscious conflicts.

Thus the therapist has a triad of aims: to relieve suffering by exercising personal professional skills, to earn a living, and to enlarge patients' understanding of themselves. The third of these aims is, in the context of psychoanalytic therapy, the result that makes the other two possible.

How Therapy Works to Achieve These Goals

In our opinion, any therapy that deserves the name "psychoanalytic" has the aim of enlarging the patient's self-understanding. As Freud (1926b) put it, "We try to restore the ego, to free it from its restrictions, and to give it back its command over the id which it lost owing to its early repressions."

Insight

We are aware that changes in the patient sometimes occur without the therapist's making an interpretation that brings the patient "insight," as Horwitz (1974) discovered in studying those successful cases of the Menninger psychotherapy research project in which the therapist relied mainly on a supportive approach, and in studying other cases in which a core conflict had not been resolved but symptoms and behavior nevertheless improved (as a result of supportive measures). Horwitz also found that nine of ten patients who received supportive therapy that had been helpful to them, maintained their improved adaptation during a 2-year follow-up period.

Although these findings seem to show that interpretation and insight do not matter, we believe that such a conclusion is unjustified. For one thing, we note that Kernberg (1977, in his foreword to Applebaum, *The Anatomy of Change*)—who, like Horwitz, studied the 42 patients in the Menninger project—reported that when highly skilled therapists were working with patients who had ego weaknesses, the therapists achieved better outcomes when they used "an approach that focused more on the transference" than when they used an approach that focused on it less

(p. x). Malan (1976, *Toward the Validation of Dynamic Psychotherapy*) had already shown that the activity of the therapist which correlated most highly with favorable outcome was the linking, by interpretation, of transference reactions with reactions to parent or sibling. For his sample of 30 brief psychotherapy and longer-term psychotherapy patients, the correlation between such interpretations and outcome was .40. Thus, in our view it is premature to abandon the hypothesis that structural change is basic to psychoanalytic therapy.

Insight need not be comprehensive.   Increased self-understanding is, we believe, essential to the lasting relief of the patient's suffering. But "insight," in an intellectual sense, need not be comprehensive. Character change and more efficient use of energy can come about without the patient's understanding completely *how* and *why* these changes take place. Indeed, both the therapist and the patient are frequently puzzled about why the patient feels better and adapts better.

Lessened repression.   Patients do not want to be burdened with repressions that rob them of gratifications that it would be safe, and socially acceptable, for them to have. At the same time, they do not want to be concerned that their impulses will cause them to lurch out of control. For example, while attending a masquerade party where one of the guests has come dressed as a policeman, the patient doesn't want to find herself or himself unaccountably going into a rage at this guest because of an unconscious anger at authority figures. She or he would prefer that these repressions would be selective, firm where needed to protect the self from destructive actions, lacking or weak where not needed. Thus maximum gratification can be achieved with the least expenditure of energy.

Greater choice.   The lifting of repressions enhances patients' ability to think and plan and releases them from the domination of unconsciously determined, repetitive patterns of behavior. L. Kubie in a classic paper, "The repetitive core of the neurosis" (1941), showed how early childhood conflicts persist into adulthood when repression has blocked their access to the person's awareness. The persisting, repressed conflicts condemn persons with neuroses to a self-destructive repetition of the behaviors that failed them as a child. Kubie pointed out that the compulsive repetition can be abolished only by an uncovering of the unconscious conflict that made the repression necessary in the first place.

When, as a result of the undoing of repression, patients become aware of the original, unconscious conflict; when as a result of this enlarged awareness they are no longer dominated by the repetition-compulsions; then patients experience a welcome sense of freedom. They no longer *have to* act as they did before, they are no longer *compelled* to repeat the same, self-defeating behaviors. They can achieve a harmonious relationship between the various parts of the self (id, ego, and superego) and with the environment, as R. Knight expressed so eloquently in his essay, "Determinism, Freedom, and Psychotherapy" (1946).

Considering these events from the standpoint of ego psychology, we may speak of the patient's achieving a greater "relative autonomy." This is the phrase that Gill and Brenman (1959), basing themselves on earlier writings by Hartmann and by Rapaport, used to describe the freeing of the activities of the ego from dependence on drives, on the one hand, or on the superego or external reality, on the other. Gill and Brenman showed that greater relative autonomy makes possible a greater flexibility in the person's behavior—a more appropriate adaptation.

Greater understanding or quick behavior change?   We are now ready to consider whether therapists should focus their attention on enlarging patients' self-understanding or on changing patients' behaviors. Our argument so far has shown that where there is unconscious conflict and repression, a lasting change in the patient's adaptation cannot be expected unless repressions are undone. We advise therapists, therefore, to fix their sights on the patient's increase in self-understanding rather than on behavioral change. Of course, such understanding must be "understanding with your guts," not intellectual wordplay.

Adaptive Changes

In the course of psychotherapy the patient moves from the more distant derivatives of core conflicts to derivatives that are closer. The patient herself or himself, who chooses what is talked about, is in charge of this movement and regulates its speed.

What is a "derivative"? It is, as Freud used this term, an expression of a repressed drive-representation. The derivative, too, may be unconscious; or, as Freud explains (1915b), it may be so removed from the original drive-representation that it can be allowed to come into consciousness. Derivatives are associatively connected with the drive-representations that they express. They are displacements from the original representation; an experimental psychologist would say that they lie along a dimension of similarity to the original stimulus, and may be explained by the principle of *stimulus generalization* (see Miller, 1960). Finally, as Fenichel (1941) emphasized, derivatives necessarily express both the drive-representation from which they derive *and* the defenses against this drive-representation. In short, they are compromise-formations.

Thus the process of undoing repressions follows a path from more distant to less distant derivatives. The more distant derivatives, when the therapist draws them to the patient's attention, provoke less anxiety and less defense than the closer ones would provoke. Fenichel (1945) therefore recommended:

> The procedure of deducing what the patient actually means and telling it to him is called interpretation. Since interpretation means helping something unconscious to become conscious by naming it at the moment it is striving to break through, effective interpretations can only be given at one specific point, namely, where the patient's immediate interest is momentarily centered. The actual shocking infantile instinctual impulses are so far removed from the possibility of being felt that, in the beginning, interpretation is not concerned with them but rather with their derivatives. (p. 25)

Notice that Fenichel is assuming that the defense against the expression of a more deeply repressed aspect of the patient's conflict is so strong that speaking to the patient about this aspect can have no impact. The other possibility is that the therapist's ill-timed interpretation does partly revoke the repression, but at the cost of a degree of anxiety that the patient cannot tolerate. If that happens, the patient may be compelled to abandon therapy or, at best, to turn away from providing any associations related to this conflict.

As the patient in the course of the therapy is dealing progressively with derivatives that are less and less displaced, he or she is at the same time achieving mastery over various aspects of his or her life. Among the derivatives of a core conflict are defenses, displacements, and sublimations. With successful therapy we not only expect ineffective repressions either to be removed or to be replaced by stable repressions; we also expect that the new set of derivatives of the conflict will allow more gratification, with less waste of energy from inefficient defensive operations. We expect that the increase in gratifications will reduce the patient's overall level of tension enough to permit sublimations to replace less productive derivatives.

Resolution of infantile neurosis.   To put the matter another way: If there is a change in the derivatives of a conflict that originated in early childhood, one could equally well speak of a "resolution" of that original conflict. Freud (1940, p. 184) called the early childhood conflicts an "early childhood [or 'infantile'] neurosis." He believed that such a neurosis would be fully resolved when the patient, if a man, had come to terms not only with his castration fear but also with his fear of passivity and homosexuality or, if a woman, had come to terms with her penis envy. (Freud, 1937b, pp. 250–253) Freud left the impression that even when psychotherapy is successful there may not be a complete dissolution of fear of passivity or of penis envy. For our part we would say that successful psychotherapy involves the resolution of the infantile neurosis either totally or in some of its aspects.

Freud's famous case of the Wolf-Man—an obsessional, deeply troubled patient who early in therapy reported a dream in which six or seven white wolves sat on the branches of a walnut tree—makes clear how resistant to change the infantile neurosis is. After 4 years in analysis with Freud, the Wolf-Man was greatly improved. Returning to his native Russia, he spent the years of the First World War there; he married, studied for a law degree, and obtained a license to practice law. Because of the revolution, he lost his home and fortune. Returning to Vienna, he had another 4 months of analysis with Freud, with the purpose of clearing up his hysterical constipation.

Seven years later, the patient developed a delusion that his nose was irreparably damaged, and he had treatment for this delusion and for related problems by Ruth Brunswick for 5 months. Eleven years later, he had a second period of analysis with Dr. Brunswick; and still later, suffering from bouts of depression, he consulted yet other psychoanalysts. It is ironic that a case believed by Freud to show with particular clarity that adult neurosis is preceded and prepared for by infantile neurosis, should also teach us that the earlier character formations are stubborn indeed. (For a fuller account of this case the reader should consult Gardiner, 1971.)

Changes in object relations.   All of these changes in self-understanding, all of these advances from more distant to less distant derivatives of a core conflict, bring about a change in the patient's object relations and an improvement in the ability to cope with life tasks. Freud, in discussing the aims of therapy, stressed the importance of better adaptation. He stated that the normal person, or the person with neurosis who has been healed by psychotherapy, has "a sufficient amount of capacity for enjoyment and of efficiency" (Freud, 1917). Saul (1958) wrote that Freud is believed to have replied, when he was asked what he considered mental health to be, "The capacity to work and to love."

Psychosexual maturity.   All object relations involve sexuality in the broad sense; some are connected with sex as narrowly defined. We would expect the patient who has profited from therapy to get more sexual satisfaction and for this sexual adaptation to show increased maturity, in terms of the psychosexual developmental scale. Although prephallic partial drives will not be abolished, and will still receive some gratification, they will be subordinated to genital aims and will be integrated under a primacy of the genital zone (Fenichel, 1941, p. 21). We believe that therapy can be helpful without the patient's achieving a genital organization; but therapy is more helpful when the patient does achieve it. When a genital organization is practical in the patient's life situation, it is, we believe, likely to be more rewarding for her or him than any less mature behavioral organization could be.

What is maturity?   Though clinicians might be able to agree that therapy should lead to greater maturity, it is less likely that they could agree on what maturity is. It might mean an enlargement of the conscious ego and a more harmonious interaction of the parts of the self (Menninger's definition). It might mean the capacity to enjoy loving and being loved and also responsible working and harmless recreation, in proper balance (Saul's [1958] definition). Offer and Sabshin, in their book *Normality* (1966), present a wide-ranging review of psychiatric and psychoanalytic views about psychological normality and maturity.

Lessening of Symptoms

Because the less-distorted derivatives allow the patient to achieve more satisfaction, there is less drive-tension, with less need for defense. As a result, there is also less need for symptoms. Symptoms disappear in successful therapy. The patient may not bother to tell the therapist that the symptoms have ceased, but they do disappear.

Reflections on the Goals of Therapy

Lack of Tension Cannot Be a Goal

Freud told us that much is to be gained if neurotic misery can be transformed into common unhappiness (Breuer & Freud, 1893–1895). He did not expect that a person can be spared from all unhappiness by being psychoanalyzed, and neither should we expect it. Life will always present us with difficulties, challenges, and frustrations; we can only learn to make the best of what life has to offer, actively working to change what we can change and resigning ourselves to the rest.

    Of course, persons helped by psychotherapy will experience much less tension than before, and when they do feel anxious, they are much more likely to feel anxious about realistic dangers. They can therefore use such anxiety to guide them to taking effective actions.

Goal-Setting: Is It Helpful?

Although insurance companies and clinics often demand an explicit statement of goals, it is really feasible to set goals only provisionally. The therapist knows that he or she wants the patient to enlarge self-understanding and, thereby, mastery over his or her life. The therapist also notices aspects of the patient's functioning that produce suffering for the patient; which, therefore, the patient might well want to change. But at the beginning of therapy the therapist doesn't know enough to be able to foresee with certainty what the consequences would be of changing this or that behavior. Better to take things as they come and to see what the patient himself or herself will decide to do, after the issues have been clarified.

In autonomous psychotherapy (to use Szasz's term) therapist and client jointly decide what their task is at any particular time. The task is, in general, to increase the patient's understanding of life. Within this framework there are particular puzzles to be solved. These change as the therapy proceeds.

Thus disturbances are dealt with as they arise rather than by having the therapist attempt to stir up conflict in order to treat it. Freud (1937b) made clear that it is inadvisable to try to stir up conflict in order to treat it. It follows, therefore, that not every potential problem of the patient can be dealt with in psychotherapy. But neither is it necessary for this to be done.

Thus, the setting of goals for psychotherapy is generally useless and is sometimes destructive of the patient's autonomy. What the therapist and the patient have to be clear about is that their aim is to increase the patient's self-understanding; put another way, to increase her or his autonomy.

Modesty in Expectations

Finally, a therapist should not expect that psychotherapy will produce perfection in a patient. After all, therapy is—as Colby (1951) put it—repair work. It takes a person who has been scarred in personal development and helps him or her to make up for some of the damage. The result is a way of living that is more satisfactory to the patient; but it is not perfect.

The culture in which the patient lives surely limits what is possible for him or her. Consider the difference between what is allowed and encouraged for American women and for Japanese women. The young woman who is at the beginning of adult life in America has many more opportunities for independence and for the development of a work career than the Japanese woman of that age does. The Japanese woman may well have greater opportunities in other directions. One could hardly hold before one's patient, or before oneself, some abstract ideal of "autonomy" or "self-realization" to which every person regardless of his or her cultural situation should aspire.

Have the Goals Been Achieved?

Psychoanalytic therapy should stop when it isn't any longer worth the time and effort. This measuring stick derives quite simply from the fundamental principle: Psychoanalysis respects the autonomy of the patient. If we respect the patient's autonomy, it follows that the patient is free to decide whether it is in *her or his* interest to continue the therapy. The patient does, however, turn to the therapist to ask her or him what the therapist thinks: "Am I ready to stop?" How does the therapist tell whether the goals they have agreed on, are achieved?

Changes in Symptoms

If the therapy is complete, the nature of the symptoms has changed. First there was a reduction in the presenting symptoms; then symptoms that were closer to the origin of the patient's conflict, and less disguised, occurred. The symptom, as we know, is a compromise-formation. As therapy had its effects, the point of compromise changed.

Transference Cure

The therapist tries to distinguish a "transference cure" from a more genuine and more lasting change. If the change is judged to be temporary and phony, the therapist is obliged to tell the patient so and to explain how this judgment was arrived at. We define transference cure (following Fenichel, 1945) as an improvement in the patient's psychological functioning deriving from her or his relationship to the therapist. The patient may be intimidated by the therapist, and thereby able to give up striving for some gratification she or he felt tempted to look for, or the patient may find satisfaction in the relationship with the therapist. The lessening of tension through avoiding temptations or through basking in satisfactions, brings a greater sense of well-being and a reduction in symptoms. We say that these effects are the result of a transference cure.

Some authors—Goldstein (1960) for example—have used the phrase "placebo effect" to describe the nonspecific processes that are associated with the patient's involvement with the therapist and the therapy, especially the patient's expectation that therapy will be helpful. The expectation that psychotherapy will be helpful is, of course, only a small part of what is going on when there is a transference cure. The gratifications that the patient receives when there is a transference cure may go far beyond the favorable expectations he or she had of the therapist and the therapy; these gratifications may include intense, oral dependence, identifications with the therapist, masochistic submission, alleviation of guilt by a tolerant authority, and so on. It seems to us that much is lost by summarizing all of this as placebo effect while failing to identify each of the specific features of the patient–therapist relationship that contributed to a temporary, undependable improvement in the patient's symptoms.

In deciding whether the patient's improvement is genuine or is a transference cure, the therapist would do well to consider:

1. whether he or she understands why the patient has changed. If not, the change may be the result of a change in defenses (i.e., a defensive maneuver) not the result of a change in the structure of the personality.
2. whether the symptoms have disappeared without any interpretation of conflicts. If there hasn't been interpretation, the change is likely to be a transference cure.
3. whether there was a dramatic, swift change, a "flight into health." Such dramatic changes are usually transference cures.
4. whether the patient has recently been avoiding dealing with important aspects of her or his life. If, for example, the patient has neglected to talk about sex for the past few weeks or months, yet the therapist knows that sexual problems were important to the patient, the sudden improvement is likely to be a transference cure.
5. whether there is a marked difference between the therapist's estimate of the patient's improvement and the patient's estimate. Where there's such a discrepancy, the improvement may be a transference cure.
6. whether there has been a shift in the quality and quantity of the patient's affective reactions. When the patient's emotional responses are calmer, deeper, and less dramatic, the change is more likely to be genuine.
7. whether there has been a change in object relations. When the patient has fewer arguments with other people, is less isolated from them, and has fewer feelings of being persecuted by others, the improvements in symptoms that are reported are more likely to be a sign of genuine change, and it is more likely that the ego has enlarged its conflict-free area and can function more autonomously.
8. whether the therapist believes there has been an increase in the capacity of the ego to synthesize effectively, that is, to reconcile competing internal demands.

In advising the therapist how to judge whether the patient's improvement is genuine, we have emphasized *internal criteria* (i.e., changes in the patient's psychological functioning as learned about by listening to what he or she says and by observing the patient in the therapy situation). We have not taken account of *external criteria* (i.e., of what friends and acquaintances of the patient think). Our emphasis is not only a counsel of convenience, in that the information relevant to internal criteria derives naturally from the therapist's work with the patient, it is also in keeping with our philosophy that the patient's autonomy should be furthered (cf. Szasz, 1974, *The Ethics of Psychoanalysis*).

Values and Psychotherapy

We close this chapter by stating concisely what our views are of the values the therapist should have. First, as we have already stated, we don't impose our values on patients. They must be free to lead their own lives (see Szasz, 1974, p. 103). Second—as we commented before—if patients' values are for the most part the values of society, (i.e., if they have a good conscience) we have no problem. If they are not, we may wish to refuse to do therapy with them. Finally, we are well aware that changes in patients as a result of psychotherapy may not lead in every detail to behaviors that are more acceptable to society. For example, removing the repression of aggression may allow a patient to decide to be more assertive, even in ways in which society does not always approve. This, we believe, is a price that must be paid for promoting autonomy.

Chapter 15

Termination: When and How to Stop Therapy

15

In this chapter we discuss the final phase of the therapy. First we raise the question, "When should the therapy come to an end?" By this we mean, "How does one decide that the therapy should stop?" This in turn raises the question, "Who should decide when the therapy comes to an end?" If we remain faithful to the principles we have espoused in previous chapters, we must advocate a commitment to the patient's autonomy: It is the patient who must decide, ultimately, when the therapy stops. Furthermore, if we are faithful to the principles previously set forth, the patient and the therapist work together in helping the patient to arrive at the right decision about when the therapy should come to an end.

Even though a collaborative decision-making process is our ideal, there are times, we believe, when it is appropriate, helpful, and necessary for the therapist alone to decide that the therapy should terminate. In these circumstances the therapist usually decides that the therapy should stop at some future time, then announces this decision to the patient. Firestein (1978) offers two examples of a constructive decision by the therapist only, that the therapy should come to an end. In one of these cases the patient was getting a great deal of pleasure from the regular sessions with the therapist. Firestein viewed the placing of a limit on the length of the therapy (by the therapist's saying, "We will stop some months from now; we will need to consider when in the fall to terminate the treatment.") as a needed and constructive maneuver. In another therapy case discussed by Firestein, a woman patient expressed a great fear that her analyst would dismiss her from therapy. She reacted to this fantasy with strong hostility. The therapist decided to set a termination date a year in the future, in order to allay the patient's fears of hasty termination. During this final year of therapy the patient was able to allow herself to experience some of her positive feelings toward the therapist.

Ferenczi (1928/1955a) believed that the patient knows when the therapy should end. To quote him, "A truly cured patient frees himself from analysis slowly but surely; so long as he wishes to come to analysis, he should continue to do so. To put it another way, one might say that the patient finally becomes convinced that he is continuing analysis only because he is treating it as a new but still a fantasy source of gratification, which in terms of reality yields him nothing. When he has slowly overcome his mourning over this discovery he inevitably looks around for other, more real sources of gratification" (p. 85).

From the therapist's viewpoint, what are the criteria for termination? We may list four such criteria. First, the patient has a greater capacity for enjoyment and for efficiency in living, as Freud (1917, p. 457) pointed out. In other words, the patient has a full capacity to work and to love. Second, when therapy has been completed the infantile neurosis has been resolved. Freud (1937b) wrote that wom-en's wish for a penis and men's fear of passivity were "bedrock," marking a successful completion of analysis when these complexes had been successfully resolved. (It had been Ferenczi [1928/1955a] who had originally proposed resolution of the Oedipus complex or of the masculinity complex as a standard for when analysis is complete.) Third, one knows that the therapy is complete when there is nothing more to analyze. Freud (1937b) put it this way: ". . . what we are asking is whether the analyst has had such a far-reaching influence on the patient that no further change could be expected to take place in him if analysis were continued" (p. 219). Later in this paper, Freud acknowledged that such a perfect result never occurs. We may assume that only a practical completeness of analytic work can be attained; that is, that the returns from further analytic work are not worth the effort that would be required. Thus in practice there is no definite beginning or end to psychotherapy.

The criteria for deciding whether the therapy is completed are necessarily criteria that have to be adapted to this particular patient, the one whom we are now considering. The judgment has to be made in relation to *this* patient, and it cannot be made in terms of general goals that apply to any patient whatsoever. (For fuller discussion of this point we refer the reader to the previous chapter on the effects of therapy.)

External events more often than not have an impact on the decision to terminate as well as on the process of termination after the decision has been made. Among the other considerations—besides an evaluation of the progress that the patient has made toward reaching her or his goals—are the following:

1. The patient or the therapist is leaving town; the patient—a mother of a newborn child—finds the appointment schedule hard to manage; the patient wants to finish her analysis before her husband finishes his. These are examples (one could give many more) of external circumstances that have an impact on the decision to bring the therapy to an end. See Firestein's discussion (1978, p. 211).

2. The patient runs out of money.

3. The patient quits as resistance to learning about herself or himself. In chapter 8, in discussing interpretation of resistance, we recommend how the therapist should deal with this; here, we simply point out that when this happens the therapy may end even though the patient's goals have not been achieved.

4. The therapist decides on termination because the patient is acting out and the therapist cannot influence this acting out by making interpretations or by insisting on the patient's refraining from it.

There is always more that could be analyzed. One stops the therapy when it is no longer worthwhile to analyze, considering the effort required. If, in view of the diminishing returns from the therapeutic work, one decides to bring the therapy to an end, one needs to be prepared to analyze and to weigh the patient's anxiety when the termination is decided on. Even though the patient knows that continuing therapy is not worth his or her while, he or she is likely to experience a good deal of anxiety about stopping the therapy.

The therapist's intuitive response to the patient is involved in the therapist's evaluation of how much the patient has changed and of when the therapy should end. The therapist senses or the patient senses that it is time to stop. It may be difficult at the time to say what considerations lead one to this judgment; often, however, one can later see that intuition led to the correct decision. We believe that there is nothing magical or counterscientific about such intuitive judgments. They simply indicate that sometimes we know more than we can put into words.

Finally, we need to point out that at times treatment has to stop even though minimal therapeutic change has occurred. Several examples of this situation are:

1. The therapy seems to stop, to hit a dead end. No new material is coming out. It may be that there is an intractable transference resistance; it may be that the patient cannot view the transference objectively despite the therapist's offering interpretation, that the patient immerses himself or herself in the transference rather than stepping back from it to examine it.

2. The resistance takes the form of acting out so that continued therapy isn't possible. The patient may keep getting into trouble so that there is no time for talk because attention is continually focused on actions that need to be taken. If the acting takes the form of the patient's missing the therapy hours, and if the therapist's attempts to prevent the patient's absences do not avail, the therapist has no choice but to call a halt to the therapy.

3. When the patient, having achieved some relief of symptoms, develops intolerable anxiety as his or her thoughts and feelings are probed more deeply into and the therapist does nothing to allay this anxiety, the therapy has to stop. Under these circumstances it may be that a vacation from therapy rather than termination is called for. When the patient's anxiety builds up to panic, one suspects that the therapist has made an error in the handling of the case. Sometimes such an error cannot be reversed; if so, therapy is not possible with the therapist who made the mistake.

4. Countertransference may lead to a situation where therapy cannot go on. For example, a therapist's need to dominate a young, unmarried mother who came to therapy with psychological difficulties as well as deficits in the skills required to be a good parent, may cause the therapist to bully this inept patient, thereby doing more harm than good.

5. Finally, it may turn out that the initial evaluation of the patient was wrong. A patient who seemed to be suffering from an anxiety neurosis, for example, turned out to have been prepsychotic; after three therapy sessions, she fled the therapy to have a brief vacation and while on this vacation decompensated into an acute, hebephrenic schizophrenia. Outpatient psychotherapy was no longer possible, because the patient had to be hospitalized for her own protection. A staff member of the hospital took over the therapy from the professional who had been doing the outpatient psychotherapy.

When an initial evaluation is wrong—it need not be so wrong as in the example just given—the patient may need another kind of treatment from the kind that the therapist wants to provide. For example, a 21-year-old, single man suffered from a closed head injury which, according to the physicians treating the effects of this injury, impaired his judgment and made it necessary for him to be made a ward of his mother. He believed that she guarded him too strictly and failed to allow him reasonable independence. He wanted to meet with a psychologist in order to get the psychologist to influence his mother to grant him more autonomy, but he had no interest whatsoever in examining his own reactions to his injury and to the restrictions that the effects of the injury had brought about. The therapist was not interested in being a judge between this man and his mother or a mediator between them. The therapist was interested only in enlarging the patient's understanding of the his own life. Because patient and therapist could not agree on the aims of the therapy, the therapy had to be abandoned.

How to Terminate the Therapy

Our first piece of advice is: Let the patient know that the therapy is coming to an end well before you believe that it should end, 3 to 6 months in advance, ideally. Don't wait until there is nothing more to deal with to announce the termination; instead, tell your patient when the therapy is going along well enough, inside and outside of therapy, that you believe that with a little more time "we will have done about all that can be done in your psychotherapy." In the chapter on personality change (chapter 14) we discussed the changes that may be expected to occur as a result of therapy; accordingly, we will not consider here what these changes are.

In our opinion the termination phase of therapy is not a time for review, nor does the shift to this phase justify departures from therapeutic (i.e., analytic) technique. The therapist gains no license to give advice, to educate, or to instruct. He or she should analyze right to the last minute of therapy. At the end of the last interview, the therapist shakes the patient's hand and wishes her or him well. This, obviously, is not analyzing. It is, we hold, a justifiable departure from analyzing.

When the therapy comes to an end, the patient's development of ever increasing ability to deal with life problems does not cease. Rather, a process that formerly included the therapist as a physically present participant now continues without her or his presence. Now, so to speak, the patient can manage his treatment by himself or herself. (The therapist continues to be present with the patient as an internalized image.) We can consider the termination phase as in part a kind of supervised practice in self-analysis. From the time that the therapist announces that she or he believes the therapy can end soon, the patient is much aware of the coming period when she or he will be on his or her own; the therapist can then help the patient see how personal resources can be used to deal with life's challenges.

Reactions of the Patient to Termination

There *must* be reactions to termination. If the patient seems to react to the announcement of a termination date in a realistic, unemotional way, we counsel against accepting this response at face value. In the termination phase one expects an exacerbation of transference reactions, a stirring up of wishes that have not been dealt with previously.

During the termination phase one sees the last residuals of the dependence that was the core of the positive transference. When the therapist says, "You don't need this any more (this therapy, this reliance on me)," the transference neurosis is no longer in a sheltered place; the patient can no longer sustain the fantasy, "Despite everything, he or she will take care of me." Accordingly, we will see the last gasp of the infantile neurosis. There may be transitory symptoms, as Ferenczi (1928/1955a, p. 86) and Firestein (1978, p. 210) have pointed out. Firestein tells us that previously undealt with wishes may come to the fore (p. 206).

The termination period is in effect a time-setting, a proposal of the therapist to set a limit on how long the therapy will continue. Accordingly, it is likely that the patient, faced with the limited time to finish the work of therapy, will be able to work much more co-operatively with the therapist and will show much less resistance. We are reminded of Freud's tactic in the case of the Wolf-Man (Freud, 1918) of announcing to this patient "that the treatment must be brought to an end at a particular fixed date, no matter how far it had advanced" (p. 11). According to Freud, "Under the inexorable pressure of this fixed limit his resistance and his fixation to the illness gave way, and now in a disproportionately short time the analysis produced all the material which made it possible to clear up his inhibitions and remove his symptoms" (p. 11).

We know, of course, that Freud's analytic work with the Wolf-Man cannot be considered thoroughly successful, if by success one requires life-long freedom from emotional disturbance. Freud wrote in 1937, "When he left me in the midsummer of 1914, with as little suspicion as the rest of us of what lay so shortly ahead, I believed that his cure was radical and permanent. In a footnote added to this patient's case history in 1923, I have already reported that I was mistaken" (1937b, pp. 217–218). Freud went on to report a period of further analysis with Freud after the end of the war and further therapy by another analyst, Dr. Ruth Mack Brunswick. The interested reader can find out still more about this patient by reading M. Gardiner's (1971) *The Wolf-Man.* This case certainly makes clear that early childhood neuroses may have very long-lasting effects that are resistant to skilled therapeutic efforts.

Among the transference reactions provoked by the termination phase are the following: (a) reactions to separation, (b) reactions to dependence, (c) reactions to sibling rivalry, and (d) reactions to parental rejection. No doubt such issues would have appeared earlier in the patient's therapy; now they arise again. As the issues come up again, they should be reworked.

Angered at the therapist for what the patient perceives as a rejection, the patient may berate the therapist for all that the therapist *hasn't* done for her or him. The therapist who appreciates that these upbraidings derive from transference will be better able to bear up under the attack.

The work of termination continues, as Firestein (1978, p. 212) brought to our attention, after the last meeting of the patient with the therapist. Firestein pictures the patient as having internalized an image of the therapist and as working, with the help of this internalized object, toward a further resolution of life difficulties.

Countertransference Reactions to Termination

The therapist, of course, has realistically appropriate reactions to the termination of therapy. He or she wonders whether a good enough job was done and whether the patient is ready to stop. With a patient who has worked well in the therapy, the therapist naturally enough regrets not continuing to work with a person it was satisfying to work with. And the therapist may have come to like the patient. Therefore to feel some anxiety and some regret over the therapy's coming to an end is not out of place.

For the therapist to avoid other, less appropriate reactions to the termination (behave therapeutically) these things need to be done:

1. He or she should have a highly sublimated therapeutic ambition. This will allow him or her to set aside his or her own formulated goals for the therapy in favor of a sense of what the patient can accomplish in a reasonable time.
2. He should have an optimally filled appointment schedule and a short waiting-list. Too little work, and he is likely to keep the patient when the patient is ready to stop; too much work, and he is likely to push the patient out the door prematurely.
3. He should arrange his work-life so that his gratifications from his work as a therapist are essentially independent of the personality of any particular patient.
4. He should be distant in time from significant termination experiences of his own.

(Firestein [1978, pp. 233–234] made these points and discussed them more fully than we have done.)

Separation anxiety may cause the therapist to prolong the therapy or to make the ending ambiguous. She or he may introduce ambiguity by using cutting-down as a way of handling the termination phase. Such a strategy denies the definition of therapy as an exploration of psychic processes rather than a procedure for the removal of symptoms. Therefore, we say to therapists: Don't set the frequency according to the intensity of the symptoms. We advise, further, that therapists not set a follow-up date (say, 6 months later). The worth of the therapy doesn't depend on what happens 6 months after its termination. Any follow-up is an invitation to the resumption of treatment.

Perhaps the most important provocation to countertransference responses is the therapist's not wanting to let go of the patient. The therapist who is heavily invested in a patient may, faced with the prospect of termination, experience a sharp sense of loss and grief. Particularly when the therapist's own life experiences related to loss and grief have not been fully resolved, the therapist may find it very difficult to deal with this necessary separation of the patient and herself or himself.

Chapter 16

How Is Therapy of Women Different?

Feminist scholars have raised questions about the psychotherapy of women that have to be considered if we are to know whether the recommendations made in earlier chapters apply to the therapy of women as well as to the therapy of men, and if we are to know how therapy should be carried out depending on whether the patient is male or female.

Because feminist scholars—like scholars in any field—do not always agree with each other, the opinions of the feminists that we cite should not be taken as presenting the views of all, or even of a majority of, feminists. Furthermore, we want to make clear that we are not citing the views of feminists in order to contradict them. Rather, we cite these views because we want to consider them seriously; and the reader will find that we agree with many of these opinions.

Freud's views on the psychology of women changed during his lifetime. In the chapter on femininity in his *New Introductory Lectures* (1933b) he softened the distinction he had previously made between the "active" male and the "passive" female; he said, "I shall conclude that you have decided in your own minds to make 'active' coincide with 'masculine' and 'passive' with 'feminine.' But I advise you against it. It seems to me to serve no useful purpose and adds nothing to our knowledge" (p. 115). Acknowledging his incomplete understanding Freud conceded in an earlier work, ". . . after all, the sexual life of adult women is a 'dark continent' for psychology" (1926b, p. 212).

Keeping in mind these limitations to our survey of feminist and of psychoanalytic views, we will proceed.

Criticisms of Psychoanalytic Theory and Therapy

Some writers (e.g., Chesler, 1972, and Friedman, 1979) have argued that Freud altogether misunderstood the psychological functioning of women. If Freud did misunderstand the psychological functioning of women, the argument runs, a therapy that is based on Freud's theory of the psychological development of women is necessarily headed in the wrong direction and must do more harm than good.

Others (e.g., Gilligan, 1982, and Lerner, 1988) have argued that there are special issues, particular aspects of human living that apply to women and not to men, or at least apply with greater pertinence to women. The therapist, these authors say, has to have a sensitivity to these particulars.

Some, indeed, have urged that the oppression of women in our society (in all societies? in most societies? in all patriarchal societies?) is so important to the woman's psychological functioning that this oppression must always be the focus of any woman's psychotherapy. Gilbert's chapter in *Women and Psychotherapy* (Brodsky & Hare-Mustin, 1980) defines feminist therapy pretty much along these lines. Rawlings and Carter (1977) advocate a feminist therapy that incorporates the political tenents of feminism. Feminist therapy, however, can either recognize the importance of the oppression of women in our society while dealing with other issues that the woman patient may face in her life, or, if the therapist is quite single-minded, focus on this issue to the exclusion of any other problems in the patient's life.

Finally, there is the question of whether it is better for a woman to get psychotherapy from a female therapist than from a male therapist. Marecek and Johnson (1980), participating in 1979 in a conference that assessed research on psychotherapy and women, reviewed the research that showed "the influence of therapists' and clients' gender on the process of therapy; . . . the influence of sex-role stereotypes on therapists' behavior toward their clients; and . . . the incidence of sexist statements and actions by therapists during the course of therapy" (p. 67). They lamented the sparseness of research on these topics, especially the lack of research that made use of observation of real therapeutic interactions. Bernstein and Warner (1984) addressed this issue in a book called *Women Treating Women: Case Material from Women Treated by Female Psychoanalysts*. This book does not attempt to answer the question "Is it better for a woman to get psychotherapy from a female therapist?" through a systematic comparison of therapy done by women and that done by men. Instead, the book presents fascinating clinical vignettes indicating some of the issues that arise in the analysis of women by women.

Did Freud Misunderstand Women?

We acknowledge that some of Freud's beliefs about the psychological development of women were erroneous. We arrive at this conclusion both from our own clinical experience of psychotherapy with women and from reading some of the extensive writings on psychoanalysis and women. We have found the discussion of these issues in *Women and Analysis* (Strouse, 1974) particularly thorough and illuminating.

When we grant that Freud made some mistakes in his theory of the psychological development of women, we do not concede that such errors make a psychoanalytic approach to the therapy of women misguided. If one takes psychoanalysis to be a scientific discipline—and we do—then it does not make sense to require total acceptance of all of Freud's hypotheses or total rejection of them. Whereas religious doctrines require total commitment of the believer, scientific theories do not. As Hempel pointed out, scientists accept a hypothesis *tentatively* on the basis of a sufficient body of confirming evidence (Hempel, 1965, p. 42). That new evidence may cause them to change their minds, thereupon regarding the hypothesis as disconfirmed, does not shake their confidence in the methods that brought them originally to accept the hypothesis, nor does it undermine their confidence in other hypotheses.

Accordingly, we ally ourselves with the views of Chasseguet-Smirgel. After pointing out that the papers in the book she edited (1964/1970) questioned Freud's ideas, she argued that to shrink from challenging those ideas would be to succumb to complacency and sterility. Then she said: "The vitality of any doctrine depends on the possibility of rethinking certain aspects without disrupting the whole structure" (p. 3).

The Moral Development of Women

In particular, we believe that Freud was wrong in saying that women have less strongly developed superegos. Granting that there are differences within each gender group in the approach of persons to morality—a fact that is well documented by the research that Loevinger (1976) and her associates have done—there may nevertheless be something to the idea that men on the average are somewhat more rigid in their application of moral rules. It is, of course, hazardous to make sweeping assertions about men in general and women in general.

Alpert and Spencer (1986) provide a review of some of the research on the development of morality in males and females, together with an evaluation of what is known about it. Although they concede that women on average may be less strict and less consistent than men in their moral judgments, they argue that differences between the sexes in making moral judgments are mostly qualitative; that is, these differences pertain to whether the man or the woman shows concern about interest in human relations or about individual autonomy and achievement. They describe Kohlberg's theory of morality as focusing on the development of autonomous rights; something that, on average, men are more inclined to be concerned about. Kohlberg acknowledged that caring, concern, and responsibility for others has not been fully assessed by his measures of moral development. Yet it is these aspects of morality, Alpert and Spencer argue, that women emphasize more than men. Accordingly they write, Kohlberg's view that males surpass females in their moral development is a biased conclusion.

Gilligan (1982) and Gilligan, Ward, and Taylor (1988) likewise argued that the moral stance of women is different, that it is more attuned to human relationships and to human caring than to abstract justice. Some researchers, however, have taken issue with Gilligan's generalization about a difference, on average, between female and male ways of thinking about moral dilemmas. In a meta-analysis of studies of morality of men and of women, Thoma (1986) found that women scored *higher* than men on Kohlberg's scale of moral judgment. Thoma accordingly concluded that the most widely used measures of moral judgment are not biased against women, and that men are not better able to reason about hypothetical dilemmas. W. Friedman, Robinson, and Friedman (1987); Gibbs, Arnold, and Burkhart (1984); Luria (1986); and Walker (1984) also were against the view that women are different in their approach to morality.

Schafer (1974) characterized the apparently greater rigidity of men as a "compulsive" approach. He believed that any such average differences between the sexes does not justify disparaging of women as "less moral." We agree.

We urge the reader to study Schafer's superb discussion of the morality of men and women, in which he makes clear the importance of distinguishing between an adaptive morality and the superego (see Blum, 1977, pp. 333–341). Schafer's final paragraph on the subject reads: "One must conclude that Freud's estimates of women's morality and objectivity are logically and empirically indefensible. In large part these estimates implement conventional patriarchal values and judgments that have been misconstrued as being disinterested, culture-free scientific observations" (Blum, p. 341).

Thus there is a point to Gilligan's argument that a male-centered point of view led Freud and some of his followers into misguided statements about feminine psychology (Gilligan, 1982, pp. 6–7). As we reflected on these matters and as we read what others had said, we found the way that Schafer presented a critical, current assessment of Freud's views on women's morality and objectivity; on women's early, prephallic development; and on Freud's sometimes confused, often inappropriate use of terms like "passive" and "feminine" to have much validity.

Activity and Passivity

We believe that there are, as Gilligan (1982) pointed out, important differences between the personalities of men and of women. (We will have more to say later on about personality differences between males and females.) Gilligan argued that a focus on the importance of human relationships, a focus derived in women from their experiences of inequality and interconnection, helps to lead to constructive resolutions of conflict between human beings and to a valuing of justice and caring (Gilligan, 1982, pp. 62–63).

Bakan (1966) drew attention to the overall difference between women and men, in which men are often more oriented to active striving, to deal with the external, physical environment, and to do so in a way that emphasizes individuality, whereas women are often more oriented to dealing with relationships among human beings. He calls the first orientation *agentic* and the second, *communal* (Bakan, 1982, pp. 102–153).

We believe that the social training of women to be more interested in interpersonal relationships and attuned to a nurturant role is not accurately described by the word *passive*, nor is the typical male preoccupation with the world outside the family accurately described as *active*. Just a little reflection should make it clear that nurturing can be very active. Nor do we believe that the training of women to be concerned about the welfare of others (sometimes sacrificing themselves for other family members) is aptly described as *masochistic*, even though women may sometimes overdo their self-sacrifice.

Accordingly, we think it inappropriate for a therapist to urge a woman to become less assertive, when the therapist—adopting the norms of his or her culture or subculture—believes that women should be submissive. We believe that it is wrong for a therapist to take a stand on whether a woman should have a career outside the home or should devote herself entirely to the household. As should be clear from all that we have said in previous chapters, we would instead advocate that the therapist explore with the patient the inner conflicts that play a part in making it hard for her to decide this issue for herself.

Penis Envy

Feminists consider the assertion that women and girls envy men and boys because males have penises and females do not to be hardly less derogatory of women than the generalization about women's inferior morality. Feminists may misunderstand what psychoanalysts are asserting here. When the psychoanalyst says that some women *believe* or *have a fantasy that* girls and women are inferior, the psychoanalyst is not thereby asserting that women are inferior. It is the troubled patient who made this irrational judgment, not the psychoanalyst.

Some psychoanalysts, however, seemed to think that all women—not just troubled women—believed that they had been deprived of a penis (believed so unconsciously, even if they consciously repudiated this belief). Freud built his explanation of the girl's turning away from "active, masculine" strivings, her acceptance of what Freud (1933b, the chapter of "Femininity" in *New Introductory Lectures*) considered to be an appropriate "passive, feminine" position, on her confronting the shocking information that boys and men had a penis and she did not. First of all, we need to ask, whether penis envy is an inevitable and typical reaction of all girls, and second, whether such envy—when it does occur—is largely based on the basic facts of anatomy or, instead, owes most of its force to societal circumstances.

We have become aware through the research done by I. Fast and her colleagues (reported in Fast, 1984), that boys and men have dissatisfactions with their capacities and achievements, and accept the limitations of their gender with as little grace as girls and women accept the limitations of their gender. In Fast's opinion every child rails against the limitations to which he or she is subjected. The issue, says Fast, is not one of how adequate one's body is, but of what one can and cannot do. Every human being wants to accept no limits on his or her selfhood; to have to put up with such limits, as we all must do, is to suffer a narcissistic affront. For the girl, the limitations she suffers by being female rather than male can be *symbolized* through envy of the penis. Horney (1926) had argued that the boy also rails against his limitations, that he has an "envy of pregnancy, childbirth, and motherhood, as well as of the breasts and of the act of suckling" (p. 337).

T. Reik (1959) pointed out some of the consequences of a woman's unconscious conviction that she is inadequate because she is female. Horney (1926) shrewdly pointed out that male psychoanalysts see the woman's dilemma pretty much from a male point of view and are, as a result, misled. Reik seems to have had some awareness of the risks of a male point of view; delightfully, he showed how the biblical story of God's creating Adam and Eve reverses the capacities of males and females. The woman in the biblical story was created out of the man's body, whereas in reality, a boy or a girl is brought out of the woman's body.

When M. Mead (1974) commented on Freud's 1933 paper on femininity, she complained that in all cultures, "without any known exception, male activity is seen as achievement; whatever women do—gathering seeds, planting, weeding, basket-making, pot-making—is valued less than when the same activity, in some other culture, is performed by men" (pp. 99–100). She also enlarged on the point that Horney (1926) had made, that our society in placing a higher value on what males do, inflicts a narcissistic wound upon girls and women. Horney argued that the "typical motives for flight into the male role—motives whose origin is the Oedipus complex—are reinforced and supported by the actual disadvantage under which women labor in social life" (p. 337). She made the point that "we must not forget that this disadvantage is actually a piece of reality and that it is immensely greater than most women are aware of." Hence, said Horney (1974), "In actual fact a girl is exposed from birth onward to the suggestion—inevitable, whether conveyed brutally or delicately—of her inferiority, an experience that constantly stimulates her masculinity complex" (p. 338).

Bardwick (1971) argued against the central importance of penis envy. First of all, she made the point, "The availability to the boy of an external, sensitive, erotic organ makes genital sex more important to him at an earlier age" (p. 11). In a somewhat contradictory vein she then said: "Those of us who have children are quite familiar with the little girl's verbalized envy of a boy's genitals, especially a brother's" (p. 12). Drawing back from this concession, she continued, "But for normal girls this is an envy without intense affect, except insofar as a girl might be jealous of a boy for some real reason. If a little girl perceives a boy as receiving preferential treatment, especially from the parents, she may grasp the idea that the origin of this difference in privilege comes from the only perceptible physical difference between them. I believe that this allows her to make her jealousy concrete, allows her to rationalize a more general envy, and that it is less threatening to her self-esteem than questioning whether his greater privileges come because he may be more loved, or nicer, or smarter" (pp. 12–13). Finally, Bardwick offered this judgment: "Because of the less intense sexual impulses in the girl, I think it probable that penis envy in neurotic girls is less a function of sexual impulses than of aggressive impulses, with a concomitant desire for castration of the boy" (p. 13).

Here we find a sensitive, thoughtful, well-informed expert on the psychology of women expressing the view that at times penis envy is important in a girl's development, that at times it gives expression to deeper-lying conflicts, and that it surely is not so straightforward a dynamic as one would suppose from reading the early accounts of it by Freud (1905). Freud put the matter thus: "Little girls do not resort to denial of this kind [against recognizing the lack of a penis in girls and women] when they see that boys' genitals are formed differently from their own. They are ready to recognize them immediately and are overcome by envy for the penis—an envy culminating in the wish, which is so important in its consequences, to be boys themselves" (p. 195).

Despite Freud's prestige, which predisposes us to accept his views unless there is strong contrary evidence, a number of contemporary psychoanalysts have come to the conclusion that usually observation of the differences between male and female sexual anatomy is not the decisive factor in a woman's developing penis envy. According to these authors (who include Torok, 1964/1970), awareness of objective anatomical differences does not account for the idealization of male genitals, and the absence of a body part—namely, the penis—does not in itself produce pathological envy or self-depreciation. Torok holds this view even though she recognizes that many female patients attribute their sense of deficiency to their lack of male genitals.

The underlying conflicts that find expression in an envy of the penis and of the male role include narcissistic injuries, deprivations of love, and provocations to envy. Grossman and Stewart (1977) pointed out that such underlying conflicts could find *metaphoric expression* in penis envy. According to these authors, the discovery of differences between the male and the female genitals is only one among many possible experiences of deprivation, all of which would lead to feelings of deprivation and self-disparagement.

Lerner (1980) reported that in her experience as a clinician, the woman who devalues femininity and desires a penis usually does so because of a disturbed relationship with her mother:

> The female child may desire a penis in order to better express her hatred toward her mother, or as a means of possessing the envied omnipotent mother and her magical attributes, or as a means of extricating herself from a dependent and frustrating relationship with mother—that is, as a desperate attempt at separation and differentiation. Penis envy may be an expression of a revolt against the narcissistic wounds inflicted by the omnipotent mother or may be the girl's attempt to protect a jealous, intrusive, maternal imago by making an unconscious "oath of fidelity" to the mother that she (the daughter) will not achieve genital fulfillment (Chasseguet-Smirgel, 1970; Torok, 1970; & Lerner, 1977). (pp. 49–50)

Lerner also pointed out that when a girl experiences her mother as dominant and controlling; as destructive, castrating, and bad, the girl may try to avoid being like her by imagining herself to be weak, powerless, and "castrated."

In the paper by Torok (1964/1970) that Lerner cites so frequently, Torok shows in a most impressive way how the little girl who had a domineering, intrusive mother, a mother who tried to meet her own needs through keeping her daughter for herself, would produce a child who felt compelled to give up her genital strivings and her basic womanliness. Such a girl would imagine that a man's penis gives power and would idealize that penis; what she could not do is accept a mutual giving with a man, that would allow both of them pleasure and mature functioning. Such a girl would renounce sexual maturity and pleasure. Her fantasy that a man's penis gives him everything serves a defensive function. It spares her from the temptation to turn away from her mother; the girl fears that the price of separating herself from her mother will be her mother's abandonment and her own annihilation.

It can be seen that in Torok's view, penis envy develops out of a distorted object-relationship with the girl's mother. It turns on the issues of control versus autonomy, separation, and the girl's movement toward a mature sexuality. And, Torok writes, the boy is faced with similar conflicts when he has a controlling mother whom he is afraid to declare his independence from, and a father whom he is afraid of challenging by asserting his own genital desires. Within this framework, the boy will defensively construct the fantasy that a woman is an inferior creature, ready to be subjugated. In this way the boy, out of his own fear of a mature sexuality, adopts what Torok (1964/1970) called "this phallo-centric prejudice, old as humanity itself" (p. 170).

Clitoral and Vaginal Orgasms

Finally, we take up the points that Sherfey (1972) emphasized. In the first chapter of her book, Sherfey disputes Freud's (1905, pp. 220–221) argument that the girl in her sexual development first experiences excitement and pleasure through the clitoris but later experiences excitement and pleasure vaginally. As Sherfey (1972) put it, "One of Freud's most useful, accepted, and enduring concepts is his theory of female psychosexual growth with its basic assumption that the female is endowed with two independent erotogenic centers; during development she must transfer the infantile erotogenic zone of the clitoris to the mature erotogenic zone of the vagina" (p. 21). Sherfey argued that the research of Masters and Johnson (1966) demonstrated a similar physiological response during clitoral masturbation and during coitus. Accordingly, Sherfey wrote, there is just one kind of orgasm and that orgasm always derives from stimulation of the clitoris. It would make no sense then to suppose that women who did not have a "vaginal orgasm" (which could not exist, Sherfey argued, because all orgasms were the same) were flawed or backward in their psychosexual development.

Moore (1977) in his chapter in Blum's book, concedes that "Sherfey establishes fairly convincingly her thesis that vaginal orgasm as distinct from clitoral orgasm does not exist *physiologically*" (p. 309). But, Moore argues, ". . . her statement that 'These findings force us to the conclusion that *there is no such thing as psychopathological clitoral fixation; there are only varying degrees of vaginal insensitivity and coital frigidity*' (p. 101) is not consistent with her own admission that 'clitoral fixation very obviously can, and very often does, interfere with vaginal functioning' (p. 42)" (p. 310).

So, Moore continues, "The crux of the matter seems to be the issue of physical versus psychic satisfaction. As in the case of her objections to the role of bisexuality in female sexuality. . . so also in regard to clitoral and vaginal erotogeneity, Sherfey overlooks the truth that the anatomical and physiological facts, though important, are of less consequence clinically than their psychic representation. Hysterical anesthesias do not conform to the anatomical distribution of nerves but to the patients' erroneous concepts of the body. Distortions of previously learned anatomical facts about the genitals are frequently observed in analytic practice, and the facts Sherfey marshals have been, she says, previously unknown, or in some instances curiously ignored or neglected even by biologists. Could more be expected of patients?" (p. 310)

Piskorz de Zimerman (1983) argued that some psychoanalysts, believing that a woman should enjoy a vaginal orgasm, psychologically damage their female patients. In the next section of the chapter we will comment on this issue.

How Should We Deal With the Inadequacies of Freud's Theory?

In the light of what we said about accepting scientific hypotheses when there is evidence for them and abandoning them when there is evidence against them, we have no choice but to give up Freud's view that women are deficient in their superego development. We must be careful, also, to distinguish between those receptive and nurturant attitudes that in most cultures are more prominent in women than in men, and the masochistic attitudes that Freud (in some of his statements) attributed to women generally. Although some women and some men are masochistic—they may express this through self-defeating actions—we see no reason to think of masochism as a naturally feminine trait. It may be that in our society girls are taught, more than boys, to sacrifice themselves for others, and to do so even when it doesn't make any sense. If, as a result of such training, women are more self-sacrificing, we believe it does not contribute to our understanding of this result to call it masochism.

Friedman (1977) in defending psychoanalysts against the charge that they try to make women submissive and discourage autonomy, offered several detailed case examples of interpretive treatment of women's excessive passivity. We recommend that the reader emulate his example: Every human being, both male and female, should be helped to overcome excessive passivity.

Freud's formulation of the penis envy hypothesis presents a more complex problem than his formulation of the "weaker superego" and "masochism" hypotheses, because he captured in this hypothesis a bundle of fantasies that play an important role in the girl's psychological development. From the partial knowledge that we now have (partial because relatively little research has been done on how boys and girls think about their bodies and on what impact this has on their psychological development), we judge that for many women, penis envy is not strong enough to play a decisive role in their adaptation. We believe that where penis envy is intense it bespeaks a pathological development, as Grossman and Stewart (1977, in Blum's book) argued. Penis envy, these authors believe, symbolizes the woman's dissatisfaction with herself; exactly what she is dissatisfied with and why remain to be discovered and cannot be taken for granted.

As for the impact of the mistaken belief that women develop a capacity for a vaginal orgasm (i.e., for the arousal leading to orgasm that depends on stimulation of the vagina) and outgrow a clitoral orgasm, we believe that what matters in the woman's psychological development has to do with her fantasies about sexuality and with her mental representations of her sexual anatomy, her sexual activity, and her sexual relationships. In our view, what matters about the woman's psychosexual development has little to do with the facts of sexual physiology and sexual anatomy.

We believe that it would be a mistake to browbeat a woman patient because she feels pleasurable sensations that she attributes to her clitoris, and yet does not have any pleasurable sensations that she attributes to her vagina. The therapist who takes fantasies and mental representations as seriously as we think he or she should, would focus on these issues: Does this woman believe that she can use her vagina as a part of providing pleasure to herself? When she has feelings of love for a man, does it give her satisfaction to have coitus? In having sexual intercourse, does she think of her vagina as a valuable part of herself?

If she disparages her genitals (unconsciously derogating herself as inferior because she is female), we believe that this self-disparagement deserves analysis. The reader can appreciate, however, that overcoming this self-disparagement has nothing to do with a focus on the sexual anatomy as an objective fact; it is the person's fantasies about the anatomy that have to be dealt with.

What Special Problems Do Women Have?

We believe that psychotherapists need to be aware of (a) the different character structures of female and male human beings, (b) the different role demands placed on females and males, and (c) the different problems that are typical of females as compared to males. Gilligan (1982) pointed out that women are typically more concerned with relationships among human beings and are more disposed to be nurturant of others. Murdock (1949, pp. 7–8) argued that the division of labor by sex had adaptive advantages for the societies that adopted such divisions. Such role prescriptions would be expected to lead to normative personality patterns for the two sexes. Erikson (1968) made a similar point when he spoke of "what [women] have always stood for privately in evolution and in history (realism of householding, responsibility of upbringing, resourcefulness in peacekeeping, and devotion to healing) . . ." (p. 262).

Terman and Miles (1936) had already shown that men and women differ markedly in their interests: men on the average are more interested in competition, aggression, business pursuits, and science and engineering; women are generally more interested in human interactions. Even today, the sexes differ along these lines in their preferences for television programs and for reading materials (in books and magazines).[1]

What implications do such sex differences in personality have for psychotherapy? These differences mean, at the very least, that a male therapist has to make a special effort to experience a female patient's living, just as the female therapist has to do in order to experience a male patient's living.

Besides the bare fact of a difference between the personality structure of males and females, there is the issue of the injustices visited on women by our society, out of its "phallo-centric prejudice," as Torok put it. The male therapist may well be inclined to discount the impact of these injustices. If he fails to give due weight to them, the female patient will have good reason to believe that he does not understand her and her life.

Accordingly, we recommend to therapists that they apply to their work with women the advice that Grier and Cobbs (1968) gave to therapists about work with Black patients, adapting that advice as needed to the circumstances of the wrongs done to women. In their chapter, "Mental Illness and Treatment," Grier and Cobbs provide a superb discussion of how the therapist needs to combine an understanding of the cultural conditions that shape a person's life and provide a framework within which that person must adapt, and of the inner conflicts that the person is struggling with. They wrote:

> Fundamentally one wonders why there should be anything singular about a Negro's mental troubles. We would like to answer that right away. There is nothing reported in the literature or in the experience of any clinician known to the authors that suggests that black people *function* differently psychologically from anyone else. Black men's mental functioning is governed by the same *rules* as that of any other

---

[1]Basow (1986) provides a fairly comprehensive review of gender differences in personality (see especially pp. 61–73 of her book). The classic review of sex differences is, of course, the work by Maccoby and Jacklin (1974). In recognizing that there are differences between men and women in their interests, we make no assertion about the origin of these differences, nor are we discussing whether such differences can be changed; we are simply pointing out some ways in which men and women, on the average, are different.

group of men. Psychological principles understood first in the study of white men are true no matter what the man's color. . . .

In sum, let us enter a plea for *clinical* clinicians who can distinguish unconscious depression from conscious despair, paranoia from adaptive wariness, and can tell the difference between a sick man and a sick nation. (pp. 154, 157–158)

They recommended that the therapist first take account of the realistic conditions of the patient's life, acknowledge these to the patient, and, having taken account of this reality, then forcefully show what remains to be explained as a personal characteristic, a result of the patient's conflicted inner life. They gave an affecting example of therapeutic work with a troubled Black woman who had paranoid symptoms, Miss Y. This woman was first seen during an acute psychotic episode. Describing the therapeutic work, Grier and Cobbs wrote:

> . . . She felt on one occasion that she (the only black person at her rather high level) was being discriminated against and being denied a promotion simply because she was black. When asked for specific evidence of this, she said that other workers less skillful than she and with shorter tenure on the job were being promoted while she remained at the same job. . . . The therapist agreed with her on the general prevalence of racial prejudice in work situations and added that it seemed more of a problem at higher job levels. She was asked about other evidence of racial discrimination and what remedies if any were available to employees. . . . As other examples of prejudice she recalled a co-worker who had been very friendly but who lately was cool and disinclined even to speak to her.
>
> . . . Such examples prompted the therapist to raise the question of her illness. She had, after all, behaved rather strangely at work on more than one occasion and her co-workers knew that she had been hospitalized for her emotional ailments. Could it be that they were afraid of her because of her symptoms?
>
> She thought for a long while and then burst into laughter. "Those bastards are not too well put together themselves! I'd probably scare the hell out of them if I said 'Boo!' And they must be really tied up in knots over what to do with this crazy nigger woman who's got such a big job!"
>
> She laughed herself breathless, and as she wiped away the tears the therapist felt tears start in his own eyes, but from a more solemn source than the tears of the laughing woman who needed to be laughed with but who needed also to be wept for. (pp. 159–160)[2]

Grier and Cobbs went on to comment, "This unhappy woman had to deal not only with the prejudices of her co-workers toward the mentally ill and toward women but with the additional factor of her being black as well. She had to separate her own pathological suspicions from the reactions of fellow workers, which were troublesome enough but, as she observed, also compounded by her being a 'crazy nigger' " (pp. 159–160).

---

[2]From *Black Rage*, by William H. Grier and Price M. Cobbs. Copyright 1968 by William H. Grier and Price M. Cobbs. Reprinted by permission of Basic Books, Inc., New York.

We believe that the strategy advised by Grier and Cobbs can and should be adapted to the situation of women, who suffer injustices because they are women. Dr. Sandra Pyke of York University in North York, Ontario, expressed a similar viewpoint in a lecture she gave at the University of Windsor (Pyke, 1984). She made the point that the woman who has suffered injustice cannot confront her own inner conflicts until she, and the therapist, have acknowledged the real injustices.

Should Every Therapy Focus on Oppression?

The reader who has carefully followed our argument to this point knows that we would not advocate that every therapy of a woman should focus on the oppression of women in our society. Nevertheless, we will spell out how we arrived at that conclusion.

First of all, psychotherapy according to psychoanalytic principles deals with what is important for the patient, for *this* patient at *this* time. The therapist attends to what the patient brings forward; he or she attempts to stay with the current flow of material and with what is preconscious or about to become preconscious. The therapist cannot be doctrinaire about what kind of material that might be. If he or she is doctrinaire, insisting on dealing with some particular material that the therapist believes to be important, the therapeutic situation is turned into one in which the therapist exercises authority over an obedient patient. Patients, male and female alike, are already too familiar with other human beings who deal with them in an authoritarian way; there is no advantage in the therapist's doing so, even in the name of "freeing her from oppression."

Second, the psychoanalytic therapist wants to deal with the patient's living as he or she experiences it, focusing on the inner life, on conflict, and to avoid doing anything to strengthen the patient's tendency to divert her (and the therapist's) attention from inner life to external events. The general trend of the therapy is from the external framework of the patient's life to the inner experience (see, for example, Dollard, Auld, & White, 1953). The therapist and the patient will misunderstand the psychodynamic processes if they attribute the problem solely to externals, just as Freud misunderstood the development of neurosis in his patients when he held to the seduction theory (see Gay, 1988, pp. 90–96).

Nevertheless, we insist on the importance of culture in defining the world in which the person lives and creating the ground in which neurosis grows. Kovel (1976) stated the matter eloquently:

> ... neurosis springs not from some mysterious estrangement from nature, nor from "immortal ambivalence," nor from suppression of mystification in the family, nor from somatic constitution, but rather from the total societal organization—in this case, advanced capitalism—as it imposes contradictions upon *all* the forms of personal life.
>
> So long as we have a dominative society with division of labor, alienation and class distinction, its splits will devolve into family life and, given the natural susceptibility of human infants, will produce neurotic characters of one kind or another.... (p. 251)

Even though the ultimate causes of neurosis are social, Kovel argued that the therapist has to deal with proximal causes. He wrote, "What the radical therapists forgot in their analysis was the distinction between the ultimate cause of a phenomenon such as neurosis and its actual manifestation. The harsh truth is that once neurotic repression sets in, whether at the behest of a repressive parent or by the alienated child's own effort to stem his feeling of inner chaos, the ensuing neurotic structure takes on a life of its own, becomes invisible. . . . Thus radical therapists—whether they be feminists, gay liberationists or straight Marxists—who fancy that a direct appeal to visible oppression will unsnarl the inner invisible twisting are simply tilting at windmills" (pp. 252–253).

Accordingly, we urge the therapist to take account of the patient's realistic life situation, to acknowledge it, but to involve herself or himself in a therapy that exposes the patient's inner life. Such a therapy, as Kovel pointed out, can bring about a helpful change in the patient's life, even if it cannot bring heaven on earth.

Should Women Treat Women?

There is, to the best of our knowledge, no definitive research to tell us whether women do better, on average, as therapists of women than men do. In Shafter's (1988) opinion, research studies have provided no evidence that male or female therapists are more likely to produce a successful therapeutic outcome. We do not mean to suggest that little has been written on this subject; the interested reader is invited to consult papers by Cavenar and Werman (1983); Felton (1986); Fenton, Robinowitz, and Leaf (1987); Goz (1973); Jones, Krupnick, and Kerig (1987); Jones and Zoppel (1982); Kaplan (1985); Kirshner, Genack, and Hauser (1978); Kulish (1984, 1986); Orlinsky and Howard (1976); Schover (1981); Shainess (1983); and Tanney and Birk (1976). Because most of these papers rely on case material rather than on systematic study of the gender variable, we believe Shafter's opinion to be correct.

Schachtel (1986) pointed out important ways in which sex roles influence the interaction between patient and therapist; but she did not offer any sweeping recommendation about whether a male or a female therapist is to be preferred. Kaplan (1979) discussed some issues affecting the therapeutic relationship that stem from the gender roles of the therapist and the patient. Lerner (1988), after listing seven purported advantages of having a female therapist for a female patient, qualified her recommendation in this way: "As is true of all generalizations, those stated here tell us nothing about the advantages or disadvantages of a particular therapist or the unique needs of an individual patient. Surely, being male does not condemn one to tunnel vision or to a rigid and unexamined adherence to patriarchal attitudes. . . ." (p. 139).

From the work of Kulish (1989) we now know that some experienced female psychoanalysts are persuaded that the analyst's gender does have an impact on the transference, especially on the sequence in which material emerges in the therapy. She pointed out, ". . . it is striking how frequently the idea of countertransference turned up" in the conversations that she had with the 17 senior female analysts whom she interviewed (p. 70). Kulish continued, "What seemed to filter through the wide variety of responses was the idea of a gender-related perceptual biasing, a sort of 'cognitive set.' Gender may serve as a basic, unconscious organizing factor around which clinical material is experienced, processed, understood, and interpreted. This processing would, in turn, interact with and influence the patient's experience of the transference, so that the various factors contributing to the final amalgam would be very difficult to decipher" (p. 70). We recommend Kulish's paper as a thoughtful survey of these issues (see also Kulish & Mayman, 1989).

Raphling and Chused (1988) believed that at times the gender of the analyst could be used as an organizer of and resistance to certain transference manifestations. They discussed the factors that contribute to the availability for analysis of cross-gender transference, and the obstacles to this analysis.

On the topic of countertransference, we want to cite Ruderman's (1986) discussion of how women therapists use their emotional reactions to their female patients, often in creative and restorative ways, in their therapy of these patients. Although Ruderman writes of countertransference, she intends much more than the unconsciously determined reactions to the patient; she wants to consider the therapist's realistic reactions to the patient as well. In her research on the feelings of analytic therapists to their patients, Ruderman identified five themes: the therapist's relationship with her or his mother, fear of success, role conflicts, envy in the countertransference, and the therapist's life stage.

The first three of these themes we take to be examples of the shared life-experience of a female therapist with a female patient, a sharing that is likely to facilitate the therapist's empathy with and understanding of the patient. Of the fourth theme Ruderman wrote, "Envy in the countertransference was associated with the reactivation in the therapist of dependency wishes, conflicts about autonomy, and mourning for lost or absent opportunities for gratification in her past life. Envy has its productive and constructive elements; if resolved, it leads to admiration and awe. It can also lead naturally to a process of mourning . . . for what was, what was not, and what can never be . . ." (p. 355).

In discussing the fifth theme, Ruderman remarked that the therapist's life stage—most of the therapists she studied were in midlife—had a strong effect. One therapist, for instance, "described her intense inner responses to her patient's youthful and flowering life," realizing that "the abundant options now available to her woman patient" had not been available to her when she had been young (p. 357). Another therapist, who in her own life now felt a particular need for the support of her family and friends, stressed to one of her patients "the importance of relationships and family ties" (p. 358). Ruderman concluded: "Finally, the female therapists in this study, and perhaps women in general, resonate in a particular way with each other. They have much to share, and many steps to climb together" (p. 360).

We need to be alert to the possibility that a male therapist can lack an appreciation of the circumstances of a woman's life, can moreover be a prisoner of the phallo-centric assumptions of our society. Sesan (1988), making use of questionnaire data, reported that the majority of the 192 former clients of 49 psychotherapists believed that they had been treated in a sex-fair manner. According to Sesan, women with the least formal education and women who had children experienced more sexual bias than other women. She found bias "in the areas of fostering traditional roles, lack of acceptance of anger, and lack of a sociocultural context in the therapy" (p. 107).

What Effect Does the Gender of the Therapist Have?

Some psychoanalytic writers believe that the gender of the therapist does not matter. These writers argue that transferences to both mother and father are elicited by either a male or a female therapist. They concede that the order in which transferences will be experienced and expressed may differ, depending on the sex of the therapist; nevertheless they insist that in due time all the transferences will appear. Blum (1977) and Zetzel (1970) write that, in their experience, oedipal transferences always adapt to the gender of the analyst. Karme (1979) says that the preoedipal transferences occur whether the therapist is female or male. She believes that female therapists rarely experience father transferences, whereas male analysts regularly experience preoedipal mother transferences. Galenson (1986) argues that transference elements of all types can be fully explored no matter what the sex of the therapist.

We ourselves are not so sure about this. We would like to see systematically gathered, empirical evidence. Until we have that kind of evidence, we will refrain from reaching any firm conclusion about whether it matters if the therapist is male or female, and how it matters. We only know that women have often done very well as the patients of male therapists, probing deeply into conflicts that touch on their gender identity; and that men have often done very well as patients of female therapists, doing the same type of probing.

Moldawsky (1986) has, in our opinion, made an important contribution to our understanding of how the gender of the therapist matters. First he quotes Mogul (1982), who after surveying more than 80 articles about the gender of the therapist concluded that the sex of the therapist matters most in face-to-face therapies that are less intensive. Presumably such therapies would emphasize the real relationship of patient and therapist more, and the transference less.

Moldawsky then quotes Person (1983), who suggested four conscious reasons for women's choice of female analysts: (a) fear of sexism from a male analyst; (b) avoidance of "faking it," that is, of feeling subject to the need to please a man; (c) fear of erotic transference and countertransference; and (d) a wish for a role model. In discussing these points, Moldawsky makes clear that the first three issues can be handled appropriately when the female patient has a male analyst if the male analyst refrains from sexist attitudes and the female patient gradually overcomes her wish to ingratiate herself to a male and her conflicting feelings in an erotic transference.

Moldawsky (1986) then proceeds to give telling examples of the preoedipal transferences that he has observed in women patients. He points out that the therapist's nonintrusive, nonjudgmental, and interested stance provides a strong provocation to the development of a preoedipal transference. He says, "Nowhere is there a more consistent nurturant atmosphere than in analysis. Hour after hour, the analyst sets aside his or her own interests and needs and devotes attention to the patient" (p. 294).

In conclusion, Moldawsky asks, "Can the female patient have the same living through experience in a preoedipal transference with a male analyst as when she is seeing a female analyst?" He answers, "I am convinced that the male analyst can help a female patient live through a preoedipal mother transference. I do not know, however, whether it is *experienced* in the same way when both members of the dyad are female. Gender should make a difference. . . . certain feelings will be facilitated with an analyst of one gender but . . . over the long term, all the conflicts will be experienced in the analytic relationship with an analyst of either sex. However, all the *feelings* may not necessarily be 'lived through.' The question for research, then, is whether or not this makes any difference" (p. 302).

Conclusion

Having reviewed some of the literature on psychoanalysis and women, and having reflected on our own experiences in doing therapy with women, we came to several judgments that may be summarized as follows:

1. Freud was mistaken in believing that the consciences of females are less well developed than the consciences of males. Although this judgment disparages women, the damage that this erroneous belief does to the therapy may sometimes be less than one would suppose.

    We draw this conclusion because we believe that no therapist is completely free of biases; no one is perfect. Yet that does not prevent therapists from doing effective work much of the time. To draw an example from Freud's therapeutic work: Even though his belief that the superego of a woman is less well developed than that of a man surely disparages women, he often admired women and valued them highly. He must have had admiration for his patient H. Doolittle (his letters to her that she reprints in her book, *Tribute to Freud*, seem to show this), for she would not have put up with condescension. Ms. Doolittle did in fact develop a strong working alliance in her therapy with Freud, as well as a personal friendship. (See her book [listed as written by "H. D.," 1956] and Friedman, 1987.) Thus we believe that it is a matter to be decided empirically: Does the therapist's misguided belief-system hinder work with the patient?

2. Freud was wrong in believing that women are more passive and more masochistic. We think that believing that passivity is natural for women may be mischievous, leading a therapist to suppose that women should refrain from appropriate self-assertion. We think that believing that women are naturally masochistic may lead a therapist to suppose that a woman has sought suffering and likes it, in the absence of any solid evidence that this is in fact so. We believe that some women, at some times, bring suffering on themselves, just as some men, at some times, do. In our opinion one should insist on evidence for such a judgment in the case at hand before accepting it.

3. There is such a thing as penis envy, and some women suffer from it. Where the intensity of penis envy leads a woman to be excessively competitive with men, and where that overcompetitiveness and hostility prevents her from achieving the loving relationship with a man that *she* wants, penis envy is indeed a problem that psychotherapy should address.

On the other hand, it has not been our experience that the majority of women—even of women who are patients—are so competitive with and hostile toward men that it interferes substantially with their relationships with men. Because we believe in looking for evidence for any characteristic before attributing that characteristic to a patient, we think it damaging to good therapy to assume automatically that every women suffers from penis envy.

4. There are many problems of living that have a special twist in the life of a woman. It should be a great advantage for any therapist, male or female, to develop a deep appreciation of the special problems that women face. Furthermore, the therapist would be well advised always to concede the realistic problems in the patient's life and then ask, "What more is there to your problem, after we've taken this into account?"

5. We do not know fully the impact of having a therapist of one gender or the other. We believe that no one is now able to give a confident answer about what difference the gender of the therapist makes. There is preliminary evidence that the therapist's gender has an impact on the readiness of the patient to express oedipal transference feelings; accordingly, this expression may come somewhat earlier or later depending on the therapist's gender. There is also preliminary evidence that preoedipal transferences will develop regardless of the therapist's gender. We acknowledge that the female therapist can serve as a model for her female patient; this may be an advantage.

We believe that when a male therapist falls into prejudices against women, allowing these to hinder his handling of the therapy, his mistaken behavior should be labeled countertransference. It is equally an instance of countertransference when a female therapist consciously or unconsciously allies herself with her female patient's complaints about bigotry based on gender and, responding to these complaints, sympathizes with her rather than analyzing these verbalizations or considering them a part of the patient's free associations. (What we said in chapter 6 about countertransference gives our recommendations about how to avoid such mistakes.)

The therapist, however, need not fall into such mistakes. When a female therapist encounters a female patient who holds forth at length about the injustices she endures as a woman, seeking to enlist the therapist as an ally in the patient's war against men—and when the therapist would not be wrong to consider this ploy of her patient to be a defensive maneuver, concealing from her patient and from the therapist an underlying conflict—then the therapist must resist the all-too-human tendency to join in with her patient in the struggle against men. The therapist's own unresolved feelings about the injustices that society has imposed on women may make it difficult for her to resist the patient's provocation.

In similar fashion, when a male therapist faces a provocative female patient who tries unconsciously to provoke a combative, antifeminist response, the therapist is well advised to keep his composure. We recall how a colleague, whose first name (Carroll) left some doubt to anyone who had only heard his name whether he was male or female, handled such provocation. When his patient, a 33-year-old woman, encountered him for the first therapy session, she exclaimed, "Oh, you're a man! I'd wanted a woman therapist. Male therapists can't really understand a woman's life."

The therapist inquired what experiences had led the patient to assume that a male therapist would lack understanding. He accepted this woman's current experience of mistrust as a real and troubling experience (not to be discounted or argued away) and took it as material for analytic understanding. His patient did agree (without coercion) to try to work with the therapist, and as it turned out, they developed a good working relationship. This patient's therapy was helpful to her, despite her initial belief that a man could not possibly understand her.

As we said in the chapter on personal responses of the therapist (chapter 9), we do not view all of the responses of the therapist to the patient as countertransference. Thus in our view it is not inevitable that the gender of the therapist will adversely affect the therapeutic process, any more or any less than it would be inevitable that other attributes of the therapist would do so. All responsible therapists will be alert for indications that the therapist's gender is having an impact on the therapeutic process and will take steps to analyze his or her reactions that give such evidence, as a means to understanding himself or herself, and the patient, more fully. Just because it is *possible* that gender may become a significant issue in the therapy, one is not justified in assuming that gender will always be an issue (and that special measures have to be taken to deal with it).

Thus the answer to the question, "Is the therapy of women different?" is yes and no. Surely the woman patient has some problems that are unique to females. She may at times feel more comfortable with a female therapist (but whether this will enable her to deal with her problems more quickly and more effectively is uncertain). And, most important, the principles of psychoanalytic therapy apply equally to females and to males.

Chapter 17

Some Controversies in Psychodynamic Psychotherapy

Freud's Conflict Model

Freud's Structural Model

Ego Psychology

Object-Relations Theory

Self Psychology

Conclusions

When the Conflict Model Falls Short
Dogmatism Is Unbecoming
The Impact of Values on Therapeutic
Strategy

17

Psychodynamic theories of human function have undergone many evolutionary (and a few revolutionary) changes in the decades since psychodynamic thinking first appeared. Along with these changes in the theory of human function have come changes in both the theory and the technique of therapy. It is useful for the psychodynamic therapist to be aware of these changes.

To the extent that one's practices now derive from earlier ideas and the techniques that implemented them, comparing these earlier ideas with current views will help one to gain a greater understanding of one's practices. To aid the reader to make such a comparison, in this chapter we will give a broad summary of historical developments in psychodynamic theory and therapy and will comment on the implications that these developments have for practice.

Among the questions raised by current controversies are these:

1. Is human behavior, pathological or otherwise, best understood as the result of intrapsychic conflict and conflict-resolution, or as the result of developmental arrest or of deficit?
2. Is the essential curative element in psychodynamic therapy interpretation, or is it attachment?
3. Are psychodynamic processes the consequence of early developed fantasies that have been repressed, or do they stem from traumatic real events that occurred during one's formative years?
4. Do persons give themselves neuroses, or should blame be placed at the doorstep of their parents?
5. Does the human organism function to achieve (psychically or otherwise) instinctual drive satisfaction, or to achieve a relationship with another person (called, technically, an "object")?
6. How is transference best conceptualized: as a repetition of archaic events from the patient's history, with the therapist experienced as an archaic object, or as a reenactment of infantile fantasies about oneself and others?
7. Is the therapeutic alliance (as written about by Greenson [1967], Zetzel [1953, 1963], and others) best understood as a form of transference manifestation (Brenner, 1976, 1982) or are the therapeutic alliance and the real relationship in the therapy entities that are separate from and different from transference?
8. Is countertransference (Racker, 1953) merely the unwanted and undesired intrusion of the therapist's unconscious conflicts into the therapy situation, or is it the therapeutically useful application of the therapist's unconscious functioning to the treatment of the patient and to the understanding of the patient's unconscious processes?

9. To what degree do the situational attributes of psychodynamic treatment (e.g., length and frequency of treatment) in fact define the therapy as psychoanalytic or not?

Freud's Conflict Model

As we consider these questions, we notice reverberations from the positions of various theorists in the history of psychoanalytic thought. We begin our review by considering one of S. Freud's earliest conceptualizations, presented in his paper on the neuropsychoses of defense (1894) and in *The Interpretation of Dreams* (1900) (see also N. Mackay's *Motivation and Explanation*, 1989, especially pp. 35–83).

Using a military metaphor, Freud posited that both the psychopathology of everyday life and the dynamics of the clinical situation were the result of conflict between drives or instinctual forces (sexual in nature) seeking expression in behavior and consciousness and opposing forces of defense (repression) that were seeking to maintain the exclusion of the instincts from consciousness. [In the Standard Edition of Freud's psychological works, Strachey has translated the German *Trieb* as "instinct." As Bettelheim (1984, pp. 103–107) pointed out, not only would "drive" be a better translation, it would also avoid the misunderstanding that Freud meant "instinct" in the sense of the instincts that guide the behavior of animals. Thus, for "instinctual forces" the reader should understand "drives."]

In general, Freud's conception was that the aims of the instinctual arousals were attached to *objects* (or, one should say, *object representations*, rather than actual persons or things), with which the instinctual aims could be satisfied. Thus fetishes were objects, parts of the anatomy were objects, and experiences of other persons at particular times were objects (e.g., the seductive mother, the threatening father).

In this early conceptualization, the person had to keep himself or herself from giving expression to the wishes, and carrying out the instinctual aims, because these wishes were closely connected with unpleasure. The person expected an unmanageable excitement or disapproval from his or her conscience or from other persons. Denied direct expression, these wishes found indirect, derivative expression in the form of symptoms, dreams, and other psychopathological formations. These expressions were, accordingly, *compromises* between the conflicted, expressive forces and repressive forces.

Because the compromises were the product of the person's infantile mental life, when they found continued expression through pathological thoughts, feelings, and actions, it seemed reasonable to hypothesize a compulsion to repeat (Freud, 1914b, p. 150). The patient recreated the archaic conflict in his or her later life situation, hoping *this time* to make the conflict come out different. We see that the concept of a repetition-compulsion provides an explanation for the appearance in therapy of reactions imported from the patient's past mental life (i.e., for transference).

The repeating in therapy of the earlier experiences, Freud believed, facilitated the interpretation of unconscious conflict because the conflict came to be represented (through derivatives) in the here-and-now. Freud's technical recommendations advising the therapist to remain neutral, to abstain from providing gratifications, and to keep anonymous and ambiguous all derived their justification from the argument that the transference could best be discerned and interpreted if the therapist did nothing that prompted the reactions of the patient in the therapy.

The conflicts about which we have been writing are deemed to be unconscious. Accordingly, Freud believed that treatment of the pathological conditions would consist primarily of making the unconscious conscious. Besides aiding the patient in recovering the unconscious contents, the therapist could use the authority attributed to him or her by the patient to exert a moral persuasion toward the abandonment of the archaic aims. The therapist would label any refusal to give up these aims as resistance. Finally, the therapist showed an attitude of curiosity rather than condemnation while observing the patient's behavior and experience. This attitude constituted a model that the patient could adopt, replacing the judgmental, disapproving attitude that had originally led to the repression of the instinctual aims. Thus treatment both provided insight into the unconscious conflict and helped the patient to become morally more objective toward unconscious intentions.

In this conceptualization of mental function, derivatives of unconscious processes find their way into consciousness; as the patient talks in the therapy, they constitute the substance of the therapeutic process. It follows that these derivatives arise in the course of therapy as a result of the processes of association. The patient unwittingly tells about his or her unconscious by producing these conscious derivatives that are associatively linked with the unconscious elements. Accordingly, *free association is the primary method (perhaps the only one) by which the therapist and the patient gain access to unconscious conflict.* Thus free association becomes the defining element of psychoanalytic therapy.

Freud's Structural Model

In later conceptualizations in which he proposed the three structures of the mind (ego, id, and superego), Freud replaced the emphasis on conscious versus unconscious and on the conflict between instinctual aims and repressive forces with explanations based on the structures. He conceived conflict as raging between these major structures (and the functions that these structures made use of). He saw the id as a repository of instinctual tendencies (which may have been phylogenetically given). These tendencies were thought to be chaotic, unorganized, and unmanaged. Freud thought of the ego not only as an experience of the self, but mainly as a collection of functions that manage the forces of the id in order to allow gratification of them or to control and regulate them. He also believed the ego to be an executive structure that implemented the necessary prohibitions and restraints that are imposed by the person's morality and conscience. (Later, he split off this aspect of ego function and called it "superego.") He thought of the ego as mediating between organism and environment: it receives stimuli from outside and then expresses the organism's intentions within the constraints of physical and social reality. The third structure in this tripartite theory, the superego, was seen as an overseer of the ego, judging both its functions and the person himself or herself. These judgments had a moral and evaluative cast. The superego expressed these judgments by evoking shame and guilt.

The structural hypothesis (as the formulation we have just presented is called) led to a somewhat different understanding of the therapeutic process. Freud summed up the therapeutic goal by saying, "Where id was, there ego shall be" (Freud, 1933a, p. 80). This goal replaced his previous one: to make the unconscious conscious. With this change in formulation, the therapeutic emphasis shifted to enabling the patient to exercise control over personal impulses, enabling him or her to give up perceiving the self as the helpless victim of psychopathology and to view himself or herself instead as master of his or her desires and achiever of appropriate gratifications within the bounds of reality, propriety, and morality. The therapeutic process could be thought of as involving the replacement of the harsh, punitive superego of the patient with the more benign, more realistic superego of the therapist (Ferenczi & Rank, 1925; see also Glover, 1955, p. 172; Ferenczi, 1928/1955b, pp. 98, 101–102; and Strachey, 1934). This hypothesis implies that therapy involves the patient's internalizing the therapist, just as she or he had earlier internalized her or his parents when forming the superego (cf. Freud, 1923, p. 34). In this view of therapy, attachment and internalization come to have equal importance with free association, interpretation, and insight in the therapeutic process and method. Evidence that Freud conducted therapy in a way that would invite such attachment and internalization has come to us in the memoirs of Freud and his technique recently published by Sterba (1982), Bettelheim (1984), and Kardiner (1977). With all the emphasis on internalization, however, conflict remained a focal concept in the structural theory of psychoanalytic therapy (Brenner, 1982).

Ego Psychology

A. Freud (1936) and H. Hartmann (1939) ushered in ego-psychology as an orientation within psychoanalytic theorizing. Trying to fulfill S. Freud's ambition to widen the scope of psychoanalysis and to make it a complete theory of human behavior, they initiated a radical change of direction. Earlier efforts at theory building had focused on the question how the individual adapts to the psychic forces of the conflicts within; the new approach focused on how the individual adapts to the world around him or her. Psychodynamic theorists and therapists shifted from studying how persons get along with themselves to studying how they get along with their environment, especially with other human beings.

A central part of this new focus was the study of the ego and its functions. Conceptions of these functions proliferated. Hartmann (1939) wrote about the adequacy of the ego to its tasks, and pointed out that in the framework of evolutionary theory we should think of the ego as guiding the person's adaptation to an "average expectable environment."

Influenced by these ideas, students of psychopathology such as Beres (1956) and Blanck and Blanck (1968, 1974, 1986) turned away from psychic conflict and emphasized the deficiencies and arrests that occurred during the development of the ego functions. When these conceptions about psychopathology were applied to the therapeutic task, those taking this approach came to consider the so-called narcissistic neuroses (schizophrenia and depression particularly) as disorders of ego function. For example, the symptoms of schizophrenia demonstrated a lack of skills in reality testing. Viewing the narcissistic neuroses in this way, one is led to propose substantial modifications in the theory of therapy and in the techniques used in it. One would see therapy as the promoter of undeveloped or underdeveloped ego skills; the therapist would serve as a kind of auxiliary ego for the patient and as a model of ego functioning from whom the patient could acquire the missing skills through learning and identification. Among the skills that were believed to be lacking in at least some of these borderline patients or patients with psychoses are reality testing, drive control, judgment, and maintenance of object relations.

Therapists holding to this view of psychopathology, giving less attention to conflict and resolution of conflict, put less emphasis on the necessity for anonymity and abstinence (which would be required in working with conflict burdened patients on the analysis of the transference). Such therapists came to be more active, more questioning, more guiding, more concerned with the realities of the patient's life than with fantasies, and more unrestrained in praising the patient for the patient's achievements. In assessing the state of the patient's ego, such therapists came to rely on a careful assessment of what the patient said; an assessment that took for granted that the patient's account of historical events was to be considered factual rather than as a set of associations, saturated with conflict like any other stream of thought. In this approach to therapy a realistic assessment is needed to find out what ego skills the patient lacks; and this assessment, once made, guides the choice of goals of the therapy. Therapists who follow such a course are thus inclined to think about the relationship between patient and therapist less in the framework of transference (as the conflict approach views transference) and more in terms of the therapist's providing a model to which the patient can attach and an object that she or he can internalize. As Alexander and French (1946) put it, therapy is a corrective emotional experience.

Object-Relations Theory

Present day therapists have come, more and more, to emphasize the importance of the patient's relationships with others. Greenberg and Mitchell (1983), for example, consider object relations to be central both to psychopathology and to therapeutic practice. Some theorists have focused on the person's experiences of attachment and separation (Bowlby, 1969, 1973, 1980; Mahler, Pine, & Bergman, 1975); on the person's defining and maintaining boundaries between self and others (Segal, 1964); on interpersonal relations as dominant elements in personality development (Sullivan, 1940); and on identity-coherence and identity-diffusion (Kernberg, 1975, 1980). Together, one may describe the contributions of these theorists as "object-relations theory." (For an excellent summary of this theory the reader is referred to Hamilton, 1988.) The theory addresses itself mainly to how the person relates himself or herself to objects, rather than to the drives themselves, their mutability, and their idiosyncratic aims. There is no disputing that relationships with other human beings are crucial to each person's development, nor that the events during the person's life that he or she remembers (or infers) give significant information about the person's individuality. Spence (1982) advocates considering the patient's report of these events as "narrative truth," not to be taken as a verifiable or refutable account of what happened; others may argue that we must find out what really happened. The present authors believe that one should focus on what these associations of the patient tell us about the patient's unconscious conflicts: They are representations of this latent material.

Because the therapeutic relationship is an object relationship, Sullivan (1940) advocated that we take it to be a sample of the patient's way of living with others, considering the therapist to be a "participant observer" (an idea taken over from social anthropology, a discipline in which the scientist gains access to the alien culture she or he wants to study by living within it). By such participant observation Sullivan believed, one could discover transference (he called it "parataxic distortion") and countertransference responses. One would not necessarily need the patient's associations to make this discovery: The patient's behavior within the therapist–patient dyad would give the relevant information. Sullivan's suggestion that the therapist can observe as well as listen has special pertinence to studying the unconscious mental life of persons such as preverbal children who cannot provide us with associations.

Just as object-relations theory emphasizes the centrality of a person's interactions with others in the formation of psychopathology, therapeutic approaches based on this theory emphasize these interactions (as stated in the writings of Cashdan [1988] and of Blanck & Blanck [1986]). These authors recommend that the therapist focus on the style of the patient's object relations, as the patient reports these (relying, we suppose, on the patient's conscious knowledge of this). The therapist is to study and to correct psychic processes, such as projective identification, that distort the relationships that the patient has with others. The therapist takes the patient's reports as more or less factual, and for the most part does not consider these reports to be associations that represent, indirectly, the patient's motivational states and perceptions (not necessarily accurate) of others.

Because within this theory transference and countertransference are dealt with as object relations without emphasis on their repetitive quality, the therapist tries to establish a natural, humane ambience rather than striving to preserve abstinence (Wolf, 1988). Interpretations are less oriented toward elucidating unconscious processes and the dynamics of intrapsychic conflicts. Instead, in making interpretations the therapist seeks to encourage discussion and examination (by both the patient and the therapist) of the nature of the relationships that the patient experiences, including the nature of the relationship with the therapist. This approach to dealing with transference has recently led to fascinating debates about when and how the therapist should disclose information about herself or himself (see Burke, 1989).

Self Psychology

Kohut (1971, 1977) and other self psychologists such as Wolf (1988), broadened and extended Freud's theory of neurosis by emphasizing the experiencing self—which Freud had dealt with partly in his concept "ego," and partly in his discussions of "narcissism," but nowhere had discussed comprehensively.

Self psychology, then, is the study of that aspect of mental functioning in which the person-as-self is the focus, and therapy based on self psychology deals with pathologies of this aspect of mental life. Kohut proposed that in the development of the self, the person requires first of all a self object (a person who provides certain functions to the baby or child) to provide him or her with the functions necessary for maintaining life: managing stimulation, controlling drive expression, and regulating esteem. As the person develops, the self object, through a process involving what are called *transmuting internalizations*, facilitates the person's taking over these activities; by doing this, the self object promotes the growth of the person and his or her enhancement of the self. Ideally, the self object is optimally empathic, making use of this empathy to decide the time and manner of promoting the transmuting internalizations as the child is ready for them. There is a risk of a narcissistic trauma to the extent of the self object's falling short of this ideal. Such traumas bring about a narcissistic personality disorder.

According to Kohut, Wolf, and others, the person suffering from a narcissistic disorder can be expected to show an *idealizing* or a *mirroring* transference in the therapy. In the idealizing transference, the patient idealizes the therapist; this enables the patient to restore his or her damaged narcissism through identification with the idealized therapist. Alternatively, the patient sees himself or herself mirrored in the therapist's eyes (figuratively), believing himself or herself to be a maximally esteemed object.

Kohut (1984) and Wolf (1988) tell us that the way to deal with these narcissistic manifestations is, first, to establish an optimally empathic experience for the patient within the treatment situation. Because the optimally empathic therapist necessarily fails, at times, to provide the empathy that the patient longs for (e.g., the therapist may take a vacation, and the patient experiences this as a stunning rejection), the patient gradually comes to assume the functions that he or she has been experiencing as provided by the therapist. The patient's taking on these functions is spoken of as his or her achieving a *transmuting internalization*. In this way the failures of empathy that took place in the patient's early life, the failures that originally produced the narcissistic personality disorder, now are overcome through an experience in therapy that fosters the patient's growth. Technically, the therapy focuses on the disturbances that the patient experiences during her or his encounter with the therapist, as the therapist oscillates between adequate and less adequate provision of empathic response (Goldberg, 1978; Schwaber, 1981). The therapist in examining these disturbances is showing, in another way, empathy with the patient; this empathic activity then furthers the patient's ability to undertake this kind of examination herself or himself. As esteem is restored through internalization of the esteem-providing function, the defenses against loss or absence of the esteem provided by the self or by the self object become less necessary. With less need for defense, there is an enhancement of the person's relations with the self and with others, both psychically and socially. An essential element of the technique of self psychology treatment is the therapist's reflecting the essence of the patient's feelings, thereby demonstrating optimal empathy. Interpretation of unconscious conflict is thus less important.

Conclusions

Having presented a brief, schematic review of various theories of psychodynamics, psychopathology, and psychotherapy, we now turn to the questions raised at the beginning of the chapter. We posed these questions in order to present the controversies that now embroil the field of psychodynamic psychotherapy.

Our first general guideline to deciding between the opposing views presented in those nine questions is to keep in mind that the oppositions assumed in the questions may be less than absolute. For example, although much of pathological behavior may be grounded in conflict, even the person whose difficulties are mostly traceable to conflict may suffer from developmental arrests and deficits in mental skills. For such a person, we would argue, analysis of conflict is essential, and attention to the arrests and deficits may prove to be a useful subsidiary therapeutic strategy, if the therapist can make use of it without compromising analytic work. Accordingly, we would view the insights of the authors who have called our attention to the arrests and deficits as valuable insights about these clinical issues and alternative viewpoints applicable to particular clinical situations (those in which arrest and deficit play an important role), but not as categorical truths that undermine the basic approach of dealing with conflict.

This reasoning can be applied, we argue, to most of the other questions as well. We want to make specific comments, however, about each of the other questions.

In our opinion question 2, which stated an opposition between interpretation as curative and attachment as curative, presents a false contradiction. As the reader of our chapters on transference, interpretation, and personal responses of the therapist knows, we believe that (a) making the unconscious conscious is essential (this is interpretation), (b) the most important interpretations are interpretations of transference, (c) the therapist knows what to interpret because of his or her emotional participation in the therapy, and (d) the patient can tolerate hearing and assimilating the interpretation because he or she feels support from the therapist. How then can one sensibly separate the interpretive process from the attachment of the patient to various persons in her or his life at an earlier time and to the therapist right now?

The proposal that because there was probably an actual traumatic event in the patient's early life, to focus on the patient's fantasies is misguided (a position that Masson [1984], among others, has taken), shows a thorough misunderstanding of mental life. The impact of the past traumas on current living is mediated through their shaping of the person's fantasies. We cannot undo the damage by gratifying now a patient who was earlier deprived, by taking care not to seduce a patient who was earlier seduced, or by joining with the patient in blaming those who had earlier harmed her or him by deprivation or seduction. Rather, we examine with the patient the impact that these fantasies—still active in his or her living—are currently having. We examine with him or her the purposes that these fantasies are serving, the goals that they are designed to attain. We also explore the behavioral and mental structure in which the fantasies developed in the person's early life (we are driven to do that as the current circumstances fail to explain the strength of the fantasies). In short, our attention is constantly on the early developed fantasies that have been repressed. We may not need to be sure whether a trauma happened or not; in any case, whether it happened or not seems to make no difference in our therapeutic strategy.

In a similar way, other controversies may matter much more for the theory of personality and the theory of psychopathology than they matter for therapeutic technique. Whether we conceptualize motivation as stemming ultimately from bodily processes we call *drives*, or conceptualize it as stemming mainly from the person's need for relationships with others influences our therapeutic approach only in so far as we might neglect object relations if we take too narrow a view of drive.

With a broadened view of drive and of the psychosexual stages—with a conception like that presented so cogently by E. Erikson in his writings (beginning with *Childhood and Society* [1950] and continuing with *Insight and Responsibility* [1964a] and *Identity: Youth and Crisis* [1968])—one would not be likely to miss the importance of the person's relationships with others. Today, perhaps, one is more likely to underplay the importance of the body and its activities than to neglect the importance of relationships.

Some of the other issues raised in the early pages of this chapter call our attention to paradoxes inherent in psychoanalytic therapy. If we ask whether persons make themselves neurotic or their parents make them so, it is clear that the parents (as guarantors of the child's continued existence and providers of what she or he needed to have in order to experience satisfactions) can be held accountable for shaping development. In that sense, they are "to blame for her or his neurosis." Yet the former child, now our patient, cannot get over the neurosis until *he or she* takes responsibility for his or her life. "How can the patient change what has been laid down by the impact of the past?" we ask (as scientific determinists should). The answer, of course, is that we urge patients to do so by an act of will. (For a discussion of "will" in psychoanalytic theory and practice, see Gill, 1989.) To save our faith in determinism, we point out to patients and to ourselves that our conviction that they are no longer bound by what was experienced years ago, that now they face a new, different situation, is offered to them; and this conviction changes them.

Some of the questions and controversies derive from failure to keep to the definition that Freud set out when he originally proposed a technical term. Consider the controversies about countertransference: If one sticks to Freud's definition of the term, it is the unwanted and unrecognized intrusion of the therapist's unconscious conflicts into the therapy situation. If one wants to speak about other aspects of the therapist's emotional responses to the patient, for the sake of clarity another word or an explanation about the current use of the word should be given. The same would apply to the definition of transference.

Finally, we may comment that Freud (1914a) argued that an approach to understanding human mental functioning could be considered psychoanalytic if it took account of unconscious processes and repression. Thus therapy that aims at the undoing of repression and that involves analysis of transference can be considered psychoanalysis. Freud pointed out (in his "On Beginning the Treatment" [1913]) that his habit of using the couch had a historical origin; at first he used the couch in order to hypnotize his patients. He argued, however, that there were advantages to using the couch: it would "prevent the transference from mingling with the patient' associations imperceptibly" (p. 134), thereby making it easier to recognize and demonstrate the transference and to define its resistant aspects. From this discussion we can judge that Freud did not believe that use of the couch defined psychoanalysis, but believed that using the couch facilitated good analytic work.

As to whether the length of therapy defines analysis, again we can ask, "What did Freud think?" In the same paper, he told how he dealt with the question that prospective patients often ask, "How long will the treatment take?" He pointed out that the length of therapy depends on how fast the patient works at it. He acknowledged, ". . . psychoanalysis is always a matter of long periods of time, of half a year or of whole years . . ." (p. 129). In comparison with the 7-year-long analyses that we have heard about and the 15 month minimum requirement for training analyses imposed by some psychoanalytic institutes, Freud's 1913 estimate of how long an analysis might be seems short.

If Freud thought then that length of time did not define whether the therapy is analysis, why should we try to do so? Not that we would argue that one should never challenge any of Freud's opinions; rather, because Freud originated psychoanalytic therapy, and because he laid so little stress on the value of making it lengthy, we would need a reasoned argument to convince us that psychoanalytic therapy must be long in order to be psychoanalytic. If a convincing argument for the necessity of lengthy therapy can be made (particularly if the argument relies on empirical studies), we stand ready to be convinced.

When the Conflict Model Falls Short

As we said earlier, for particular patients whose difficulties can mainly be explained by the conflict model, the facts may show, nevertheless, that some aspects of their pathology is explainable in terms of other models (e.g., ego psychology, object relations theory, and self psychology). We can picture conflicted persons coming for therapy feeling, consciously, that they *cannot* (as opposed to *unconsciously will not*) function as they desire. These patients present their conflict-resolutions (i.e., the "pathological" compromises that they have arrived at) in the form of difficulties that they have in getting along with others and themselves. Would not such persons also feel that their self-esteem has been significantly damaged because of the difficulties that they are experiencing in their functioning? All of these (not necessarily contradictory) viewpoints can and do play a part in our thinking about treating conflicted persons.

Such a catholicity of vision is sometimes not enough. It happens at times, with some patients, that when we apply the techniques implied by the conflict model we run into a therapeutic impasse. The therapy stalls. Interpretations of unconscious dynamics seem to be without effect. Discussions between the patient and the therapist about the impasse do not alter it. Consultation with another therapist turns out to be essentially unhelpful. At this point, declarations that the patient has gradually or suddenly become "unanalyzable" add nothing to the therapist's understanding of what is happening.

Such an impasse should be taken as an empirical demonstration that the therapist may not be able to help the patient within the conflict model. The therapist may then decide to change the concepts and the techniques that are being used. For example, she or he and the patient might agree that the therapy should be directed not at uncovering conflict but at enhancing the patient's adaptational skills (skills in dealing with the therapist and with other persons in her or his life). The hoped for result would be an improvement in how well the patient gets along with others.

If the therapeutic impasse has damaged the therapeutic alliance irreparably, the therapist is not in a position to continue the therapy by changing her or his technical orientation, even if the therapist has the knowledge and skill to do so. When there has been such damage to the alliance, the therapist has to discuss with the patient whether the patient should be referred to a therapist of another theoretical persuasion.

We believe that it is unrealistic to expect that a therapist who works within a particular conceptual framework will be able to work well with any patient who comes along. Sometimes a patient has to consult and try out more than one therapist before finding a workable match. We do not decry this state of affairs; it comes with the territory.

Dogmatism Is Unbecoming

Thus, therapy is not a uniform procedure to be applied identically to all persons, a procedure expected to have the same results for each of these persons. It is, instead, a highly idiosyncratic enterprise in which the therapist can be offered only the most general principles to guide her or him. Despite these uncertainties, we hold that the therapist can make good use of theories concerning psychology in general, concerning psychopathology in particular, and concerning therapy most particularly.

We believe also that the therapist should decide whether a particular style of therapy can work with the patient at hand by giving the therapy a try rather than by relying on sweeping generalizations such as, "One cannot do interpretive therapy with persons afflicted with schizophrenia" or "Alcoholics have to be resocialized before they can enter dynamic psychotherapy."

The Impact of Values on Therapeutic Strategy

Lacking evidence drawn from empirical studies about some of these issues (e.g., the frequency of inner conflicts and developmental arrests), how can we choose between opposing explanations of psychopathology? In deciding what position to take on these questions we find ourselves driven to consider our values. For therapy does not take place in a vacuum. It cannot be free of the values of the patient, of the therapist, and of the society in which they live. Accordingly we find it helpful to be explicit about our values as we think about the therapy that we do and about our reasons for choosing one strategy rather than another. Some of our values are:

1. We believe that when a person has attained adulthood, he or she has the right to act as human beings act, to be as human beings are, and to take the consequences of these actions.
2. We cannot accept the idea that others besides the patient, either as individuals or as representatives of institutions, have the right to deprive an adult person of the freedom to experience consequences—no matter how benevolent the impulse to spare the person these consequences may seem.
3. Tyranny, we believe, is almost always imposed in the name of benevolence.
4. We further hold that an adult person is entitled to the assumption that he or she possesses whatever capabilities are needed to live life the way he or she wants, until he or she has demonstrated (by actions) that these capacities are lacking.

Thus we recommend starting therapy with the assumption that the conflict model is applicable and that an autonomous psychotherapy (to use Szasz's phrase; a style of therapy suited to the conflict model) will be effective. One should *first* hypothesize that the patient cannot get along with herself or himself or with others because he or she is getting along with herself or himself and with others according to *hidden* objectives and agendas that are suited to bringing about the resolution of archaic conflicts. One should wait until this hypothesis is proven wrong to propose that the patient *cannot* get along with herself or himself and with others.

Our therapeutic theory and practice are based on the values that we exposed above, and on their implications. One implication is that one should begin in any therapy with the least intrusive style of intervention, and should turn to more intrusive techniques only when the less intrusive have been found wanting. In doing this, we accord the patient the expectation that he or she will be as fully responsible for the therapy as the therapist is for the therapist's participation in it. We should expect the patient to possess the capacity for tolerating those characteristics of the therapeutic situation that distinguish it radically from all other social situations. The patient has to recognize that the therapeutic situation is an artificial one and that it has been designed and created only to further the aims of the therapy.

In the long run, we believe that both the patient and the therapist will find it more satisfying to adhere to this set of principles. The therapist will not get obedience and gratitude, but she or he will get the satisfaction of seeing the development of a more competent, better integrated human being. The patient will not get advice, orders, or easy sympathy, but he or she will exercise competencies, reaching out to the world around, and inwardly experience a greater sense of harmony.

References

Alexander, F., & French, T. M. (Eds.). (1946). *Psychoanalytic therapy: Principles and application*. New York: The Ronald Press Company.

Alpert, J. L. (Ed.). (1986). *Psychoanalysis and women: Contemporary reappraisals*. Hillsdale, NJ: The Analytic Press.

Alpert, J. L., & Spencer, J. B. (1986). Morality, gender, and analysis. In J. L. Alpert (Ed.), *Psychoanalysis and women: Contemporary reappraisals* (pp. 83–111). Hillsdale, NJ: The Analytic Press.

American Psychiatric Association. (1987). *Diagnostic and statistical manual of mental disorders* (3rd ed., rev.). Washington, DC: Author.

American Psychological Association. (1981). *Ethical principles of psychologists*. Washington, DC: American Psychological Association.

Bakan, D. (1966). *The duality of human existence: An essay on psychology and religion*. Chicago: Rand McNally & Company.

Bardwick, J. M. (1971). *Psychology of women: A study of bio-cultural conflicts*. New York: Harper & Row.

Bardwick, J. M. (1979). *In transition: How feminism, sexual liberation, and the search for self-fulfillment have altered America*. New York: Holt Rinehart, and Winston.

Basch, M. F. (1980). *Doing psychotherapy*. New York: Basic Books.

Basow, S. A. (1986). *Gender stereotypes: Traditions and alternatives* (2nd ed.). Monterey, CA: Brooks/Cole.

Beres, D. (1956). Ego deviation and the concept of schizophrenia. *The Psychoanalytic Study of the Child, 11*, 164–235.

Bernstein, A. E., & Warner, G. M. (1984). *Women treating women: Case material from women treated by female psychoanalysts*. New York: International Universities Press.

Bettelheim, B. (1984). *Freud and man's soul*. New York: Random House. (Originally published New York: Knopf, 1982)

Bion, W. R. (1961). *Experiences in groups*. New York: Basic Books.

Blanck, G., & Blanck, R. (1974). *Ego psychology: Theory and practice*. New York: Columbia University Press.

Blanck, R., & Blanck, G. (1968). *Marriage and personal development*. New York: Columbia University Press.

Blanck, R., & Blanck, G. (1986). *Beyond ego psychology: Developmental object relations theory*. New York: Columbia University Press.

Blum, H. P. (Ed.). (1977). *Female psychology: Contemporary psychoanalytic views*. New York: International Universities Press.

Bowlby, J. (1969). *Attachment and loss: Vol. 1. Attachment*. New York: Basic Books.

Bowlby, J. (1973). *Attachment and loss: Vol. 2. Separation: Anxiety and anger*. New York: Basic Books.

Bowlby, J. (1980). *Attachment and loss: Vol. 3. Loss: Sadness and depression*. New York: Basic Books.

Brenner, C. (1973). *An elementary textbook of psychoanalysis*. (rev. ed.) New York: International Universities Press.

Brenner, C. (1976). *Psychoanalytic technique and psychic conflict*. New York: International Universities Press.

Brenner, C. (1982). *The mind in conflict*. New York: International Universities Press.

Breuer, J., & Freud, S. (1893–1895). *Studies on hysteria.* In J. Strachey (Ed. and Trans.), *The standard edition of the complete psychological works of Sigmund Freud* (Vol. 2). London: Hogarth Press. (Translated work published 1955)

Brodsky, A. M., & Hare-Mustin, R. (Eds.). (1980). *Women and psychotherapy: An assessment of research and practice.* New York: Guilford.

Burke, W. F. (1989, August). Validation of countertransference reactions. In W. F. Burke (Chair), *Countertransference: Validation and disclosure in the therapeutic interaction.* Symposium conducted at the meeting of the American Psychological Association, New Orleans, LA.

Cashdan, S. (1988). *Object relations therapy.* New York: Norton.

Cavenar, J. O., & Werman, D. S. (1983). The sex of the psychotherapist. *American Journal of Psychiatry, 40,* 85–87.

Chasseguet-Smirgel, J. (1970). *Female sexuality: New psychoanalytic views.* Ann Arbor: The University of Michigan Press. (Original work, *Recherches psychanalytiques nouvelles sur la sexualité féminine,* published 1964)

Chesler, P. (1972). *Women and madness.* Garden City, NY: Doubleday.

Colby, K. M. (1951). *A primer for psychotherapists.* New York: The Ronald Press Company.

Davanloo, H. (Ed.). (1978a). *Basic principles and techniques in short-term dynamic psychotherapy.* New York: SP Medical & Scientific Books.

Davanloo, H. (1978b). Evaluation, criteria for selection of patients for short-term dynamic psychotherapy: A metapsychological approach. In H. Davanloo (Ed.), *Basic principles and techniques in short-term dynamic psychotherapy* (pp. 9–34). New York: SP Medical & Scientific Books.

Deutsch, F., & Murphy, W. F. (1955). *The clinical interview.* New York: International Universities Press.

Dollard, J., Auld, F., Jr., & White, A. M. (1953). *Steps in psychotherapy: Study of a case of sex-fear conflict.* New York: Macmillan.

Dollard, J., and Miller, N. E. (1950). *Personality and psychotherapy: An analysis in terms of learning, thinking, and culture.* New York: McGraw-Hill.

Edelson, M . (1984). *Hypothesis and evidence in psychoanalysis.* Chicago: University of Chicago Press.

Edelson, M. (1988). *Psychoanalysis: A theory in crisis.* Chicago: University of Chicago Press.

Eissler, K. R. (1953). The effect of the structure of the ego on psychoanalytic technique. *Journal of the American Psychoanalytic Association, 1,* 104–143.

Erikson, E. H. (1950). *Childhood and society.* New York: Norton.

Erikson, E. H. (1964a). *Insight and responsibility: Lectures on the ethical implications of psychoanalytic insight.* New York: Norton.

Erikson, E. H. (1964b). Reflections on womanhood. *Daedalus, 2,* 582–606.

Erikson, E. H. (1968). *Identity: Youth and crisis.* New York: Norton.

Fast, I. (1984). *Gender identity: A differentiation model.* Hillsdale, NJ: The Analytic Press.

Felton, J. R. (1986). Sex makes a difference: How gender affects the therapeutic relationship. *Clinical Social Work Journal, 14,* 127–138.

Fenichel, O. (1941). *Problems of psychoanalytic technique* (D. Brunswick, Trans.). New York: The Psychoanalytic Quarterly.

Fenichel, O. (1945). *The psychoanalytic theory of neurosis.* New York: Norton.

Fenton, W. S., Robinowitz, C. B., & Leaf, P. J. (1987). Male and female psychiatrists and their patients. *American Journal of Psychiatry, 144,* 358–361.

Ferenczi, S. (1955a). The problem of the termination of the analysis (E. Mosbacher, Trans.). In M. Balint (Ed.), *Final contributions to the problems and methods of psycho-analysis* (pp. 77–86). New York: Basic Books. (Original work published 1928)

Ferenczi, S. (1955b). The elasticity of psycho-analytic technique (E. Mosbacher, Trans.). In M. Balint (Ed.) *Final contributions to the problems and methods of psycho-analysis* (pp. 87–101). New York: Basic Books. (Original work published 1928)

Ferenczi, S., & Rank, O. (1925). *The development of psycho-analysis.* New York: Nervous and Mental Disease Publishing Company. (Original work published 1924)

Fierman, L. B. (Ed.). (1965). *Effective psychotherapy: The contribution of Hellmuth Kaiser.* New York: The Free Press.

Firestein, S. K. (1978). *Termination in psychoanalysis.* New York: International Universities Press.

Freud, A. (1936). *The ego and the mechanisms of defense* (C. Baines, Trans.). New York: International Universities Press. (Translated work published 1946)

Freud, A. (1946). *The psycho-analytical treatment of children.* London: Imago Publishing Co.

Freud, S. (1894). The neuro-psychoses of defence. In J. Strachey (Ed. and Trans.), *The standard edition of the complete psychological works of Sigmund Freud* (Vol. 3, pp. 43–61). London: Hogarth Press. (Translated work published 1962)

Freud, S. (1900). *The interpretation of dreams.* In J. Strachey (Ed. and Trans.), *The standard edition of the complete psychological works of Sigmund Freud* (Vols. 4–5). London: Hogarth Press. (Translated work published 1953)

Freud, S. (1905). Three essays on the theory of sexuality. In J. Strachey (Ed. and Trans.), *The standard edition of the complete psychological works of Sigmund Freud* (Vol. 7, pp. 125–243). London: Hogarth Press. (Translated work published 1953)

Freud, S. (1909). Notes upon a case of obsessional neurosis. In J. Strachey (Ed. and Trans.), *The standard edition of the complete psychological works of Sigmund Freud* (Vol. 10, pp. 153–249). London: Hogarth Press. (Translated work published 1955)

Freud, S. (1910a). Five lectures on psychoanalysis. In J. Strachey (Ed. and Trans.), *The standard edition of the complete psychological works of Sigmund Freud* (Vol. 11, pp. 3–55). London: Hogarth Press. (Translated work published 1957)

Freud, S. (1910b). The future prospects of psycho-analytic therapy. In J. Strachey (Ed. and Trans.), *The standard edition of the complete psychological works of Sigmund Freud* (Vol. 11, pp. 139–151). London: Hogarth Press. (Translated work published 1957)

Freud, S. (1912). The dynamics of transference. In J. Strachey (Ed. and Trans.), *The standard edition of the complete psychological works of Sigmund Freud* (Vol. 12, pp. 97–108). London: Hogarth Press. (Translated work published 1958).

Freud, S. (1913). On beginning the treatment. In J. Strachey (Ed. and Trans.), *The standard edition of the complete psychological works of Sigmund Freud* (Vol. 12, pp. 121–144). London: Hogarth Press. (Translated work published 1958).

Freud, S. (1914a). On the history of the psycho-analytic movement. In J. Strachey (Ed. and Trans.), *The standard edition of the complete psychological works of Sigmund Freud* (Vol. 14, pp. 3–66). London: Hogarth Press. (Translated work published 1957)

Freud, S. (1914b). Remembering, repeating, and working-through. In J. Strachey (Ed. and Trans.), *The standard edition of the complete psychological works of Sigmund Freud* (Vol. 12, pp. 145–156). London: Hogarth Press. (Translated work published 1958)

Freud, S. (1915a). Observations on transference-love. In J. Strachey (Ed. and Trans.), *The standard edition of the complete psychological works of Sigmund Freud* (Vol. 12, pp. 157–171). London: Hogarth Press. (Translated work published 1958)

Freud, S. (1915b). Repression. In J. Strachey (Ed. and Trans.), *The standard edition of the complete psychological works of Sigmund Freud* (Vol. 14, pp. 141–158). London: Hogarth Press. (Translated work published 1957)

Freud, S. (1915c). The unconscious. In J. Strachey (Ed. and Trans.), *The standard edition of the complete psychological works of Sigmund Freud* (Vol. 14, pp. 159–204). London: Hogarth Press. (Translated work published 1957)

Freud, S. (1917). *Introductory lectures on psycho-analysis* (Part 3). In J. Strachey (Ed. and Trans.), *The standard edition of the standard edition of the complete psychological works of Sigmund Freud* (Vol. 16). London: Hogarth Press. (Translated work published 1963)

Freud, S. (1918). From the history of an infantile neurosis. In J. Strachey (Ed. and Trans.), *The standard edition of the complete psychological works of Sigmund Freud* (Vol. 17, pp. 3–122). London: Hogarth Press. (Translated work published 1955)

Freud, S. (1923). *The ego and the id.* In J. Strachey (Ed. and Trans.), *The standard edition of the complete psychological works of Sigmund Freud* (Vol. 17, pp. 3–66). London: Hogarth Press. (Translated work published 1961)

Freud, S. (1925). Some psychical consequences of the anatomical distinction between the sexes. In J. Strachey (Ed. and Trans.), *The standard edition of the complete psychological works of Sigmund Freud* (Vol. 19, pp. 243–258). London: Hogarth Press. (Translated work published 1961)

Freud, S. (1926a). *Inhibitions, symptoms, and anxiety.* In J. Strachey (Ed. and Trans.), *The standard edition of the complete psychological works of Sigmund Freud* (Vol. 20, pp. 179–258). London: Hogarth Press. (Translated work published 1959)

Freud, S. (1926b). The question of lay analysis. In J. Strachey (Ed. and Trans.), *The standard edition of the complete psychological works of Sigmund Freud* (Vol. 20, pp. 179–258). London: Hogarth Press. (Translated work published in 1959)

Freud, S. (1933a). *New introductory lectures on psycho-analysis*. In J. Strachey (Ed. and Trans.), *The standard edition of the complete psychological works of Sigmund Freud* (Vol. 22, pp. 3–182). London: Hogarth Press. (Translated work published 1964)

Freud, S. (1933b). Femininity. In J. Strachey (Ed. and Trans.), *The standard edition of the complete psychological works of Sigmund Freud* (Vol. 22, pp. 112–135). London: Hogarth Press. (Translated work published 1964)

Freud, S. (1937a). Constructions in analysis. In J. Strachey (Ed. and Trans.), *The standard edition of the complete psychological works of Sigmund Freud* (Vol. 23, pp. 255–269). London: Hogarth Press. (Translated work published 1964)

Freud, S. (1937b). Analysis terminable and interminable. In J. Strachey (Ed. and Trans.), *The standard edition of the complete psychological works of Sigmund Freud* (Vol. 23, pp. 209–253). London: Hogarth Press. (Translated work published 1964)

Freud, S. (1940). *An outline of psycho-analysis*. In J. Strachey (Ed. and Trans.), *The standard edition of the complete psychological works of Sigmund Freud* (Vol. 23, pp. 141–207). London: Hogarth Press. (Translated work published 1964)

Friedman, H. J. (1977). Special problems of women in psychotherapy. *American Journal of Psychotherapy, 31*, 405–416.

Friedman, S. S. (1979). *A woman's guide to therapy*. Englewood Cliffs, NJ: Prentice-Hall.

Friedman, S. S. (1987). Collaboration and intimacy in the relationship of H. D. and Freud. *Literature & Psychology, 33*, 89–108.

Friedman, W. J., Robinson, A. B., & Friedman, B. L. (1987). Sex differences in moral judgments? A test of Gilligan's theory. *Psychology of Women Quarterly, 11*, 37–46.

Galenson, E. (1986). "Indoctrination vs. insight: Radical feminist and psychoanalytically oriented psychotherapy oriented psychotherapy:" A case report: Discussion. *Dynamic Psychotherapy, 4*, 51–52.

Gardiner, M. (Ed.) (1971). *The Wolf-Man by the Wolf-Man*. New York: Basic Books.

Gay, P. (1988). *Freud: A life for our time*. New York: Norton.

Gibbs, J. C., Arnold, K. D., & Burkhart, J. E. (1984). Sex differences in the expression of moral judgment. *Child Development, 55*, 1040–1043.

Gilbert, L. A. (1980). Feminist therapy. In A. M. Brodsky and R. T. Hare-Mustin (Eds.), *Women and psychotherapy: An assessment of research and practice* (pp. 245–265). New York: Guilford.

Gill, H. S. (1989). The will in psychoanalytic theory and practice. *British Journal of Medical Psychology, 62*, 1–11.

Gill, M. M., & Brenman, M. (1959). *Hypnosis and related states: Psychoanalytic studies in regression*. New York: International Universities Press.

Gilligan, C. (1982). *In a different voice*. Cambridge, MA: Harvard University Press.

Gilligan, C. , Ward, J. V., & Taylor, J. M. (Eds.) (1988). *Mapping the moral domain*. Cambridge, MA: Harvard University Press.

Glover, E. (1931). The therapeutic effect of inexact interpretation: A contribution to the theory of suggestion. *International Journal of Psycho-Analysis, 12*, 397–411.

Glover, E. (1955). *The technique of psycho-analysis*. New York: International Universities Press.

Goldberg, A. (1978). *The psychology of the self: A casebook*. New York: International Universities Press.

Goldstein, A. P. (1960). Patient's expectancies and non-specific therapy as a basis for (un)spontaneous remission. *Journal of Clinical Psychology, 16*, 399–403.

Goz, R. (1973). Women patients and women therapists: Some issues that come up in psychotherapy. *International Journal of Psychoanalytic Psychotherapy, 2*, 298–319.

Greenberg, J., & Mitchell, S. (1983). *Object relations in psychoanalytic theory*. Cambridge, MA: Harvard University Press.

Greenson, R. R. (1967). *The technique and practice of psychoanalysis: Vol. 1*. New York: International Universities Press.

Grier, W. H., & Cobbs, P. M. (1968). *Black rage*. New York: Basic Books.

Grossman, W. J., & Stewart, W. A. (1977). Penis envy: From childhood wish to developmental metaphor. In H. P. Blum (Ed.), *Female psychology: Contemporary psychoanalytic views* (pp. 193–212). New York: International Universities Press.

Grünbaum, A. (1984). *The foundations of psychoanalysis: A philosophical critique.* Berkeley and Los Angeles, CA: University of California Press.

H. D. (1956). *Tribute to Freud.* New York: Pantheon.

Hamilton, N. G. (1988). *Self and others: Object relations theory in practice.* Northvale, NJ: Jason Aronson.

Hartmann, H. (1939). *Ego psychology and the problem of adaptation* (D. Rapaport, Trans.). New York: International Universities Press.

Hempel, C. G. (1965). *Aspects of scientific explanation and other essays in the philosophy of science.* New York: The Free Press.

Horney, K. (1926). The flight from womanhood: The masculinity complex in women as viewed by men and by women. *International Journal of Psycho-Analysis, 7,* 324–339.

Horwitz, L. (1974). *Clinical prediction in psychotherapy.* New York: Jason Aronson.

Johnson, C. L. (1989, August). Transference and countertransference themes in the treatment of false-self disorders. In W. F. Burke (Chair), *Countertransference: Validation and disclosure in the therapeutic interaction.* Symposium conducted at the meeting of the American Psychological Association, New Orleans, LA.

Jones, E. E., Krupnick, J. L., & Kerig, P. K. (1987). Some gender effects in brief psychotherapy. *Psychotherapy, 24,* 336–352.

Jones, E. E., & Zoppel, C. L. (1982). Impact of client and therapist gender on psychotherapy process and outcome. *Journal of Consulting and Clinical Psychology, 50,* 259–272.

Jones, E. (1959). *Free associations: Memories of a psycho-analyst.* New York: Basic Books.

Kaplan, A. G. (1979). Toward an analysis of sex-role-related issues in the therapeutic relationship. *Psychiatry, 42,* 112–120.

Kaplan, A. G. (1985). Female or male therapists for women patients: New formulations. *Psychiatry, 48,* 111–121.

Kardiner, A. (1977). *My analysis with Freud: Reminiscences.* New York: Norton.

Karme, L. (1979). The analysis of a male patient by a female analyst: The problem of the negative oedipal transference. *International Journal of Psycho-Analysis, 60,* 253–261.

Karon, B. P., & VandenBos, G. R. (1981). *Psychotherapy of schizophrenia: The treatment of choice.* New York: Jason Aronson.

Kernberg, O. F. (1975). *Borderline conditions and pathological narcissism.* New York: Jason Aronson.

Kernberg, O. F. (1977). Foreword. In S. Appelbaum (Ed.) *The anatomy of change* (pp. vii–xiii). New York: Plenum.

Kernberg, O. F. (1980). *Internal world and external reality.* New York: Jason Aronson.

Kirshner, L. A., Genack, A., & Hauser, S. T. (1978). Effects of gender on short-term psychotherapy. *Psychotherapy: Theory, Research, and Practice, 15,* 158–167.

Kline, P. (1984). *Psychology and Freudian theory: An introduction.* London and New York: Methuen.

Knight, R. P. (1946). Determinism, "freedom," and psychotherapy. *Psychiatry, 9,* 251–262.

Kohut, H. (1971). *The analysis of the self.* New York: International Universities Press.

Kohut, H. (1977). *The restoration of the self.* New York: International Universities Press.

Kohut, H. (1984). *How does analysis cure?* Chicago: University of Chicago Press.

Kovel, J. (1976). *A complete guide to therapy: From psychoanalysis to behavior modification.* New York: Pantheon Books.

Kubie, L. S. (1941). The repetitive core of the neurosis. *Psychoanalytic Quarterly, 10,* 23–43.

Kubie, L. S. (1950). *Practical and theoretical aspects of psychoanalysis.* New York: International Universities Press.

Kubie, L. S. (1953). Some unsolved problems of the scientific career. *American Scientist, 61,* 596–613.

Kubie, L. S. (1954). Some unsolved problems of the scientific career (part 2). *American Scientist, 62,* 104–112.

Kulish, N. M. (1984). The effect of the sex of the analyst on transference: A review of the literature. *Bulletin of the Menninger Clinic, 48,* 95–110.

Kulish, N. M. (1986). Gender and transference: The screen of the phallic mother. *International Review of Psycho-Analysis, 13,* 393–404.

Kulish, N. M. (1989). Gender and transference: Conversations with female analysts. *Psychoanalytic Psychology, 6,* 59–71.

Kulish, N. M., & Mayman, M. (1989, April). A research study of gender-linked determinants of transference and countertransference. In D. Harder (Chair), *The contributions of re-*

search to the psychoanalytic process. Symposium conducted at the spring meeting of the Division of Psychoanalysis, American Psychological Association, Boston, MA.

Langs, R. (1973). *The technique of psychoanalytic therapy: Vol. 1.* New York: Jason Aronson.

Lerner, H. E. (1977). Parental mislabeling of female genitals as a determinant of penis envy and learning inhibitions in women. In H. P. Blum (Ed.), *Female psychology: Contemporary psychoanalytic views* (pp. 269–283). New York: International Universities Press.

Lerner, H. E. (1980). Penis envy: Alternatives in conceptualization. *Bulletin of the Menninger Clinic, 44*, 39–48.

Lerner, H. G. (1988). *Women in therapy.* Northvale, NJ: Jason Aronson.

Lerner, H. D. (1989, August). Borderline patients and the paradox of countertransference. In W. F. Burke (Chair), *Countertransference: Validation and disclosure in the therapeutic interaction.* Symposium conducted at the meeting of the American Psychological Association, New Orleans, LA.

Loevinger, J. (1976). *Ego development.* San Francisco: Jossey-Bass.

Luborsky, L. (1984). *Principles of psychoanalytic psychotherapy: A manual for supportive-expressive treatment.* New York: Basic Books.

Luborsky, L., Crits-Christoph, P., Mintz, J., & Auerbach, A. (1988). *Who will benefit from psychotherapy? Predicting therapeutic outcomes.* New York: Basic Books.

Luborsky, L., & Crits-Christoph, P. (1990). *Understanding transference: The CCRT method.* New York: Basic Books.

Luria, Z. (1986). A methodological critique. *Signs: Journal of Women in Culture and Society, 11*, 316–321.

Maccoby, E. E., & Jacklin, C. N. (1974). *The psychology of sex differences.* Stanford, CA: Stanford University Press.

Mackay, N. (1989). *Motivation and explanation: An essay on Freud's philosophy of science.* Madison, CT: International Universities Press.

Mahl, G. F. (1968). Gestures and body movements in interviews. In J. M. Shlien (Ed.), *Research in psychotherapy: Vol. 3* (pp. 295–346). Washington, DC: American Psychological Association.

Mahl, G. F. (1987). *Explorations in nonverbal and vocal behavior.* Hillsdale, NJ: Lawrence Erlbaum Associates.

Mahler, M. S., Pine, F., & Bergman, A. (1975). *The psychological birth of the human infant: Symbiosis and individuation.* New York: Basic Books.

Malan, D. H. (1963). *A study of brief psychotherapy.* London: Tavistock.

Malan, D. H. (1976). *Toward the validation of dynamic psychotherapy: A replication.* New York: Plenum.

Malan, D. H. (1979). *Individual psychotherapy and the science of psychodynamics.* London: Butterworths.

Mann, J. (1973). *Time-limited psychotherapy.* Cambridge, MA: Harvard University Press.

Marecek, J., & Johnson, M. (1980). Gender and the process of therapy. In A. M. Brodsky & R. T. Hare-Mustin (Eds.), *Women and psychotherapy* (pp. 67–93). New York: Guilford.

Masson, J. M. (1984). *The assault on truth: Freud's suppression of the seduction theory.* New York: Farrar, Straus, and Giroux.

Masters, W. H., & Johnson, V. E. (1966). *Human sexual response.* Boston: Little-Brown.

Mead, M. (1974). On Freud's view of female psychology. In J. Strouse (Ed.), *Women & analysis* (pp. 95–106). New York: Grossman.

Menninger, K. (1958). *Theory of psychoanalytic technique.* New York: Basic Books.

Menninger, K., & Holzman, P. S. (1973). *Theory of psychoanalytic technique* (2nd ed.). New York: Basic Books.

Miller, N. E. (1959). Liberalization of basic S-R concepts: Extensions to conflict behavior, motivation, and social learning. In S. Koch (Ed.), *Psychology: A study of a science: Vol. 2. General systematic formulations, learning, and special processes* (pp. 196–292). New York: McGraw-Hill.

Miller, N. E. (1960). Theory and experiment relating psychoanalytic displacement to stimulus-response generalization. *Journal of Abnormal and Social Psychology, 43*, 155–178.

Mogul, K. M. (1982). Overview: The sex of the therapist. *American Journal of Psychiatry, 139*, 1–9.

Moldawsky, S. (1986). When men are therapists to women: Beyond the oedipal pale. In T. Bernay and D. W. Cantor (Eds.), *The psychology of today's woman: New psychoanalytic visions* (pp. 291–303). Hillsdale, NJ: The Analytic Press.

Moore, B. E. (1977). Psychic representation and female orgasm. In H. P. Blum (Ed.), *Female psychology: Contemporary psychoanalytic views* (pp. 305–330). New York: International Universities Press.

Mowrer, O. H., & Ullman, A. D. (1945). Time as a determinant in integrative learning. *Psychological Review, 52,* 61–90.

Murdock, G. P. (1949). *Social structure.* New York: Macmillan.

Nemiah, J. C. (1961). *Foundations of psychopathology.* New York: Oxford University Press.

Offer, D., & Sabshin, M. (1966). *Normality: Theoretical and clinical concepts of mental health.* New York: Basic Books.

Orlinsky, D. E., & Howard, K. I. (1976). The effects of sex of therapist on the therapeutic experiences of women. *Psychotherapy: Theory, Research, and Practice, 13,* 82–88.

Perls, F. S. (1947). *Ego hunger and aggression: A revision of Freud's theory and method.* London: G. Allen and Unwin.

Perls, F. S., Hefferline, R. F., & Goodman, P. (1951). *Gestalt therapy: Excitement and growth in the human personality.* New York: Dell.

Person, E. S. (1983). Women in therapy: Therapist gender as a variable. *International Review of Psycho-Analysis, 10,* 193–204.

Piskorz de Zimerman, S. (1983). La mujer segun el psicoanalisis [The female as viewed by psychoanalysis]. *Revista de Psicoanalisis, 40,* 1155–1172.

Pyke, S. (1984, March 27). *Psychotherapy for women: Feminist perspectives.* [Lecture, University of Windsor, Windsor, Ontario].

Racker, H. (1953). A contribution to the problem of counter-transference. *International Journal of Psycho-Analysis, 34,* 313–324.

Rapaport, D. (1967). The scientific methodology of psychoanalysis. In M. M. Gill (Ed.), *The collected papers of David Rapaport* (pp. 165–220). New York: Basic Books.

Raphling, D. L., & Chused, J. F. (1988). Transference across gender lines. *Journal of the American Psychoanalytic Association, 36,* 77–104.

Rawlings, E. I., & Carter, D. K. (1977). Feminist and nonsexist psychotherapy. In E. I. Rawlings & D. I. Carter (Eds.), *Psychotherapy for women: Treatment toward equality* (pp. 49–76). Springfield, IL: Charles C. Thomas.

Reich, A. (1951). On counter-transference. *International Journal of Psycho-Analysis, 32,* 25–31.

Reich, W. (1945). *Character analysis* (2nd ed.) (T. P. Wolfe, Trans.). New York: Orgone Institute Press. (Original work published 1933)

Reik, T. (1959). *Of love and lust.* New York: Grove.

Rieker, P. P., & Carmen, E. (Hilberman) (Eds.). (1984). *The gender gap in psychotherapy.* New York: Plenum.

Ruderman, E. B. (1986). Creative and reparative uses of countertransference by women psychotherapists treating women patients: A clinical research study. In T. Bernay & D. W. Cantor (Eds.), *The psychology of today's woman: New psychoanalytic visions* (pp. 339–363). Hillsdale, NJ: The Analytic Press.

Salmon, W. C. (1959). Psychoanalytic theory and evidence. In S. Hook (Ed.), *Psychoanalysis, scientific method, and philosophy* (pp. 252–267). New York: New York University Press.

Saul, L. J. (1958). *Technic and practice of psychoanalysis.* Philadelphia: Lippincott.

Schachtel, Z. (1986). The "impossible profession" considered from a gender perspective. In J. L. Alpert (Ed.), *Psychoanalysis and women: Contemporary reappraisals* (pp. 237–255). Hillsdale, NJ: The Analytic Press.

Schafer, R. (1974). Problems in Freud's psychology of women. *Journal of the American Psychoanalytic Association, 22,* 459–485.

Schafer, R. (1984). *The analytic attitude.* New York: Basic Books.

Schover, L. R. (1981). Male and female therapists' responses to male and female client sexual material: An analogue study. *Archives of Sexual Behavior, 10,* 477–492.

Schwaber, E. A. (1981). Narcissism, self psychology, and the listening perspective. *Annual of Psychoanalysis, 9,* 115–131.

Searles, H. F. (1965). *Collected papers on schizophrenia and related subjects.* New York: International Universities Press.

Segal, H. (1964). *Introduction to the work of Melanie Klein.* New York: Basic Books.

Sesan, R. (1988). Sex bias and sex-role stereotyping in psychotherapy with women: Survey results. *Psychotherapy, 25,* 107–116.

Shafter, R. (1988). When the therapist is female: Transference, countertransference, and reality. *Issues in Ego Psychology, 11,* 32–42.

Shainess, N. (1983). Significance of match in sex of analyst and patient. *American Journal of Psychoanalysis, 43,* 205–217.

Sharpe, E. F. (1947). The psychoanalyst. *International Journal of Psycho-Analysis, 28,* 1–6.

Sherfey, M. J. (1972). *The nature and evolution of human sexuality.* New York: Random House.

Sifneos, P. E. (1972). *Short-term psychotherapy and emotional crisis.* Cambridge, MA: Harvard University Press.

Sifneos, P. E. (1979). *Short-term dynamic psychotherapy: Evaluation and technique.* New York: Plenum.

Silverman, H. (1963). Commitment: Aspects of a variable in the training and functioning of the clinical psychologist. *Journal of Clinical Psychology, 19,* 497–501.

Spence, D. P. (1982). *Narrative truth and historical truth: Meaning and interpretation in psychoanalysis.* New York: Norton.

Sterba, R. (1929). The fate of the ego in analytic therapy. *International Journal of Psycho-Analysis, 37,* 380–385.

Sterba, R. (1930). Zur Problematik der Sublimerungslehre. [On the problem of the theory of sublimation]. *Internationale Zeitschrift für Psychoanalyse, 16,* 370–377.

Sterba, R. F. (1940). The dynamics of the dissolution of the transference resistance. *Psychoanalytic Quarterly, 9,* 363–379.

Sterba, R. F. (1982). *Reminiscences of a Viennese psychoanalyst.* Detroit, MI: Wayne State University Press.

Strachey, J. (1934). The nature of the therapeutic action of psycho-analysis. *International Journal of Psycho-Analysis, 15,* 127–159.

Strouse, J. (Ed.) (1974). *Women & analysis.* New York: Grossman.

Strupp, H. H., & Binder, J. L. (1984). *Psychotherapy in a new key: A guide to time-limited dynamic psychotherapy.* New York: Basic Books.

Sullivan, H. S. (1940). *Conceptions of modern psychiatry.* New York: Norton.

Szasz, T. S. (1956). On the experience of the analyst in the psychoanalytic situation. *Journal of the American Psychoanalytic Association, 4,* 197–223.

Szasz, T. (1974). *The ethics of psychoanalysis.* New York: Basic Books.

Tanney, M. F., & Birk, J. M. (1976). Women counselors for women clients? A review of the research. *Counseling Psychologist, 6,* 28–32.

Tansey, M. J. (1989, August). The uses and abuses of countertransference disclosure. In W. F. Burke (Chair), *Countertransference: Validation and disclosure in the therapeutic interaction.* Symposium conducted at the meeting of the American Psychological Association, New Orleans, LA.

Tarachow, S. (1963). *An introduction to psychotherapy.* New York: International Universities Press.

Terman, L. M., & Miles, C. C. (1936). *Sex and personality: Studies in masculinity and femininity.* New York: McGraw-Hill.

Thoma, S. (1986). Estimating gender differences in the comprehension and preferences of moral issues. *Developmental Review, 6,* 165–180.

Torok, M. (1970). The significance of penis envy in women. In J. Chasseguet-Smirgel, *Female sexuality: New psychoanalytic views* (pp. 135–170). Ann Arbor: The University of Michigan Press. (Original work published 1964)

Tower, L. E. (1956). Countertransference. *Journal of the American Psychoanalytic Association, 4,* 224–255.

Waelder, R. (1960). *Basic theory of psychoanalysis.* New York: International Universities Press.

Walker, L. J. (1984). Sex differences in the development of moral reasoning: A critical review. *Child Development, 55,* 677–691.

Wetzler, S. (1985). The historical truth of psychoanalytic reconstructions. *International Review of Psycho-Analysis, 12,* 187–197.

Winnicott, D. W. (1960). The theory of the parent-infant relationship. *International Journal of Psycho-Analysis, 41,* 585–595.

Wolf, E. S. (1988). *Treating the self: Elements of clinical self psychology.* New York: Guilford.

Zetzel, E. R. (1953). Panel report: The traditional psychoanalytic technique and its variations. *Journal of the American Psychoanalytic Association, 1,* 526–537.

Zetzel, E. R. (1963). The significance of the adaptive hypothesis for psychoanalytic theory and practice. *Journal of the American Psychoanalytic Association, 11,* 652–660.

Zetzel, E. R. (1970). The doctor-patient relationship in psychiatry. In E. R. Zetzel (Ed.), *The capacity for emotional growth* (pp. 139–155). New York: International Universities Press.

Index